.

U.S. LAW AFFECTING AMERICANS LIVING AND WORKING ABROAD

———

A REPORT

TO THE

COMMITTEE ON FOREIGN RELATIONS
UNITED STATES SENATE

University Press of the Pacific
Honolulu, Hawaii

U. S. Law Affecting Americans Living and Working
Abroad

A report from
President Jimmy Carter

to the Committee on Foreign Relations
United States Senate

ISBN: 0-89499-123-X

Copyright © 2001 by University Press of the Pacific

Reprinted from the 1980 edition

University Press of the Pacific
Honolulu, Hawaii
http://www.universitypressofthepacific.com

LETTER OF TRANSMITTAL

JULY 2, 1980.

Hon. FRANK CHURCH,
Chairman, Committee on Foreign Relations,
U.S. Senate.

DEAR MR. CHAIRMAN: In 1978 and again in 1979, I drafted and sponsored legislation intended to bring governmental attention to bear on the question of how U.S. law affects American citizens living and working abroad. Numbering well over one million and representing the United States around the world in all aspects of commerce, these overseas Americans constitute an important national asset. Recently, however, U.S. law governing the rights and obligations of these citizens has fallen subject to increasing criticism—first, as to its fairness; and second, as to its wisdom, at a time when America's international economic competitiveness, which depends heavily on effective business activity by U.S. citizens abroad, is under severe challenge. I therefore deemed it important that the policy implicit in this diverse body of law be subjected to a fresh and comprehensive examination.

Recognizing that laws governing U.S. citizens abroad fall under a variety of legislative and executive branch jurisdictions, I concluded that such an effort could be generated most effectively by a legal provision requiring the President, drawing upon the diverse resources of the executive branch, to conduct a thorough study. My first proposal, enacted in 1978 as Section 611 of Public Law 95–426, was designed to focus scrutiny on the question of whether our laws discriminate against Americans who chose to—or, for business reasons, must—reside overseas, as against those who reside within the borders of the United States. Subsequently, however, I decided that the study should be explicitly broadened to include the question of whether our laws place Americans abroad at a competitive disadvantage vocationally in the foreign countries where they may be living. Accordingly, I initiated last year an amendment, enacted as Section 407 of Public Law 96–60, which expanded the scope of the original requirement to include an examination of laws which treat Americans living abroad in a way that may cause them a disadvantage relative to the treatment accorded by other major trading countries to their citizens abroad.

In response to the initial requirement and its subsequent amendment, the President has submitted to Congress two reports. Although far from adequate to complete the task, these reports can, I believe, serve as the basis for further consideration of this important subject—and for appropriate action. Toward that end, I request that they be printed so as to be readily available to Members and to the American public.

GEORGE MCGOVERN,
United States Senator.

CONTENTS

I. SECTION 611, PUBLIC LAW 95–426 AS AMENDED BY SECTION 407, PUBLIC LAW 96–60

EQUITABLE TREATMENT OF UNITED STATES CITIZENS LIVING ABROAD

SEC. 611. (a) The Congress finds that—

(1) United States citizens living abroad should be provided fair and equitable treatment by the United States Government with regard to taxation, citizenship of progeny, veterans' benefits, voting rights, Social Security benefits, and other obligations, rights, and benefits; and

(2) United States statutes and regulations should be designed so as not to create competitive disadvantage for individual American citizens living abroad or working in international markets.

(b) Not later than January 20, 1980, the President shall transmit to the Speaker of the House of Representatives and the chairman of the Committee on Foreign Relations of the Senate a report which—

(1) identifies all United States statutes and regulations which treat United States citizens living abroad differently from United States citizens residing within the United States, or which may cause, directly or indirectly, competitive disadvantage for Americans working abroad relative to the treatment by other major trading nations of the world of their nationals who are working outside their territory;

(2) evaluates each such discriminatory practice; and

(3) recommends legislation and any other remedial action the President finds appropriate to eliminate unfair or competitively disadvantaging treatment of Americans living or working abroad.

II. FIRST PRESIDENTIAL REPORT

THE WHITE HOUSE,
Washington, August 27, 1979.

Hon. FRANK CHURCH,
Chairman, Committee on Foreign Relations,
U.S. Senate, Washington, D.C.

DEAR MR. CHAIRMAN: The enclosed report, prepared in compliance with Section 611 of Public Law 95–426 identifies six Federal statutory and regulatory provisions which discriminate against United States citizens living abroad. The Executive branch has evaluated those provisions and has concluded that changes are warranted in order to resolve certain inequities involving citizenship and veterans and social security benefits. The report also reviews twenty-eight other issues raised by some Americans living abroad concerning their rights and obligations as U.S. citizens.

This report is the result of a painstaking and earnest review of the many legal provisions affecting our citizens residing abroad. The test for discrimination used was to compare the effect of those provisions on U.S. citizens residing abroad with U.S. citizens living in the United States.

I believe the report responds in a responsible manner to the concern about the situation of Americans residing abroad. I am aware that section 407 of H.R. 3363 just recently enacted, broadens the scope of the report to include the "competitive disadvantage" of Americans abroad compared to nationals of other major trading partners and extends the report's transmittal date until January 20, 1980. Because this report was completed and awaiting my transmittal at the time section 407 was enacted, I believe it best to transmit it now to the Congress for its consideration. I have, moreover, requested the Secretary of the Treasury to prepare an additional report on the taxation of American citizens living abroad compared to the treatment by our major trading partners of their citizens living abroad and to identify any competitive disadvantages that may ensue.

The Administration will continue to work to resolve discriminatory provisions in regulations and in agency procedures affecting Americans living abroad; I am hopeful that inequities which are subject to legislative remedy will likewise be resolved.

Sincerely,

JIMMY CARTER.

(2)

REPORT ON EQUITABLE TREATMENT OF UNITED STATES CITIZENS LIVING ABROAD

(As required by Section 611, Pubilc Law 95–426)

INTRODUCTION

The Foreign Relations Authorization Act for fiscal year 1979 (Public Law 95–426), signed into law on October 7, 1978, contained the following provision:

Section 611(a) The Congress finds that—

(1) United States citizens living abroad should be provided fair and equitable treatment by the United States Government with regard to taxation, citizenship of progeny, veterans' benefits, voting rights, Social Security benefits, and other obligations, rights, and benefits; and

(2) such fair and equitable treatment would be facilitated by a periodic review of the statutes and regulations affecting Americans living abroad.

(b) Not later than January 20, 1979, the President shall transmit to the Speaker of the House of Representatives and the chairman of the Committee on Foreign Relations of the Senate a report which—

(1) identifies all United States statutes and regulations which discriminate against United States citizens living abroad;

(2) evaluates each such discriminatory practice; and

(3) recommends legislation and any other remedial action the President finds appropriate to eliminate unfair or inequitable treatment of Americans living abroad.

To comply with this mandate, the Office of Management and Budget requested seventeen agencies to review existing laws and regulations and to identify those which were discriminatory in nature. Subsequently, views of nine agencies were sought regarding a compendium of issues prepared by American Citizens Abroad, a private group based in Geneva. That compendium is a well-prepared, comprehensive collection of citizens' concerns, most of which deal with claims of unfair treatment. The compendium was helpful in identifying those issues of concern to a number of Americans living abroad. Comments from other private groups and private individuals were also received and considered. The personal quality of many letters provided a context in which the issues could be better understood.

The scope of this report is consistent with the Section 611 requirement to identify laws and regulations which discriminate against Americans abroad. Implicit in this requirement are comparisons between Americans living abroad and living in the United States. A number of issues raised by those living abroad, however, compared the treatment accorded them by Federal law with the treatment accorded by other governments to their citizens living abroad. This report does not address those comparisons. It is difficult to claim that American law is discriminatory because it treats Americans living abroad differently from the way French law treats French citizens living abroad or British law treats British citizens living abroad. Such an approach would require choosing among several different foreign laws for a comparative standard for American law. It is doubtful that the American public domiciled in the United States would understand why the standards of foreign law should be applied to American law to accord special treatment for Americans living abroad.

One of the most frequent issues raised by Americans living abroad has been that of taxation of personal income earned abroad. Many correspondents objected to the tax revisions included in the Foreign Earned Income Act, enacted last year. It is frequently alleged that those revisions, especially in the income exclusion provision, will have detrimental effects on the ability of American business to hire American citizens to work abroad, which in turn may result in reduced American exports or reduced profits earned abroad by American business. This report does not address this matter because its purpose is to focus on the issue of discrimination; because the Commerce Department and the Senate Committee on Banking, Housing and Urban Affairs have recently studied U.S. export policy in depth; and because, after protracted consideration by Congress and the Administration, the new tax law was enacted just months ago.

Section I of this report identifies statutory and regulatory provisions found to be discriminatory; Section II reviews several issues which did not reveal discrimination toward Americans living abroad. Extended time and effort were necessary to prepare the report because of the wide-ranging and complicated nature of many of the issues.

Section I.—Discriminatory Provisions

1. LOSS OF CITIZENSHIP GUARANTEES BY CHILDREN WHEN PARENTS FILE FOR FOREIGN CITIZENSHIP ABROAD

Citation of law/regulation

Immigration and Nationality Act of 1952, Section 349(a)(1) (8 U.S.C. 1460).

Explanation and evaluation of effect on Americans living abroad

The Act specifies that a United States citizen, who, while under age twenty-one acquires foreign nationality upon an application of a parent or through naturalization of the parent, will lose United States citizenship if such person fails to enter the United States to establish a permanent residence prior to his twenty-fifth birthday. Loss of citizenship, however, does not occur automatically; it can occur only when it is clear that the subject willfully failed to comply with the requirement for the express purpose of transferring or abandoning allegiance. Evidentary requirements to support a finding of intent to transfer or abandon allegiance are very high. As a result, few findings of loss of citizenship are made under this section, and these provisions no longer serve to revoke a person's citizenhip unless the citizen wishes to lose citizenship.

Recommended action

Although this provision of law is no longer viable, it still remains in force and, when applicable, must be administered. To avoid the difficulties and inequalities that the law imposes on young American citizens by requiring their return to the United States before the age of twenty-five and in view of the fact that Congress has repealed a similar proviso in Section 301 of the Act, the Justice Department will propose legislation to amend Section 349(a)(1) to provide that loss of nationality shall occur only when a citizen applies for naturalization in a foreign state on his own behalf after age twenty-one.

2. TRANSMISSION OF CITIZENSHIP TO CHILDREN BORN ABROAD

Citation of law/regulation

Immigration and Nationality Act of 1952, Section 301 (8 U.S.C. 1412).

Explanation and evaluation of effect on Americans living abroad

Section 301 of the Immigration and Nationality Act imposes limitations on the ability of United States citizen parents to transmit citizenship to children born abroad. This is particularly true in cases involving one citizen parent and an alien spouse. In such an instance, the citizen parent must have been physically present in the United States for ten years, at least five of which were after the age of fourteen. The congressional purpose in enacting these restrictions was to prevent the perpetuation of successive generations of absentee United States citizens whose ties and loyalty to the United States might be questionable. That underlying goal of the transmission of citizenship requirement is reasonable and the means chosen to attain the goal are rational.

Recommended Action

In the last session of Congress, a bill (S. 2314) was introduced which would reduce to two years the period of residence in the United States necessary to transmit United States citizenship to a child born abroad. That bill was supported by the Administration. The Administration will support a lightly revised version which is expected to be introduced in the current session of Congress.

3. APO PRIVILEGES FOR CERTAIN SCHOOLS SPONSORED BY AMERICANS ABROAD

Citation of law/regulation

Department of Defense Directive 4525.5.

Explanation and evaluation of effect on Americans living abroad

In March 1978, the Department of Defense revised DOD Directive 4525.5 to delete about seventy non-Defense Department tuition fee schools from the list of organizations authorized the use of the Military Postal Service (MPS). This change was one of several made following a number of reviews of the steadily increasing overseas mail volume which had resulted in costs rising to $78 million annually.

Because the MPS was established for the purpose of supporting the active U.S. Armed Forces deployed abroad, the Defense Department decided to delete from the list of eligible users of the system all individuals and organizations not operating in direct support of the

Defense mission. The non-Defense Department tuition fee schools were only one group among the several organizations eliminated from the list of eligible users. The Defense Department's action also reflected the views of the House Committee on Post Office and Civil Service, which has recommended "that the Department of Defense in concert with the Postal Service take the necessary action to insure that each user of the MPS will pay a fair share of the cost of maintaining the system." A significant consideration affecting the Defense decision in this matter was the fact that dependent children of military personnel and Defense Department employees in these schools frequently represent less than one percent of the total enrollment.

Remedial action taken

Although the curtailment of MPS service applied to all non-Defense tuition fee schools, the Department of Defense has agreed that these schools, having Defense Department and other U.S. Government dependents enrolled, are authorized to use the MPS for first class letter mail weighing less than sixteen ounces and containing official school correspondence, test materials, student records, etc. In addition, the Defense Department has agreed to continue to review individual requests for reinstatement of full service based upon exceptional circumstances.

4. VOCATIONAL REHABILITATION BENEFITS TO VETERANS LIVING ABROAD

Citation of law/regulation

38 U.S.C. 1502; 38 C.F.R. 21.20(c).

Explanation and evaluation of effect on Americans abroad

Current law provides that vocational rehabilitation may not be afforded outside of the United States to a veteran on account of post-World War II service, if the veteran at the time of such service was not a citizen of the United States. Additionally, Veterans Administration regulation limits the availability of vocational rehabilitation training in a foreign country, other than the Philippines, by specifying that such training may be authorized only if adequate training for the selected objective is not available in the United States or its possessions and if training is pursued under the direct supervision of a representative of the Veterans Administration.

The regulatory restriction on foreign training is based on the fact that, with few exceptions, the training needs of veterans can be met in this country, and that the Veterans Administration must be in a position to furnish assistance and monitor progress during the period of rehabilitation training. This latter restriction has essentially ruled out the possibility of foreign training because the Veterans Administration has no offices in foreign countries other than the Philippines.

Recommended loan

The Veterans Administration has recently proposed legislation which will remove the restrictions noted above and give the Administrator greater flexibility in meeting the veteran's legitimate rehabilitation needs. If those cases where vocational rehabilitation is provided outside the United States, the Veterans Administration will make arrangements through contract or otherwise for necessary training assistance and supervision.

5. SEVEN-DAY EARNINGS TESTS FOR SOCIAL SECURITY BENEFICIARIES ABROAD

Citation of law/regulation

Social Security Act, Section 203 (42 U.S.C. 403).

Explanation and evaluation of effect on Americans abroad

Americans abroad who receive retirement benefits under the social security program may have their benefits reduced if they engage in certain levels of gainful post-retirement employment. If such employment is covered under social security the reduction will be related, as it is in the United States, to the amount they earn. If retirees' employment abroad is not covered under social security (i.e., if the retirees work for a foreign government or foreign firm), for each month in which they work for seven days or more, they lose the entire month's benefit. This seven-day foreign work test was adopted to avoid the variation in benefit reduction in different countries resulting from prevailing wage rates and foreign exchange rates.

Relating the benefit reduction to a test, either of time worked or of wages earned, is a difficult problem because the retirement benefit is geared to a standard of living and a prevailing wage rate in the United States. Thus, compared to a graduated, dollar-denominated benefit reduction, the worker under the seven day test will gain in some countries and lose in others, depending upon how much he is able to earn during that period and the current cost of living in those countries.

Recommended action

A provision in the Administration's proposed 1979 amendments to the Social Security Act would change the seven-day work test to a forty-five-hour work test. The purpose of the proposed change is to allow a greater flexibility in the allocation of work during the month, so that a retiree engaged in noncovered emyloyment abroad could work up to forty-five-hours per month and still receive full benefits. The proposed change would not alter the problem of dollar-denominated vs. time-denominated benefit reductions.

6. SOCIAL SECURITY PROTECTION FOR AMERICANS ABROAD

Citation of law/regulation

Social Security Act, Section 210(a) (42 U.S.C. 410(a)).

Explanation and evaluation of effect on Americans abroad

U.S. citizens abroad who have some quarters of social security coverage earned in the United States may have difficulty in earning full coverage unless they are covered while working for foreign firms, governments and international organizations abroad. In those cases where the foreign firm is the subsidiary of a U.S. corporation, employees who are U.S. citizens may be covered under U.S. social security if the corporation agrees to pay the employer's tax, to withhold taxes from the employees, to report wages, etc., and if all U.S. employees of the subsidiary are covered. On the other hand, U.S. social security coverage is mandatory for U.S. citizens working for a U.S. corporation or business, or a self-employed U.S. citizen operating as a U.S. businessman in a foreign country, whether or not foreign social security coverage is also mandatory. Some citizens abroad recommend that participation in social security be made voluntary in such situations in which coverage is excluded or where double coverage occurs.

A basic problem with any voluntary participation scheme is adverse selection. Those persons who would volunteer to participate in social security would tend to be those who would receive the largest returns on their contributions, thereby unduly increasing the cost of the program. It would be unfair to burden those who are compulsorily covered with the increases in cost resulting from a special provision permitting voluntary coverage for Americans residing abroad. It would also be unfair to those in the United States who wish to be exempt from social security coverage.

The U.S. Government cannot compel foreign corporations, foreign governments, or international organizations to participate in the social security program or to pay the employer's share of the social security tax, nor can it compel a foreign subsidiary of a domestic corporation to pay social security contributions. Present social security law provides for "contract coverage" for the U.S. employees of a foreign subsidiary, whereby the domestic parent corporation arranges for coverage by entering into an agreement with the Secretary of the Treasury to be responsible for payment of all social security taxes on the employees' wages. In order to avoid adverse selection, the parent corporation must provide coverage for all American employees of the foreign subsidiary.

If coverage were extended to American employees of foreign corporations, foreign governments, international organizations, and foreign subsidiaries on an individual voluntary basis, there would be a question of establishing an appropriate contribution rate for them in order to avoid distorting costs to the social security trust funds. The choice would be between imposing on the employee both the employee's and the employer's tax or treating him as a self-employed individual and requiring him to pay the self-employment tax, which is approximately $1\frac{1}{2}$ times the employee tax. In either case, the individual's payments would be relatively high, thus lessening the attractiveness of voluntary participation, especially in view of the contributions he might already be required to make to the other country's system.

The inability to compel compliance by foreign employers and international organizations also means that reliance would have to be placed on the employee to comply with social security reporting requirements. Although individuals electing voluntary coverage would presumably report their earnings, there is potential for abuse.

Recommended action

The Social Security Administration believes that the problem of gaps in U.S. social security protection for American citizens working outside the United States can be remedied by totalization agreements. The 1977 amendments to the Social Security Act authorized the President to enter into these bilateral agreements to provide for limited coordination between the social security systems of the United States and other countries. Under an agreement, coverage and earnings from both countries may be combined to establish eligibility for, and entitlement to, benefits; furthermore, dual coverage and taxation for the same work is eliminated and the problem of adverse selection is avoided. A totalization agreement is already in effect between the United States and Italy; negotiations for similar agreements have been completed with West Germany, and are underway with Switzerland, Canada, Israel, and the United Kingdom. Additional agreements are contemplated; however, they do require substantial time to develop and ratify.

SECTION II.—REVIEW OF ADDITIONAL ISSUES AFFECTING AMERICANS ABROAD

CITIZENSHIP

Retention requirements for citizens born abroad

Amendment 14, section 1 of the Constitution of the United States grants citizenship status to all persons born or naturalized in the United States and subject to the jurisdiction thereof. The citizenship status of a person born or naturalized in the United States cannot be withdrawn or taken away by Congress, except that naturalization may be revoked for cause in accordance with section 340 of the Immigration and Naturalization Act. Citizenship can only be relinquished voluntarily by a citizen (*Afroyim* v. *Rusk*, 387 U.S. 253 (1967)). Article 1, Section 8 empowers the Congress to establish a uniform rule of naturalization. The Congress of the United States has established laws creating, modifying and otherwise regulating the acquisition of United States citizenship status by persons born outside the continental United States. The power of Congress to so legislate was upheld by the Supreme Court in the case of *Rogers* v. *Bellei*, 401 U.S. 815 (1971). Thus, Congress can establish laws relating to the acquisition or retention of United States citizenship for individuals born abroad as U.S. citizens.

For many years, section 301(b) of the Immigration and Nationality Act of 1952 required children born abroad of a United States citizen parent and an alien spouse to be physically present in the United States for a period of five years, later reduced to two years, between ages fourteen and twenty-eight in order to retain their United States citizenship. This requirement was repealed by Public Law 95–432, effective October 10, 1978. There are no longer any provisions of law which discriminate against citizens born abroad with respect to retention or loss of citizenship. During the hearings on the bill, Congress considered arguments for and against retroactive repeal of section 301(b), and found sufficient reasons for repealing the statute prospectively only. The arguments against retroactive repeal were grounded on difficulties, legal and administrative, inherent in restoring citizenship status to persons who have previously lost it, and in the "ripple effect" that such action would have on derivative citizenship claims, tax obligations, and social security benefits. Reconsideration of this matter has resulted in the conclusion that the Administration should not seek a revision in the recent legislation enacted by the Congress.

Loss of nationality for naturalized citizens who go abroad within five years of naturalization

Section 340(d) of the Immigration and Nationality Act states that a naturalized person who establishes a permanent residence abroad within five years of the date of naturalization is presumed to have lacked the requisite intent to reside permanently in the United States when he or she was naturalized. This presumption can be overcome by countervailing evidence.

A lawful admission to the United States for permanent residence is one of the key requirements for naturalization under sections 316 and 318 of the Act. The only exception to this rule applies to certain members of the Armed Forces or veterans who have served honorably during periods of hostility. It is clear that Congress contemplated that permanent residents who are naturalized would remain permanent residents of our country. Thus, section 340(d) sets up a presumption that one who takes up permanent residence abroad within five years of naturalization obtained the naturalization by concealing a material fact or by willful misrepresentation when he did not reveal his true intentions with respect to residence. Exceptions are accorded naturalized citizens who establish residence abroad within five years because of assignment by an American employer or because of unforeseen circumstances arising subsequent to naturalization; e.g., serious illness in the family. On the other hand, if it becomes apparent that a naturalized citizen did establish residence abroad for other than compelling reasons, revocation proceedings may be instituted by the Justice Department. Judicial procedures and rules of proof apply in such proceedings, which are rarely convened; hardly more than ten to twelve cases arise each year.

It is clear that Congress did not intend to extend naturalization benefits to those whose intention was to reside permanently abroad rather than in the United States. Limiting naturalization to those who intend to reside in the United States permanently is not discriminatory simply on the basis that a natural-born citizen does not have to have such an intent. Naturalized citizens are required to meet other requirements that are not imposed on natural born citizens, such as literacy in the English language, good moral character, and certain periods of residence and physical presence in the United States. It seems reasonable, in conferring the benefit of citizenship through naturalization, to take account of whether or not the individual seeking citizenship intends to maintain a permanent residence in this country. The five-year residence obligation is designed to gauge this intent.

Naturalization of alien spouses

Section 316 of the Immigration and Nationality Act requires five years lawful and continuous permanent residence as a prerequisite to naturalization. The five-year period of residence is reduced to three years in those instances where the alien has been married to a United States citizen spouse during that time. Section 316(b) provides that, generally, absence for a continuous period of one year or more will break the continuity of residence required.

In recognition of the fact that many United States citizen spouses are regularly assigned abroad in the course of their employment, and that these assignments are for extended periods of time, Congress enacted section 319(b) which waives the three-year residence requirement in those cases where the citizen spouse is directed abroad on a regular (as opposed to temporary) assignment of the type set forth in the statute. Under the statute, many military spouses and those married to employees of organizations or firms defined in the subsection have been naturalized early to accompany or join the employed person abroad. The statute requires such persons to declare their intention to resume permanent residence in the United States upon termination of the tour of duty abroad.

Section 319(b) attempts to define certain types of obligatory employment abroad which furthers the interests of the United States Government. It was not the intention of Congress to benefit those who choose to go abroad to run their own businesses, work for foreign employers, or for leisure purposes. If all spouses of United States citizens living abroad were entitled to immediate naturalization, discrimination would be effected against those United States citizens who choose to live in this country and whose spouses have to fulfill the three-year residence requirement provided in section 319.

Preference to certain individuals in transmission of citizenship to children

Section 301(g) of the Immigration and Nationality Act gives benefits with respect to the transmission of citizenship requirements to certain individuals, such as military personnel and government employees who may be abroad involuntarily at the direction of the United States Government, and those working for an international organization. These persons can count time spent abroad in the service of the United States Government or an international organization as a period of physical presence in the United States for purposes of transmission of citizenship. In making a distinction between persons residing abroad voluntarily and those serving abroad with the Government or an international organization, Congress was carrying out a legitimate purpose and had sound basis for its distinctions. The enactment of the legislation liberalizing the general requirements for transmission of citizenship, as cited in Section I of this report, would significantly lessen the difference in treatment between those abroad who are in the service of the U.S. Government or international organizations and other Americans living abroad.

Congressional representation for Americans abroad

A nonvoting representative in the Congress for all Americans living in foreign countries has been suggested by some. The constitutional basis for representation in the Congress for the District of Columbia, Guam and the Virgin Islands are those clauses of the Constitution granting to Congress power over the District of Columbia and the territories of the United States. To create a representative in the national legislature of individuals in areas of the world over which the United States has no sovereignty would alter the basic scheme of national representation as it presently exists.

Eligibility of persons born abroad to run for the Office of President of the United States

Article II, Section 1 of the Constitution limits eligibility of the Office of President to "natural-born citizens" of the United States.

The meaning of term "natural-born citizen" has never been definitively determined. Its meaning has been argued for years and legal authorities are divided on the issue. Because of the legal complexities inherent in this issue and the skills and judgment required to interpret relevant provisions of law, it is appropriate and advisable to look to the courts for its resolution.

EDUCATION

Education allowances for U.S. Government employees

When the Congress authorized education allowances for the dependents of U.S. Government employees abroad attending primary and secondary schools, the Congress indicated its intent that Department of Defense schools be utilized where they existed for all employee dependents and that education allowances not be paid, except in certain limited cases, if dependents are not enrolled in the available Defense schools. Some U.S. employees object to this policy and argue that it inhibits their freedom to choose appropriate schools for their children.

The choice afforded employees abroad where Defense schools exist is the same as the choice they would face at home, namely, either to utilize a publicly-supported school at no direct cost or a reimbursed cost or to pay for attendance at a private or other school not supported by the U.S. taxpayers. Education allowances are provided only in cases where there is no such choice.

Education for children of nongovernmental employees abroad

Some have proposed that the Federal Government contribute in some direct way to the education of children of all Americans living abroad, pointing out that some other governments make substantial budget expenditures for this purpose

The United States Government, under the authority of the Fulbright-Hays and Foreign Assistance Acts has for some time provided support to many American-sponsored primary and secondary schools abroad. This program is administered by the Department of State. The Congress annually appropriates funds to the State Department, the Agency for International Development, and the International Communication Agency to finance this support. As in the United States, no Federal funds (except for special cases of compensatory education for disadvantaged children) are provided for tuition grants to private schools. Such grants would raise a serious constitutional question in many cases.

Financial aid for Americans attending foreign higher education institutions

Federal aid for higher education is intended to ensure equal educational opportunity for all students. Under current law, assistance for study at foreign institutions is available only under the Guaranteed Student Loan Program. It has been suggested that Americans studying at foreign institutions should be made eligible for all HEW student financial assistance programs. If this were the case, foreign institutions would have to be willing to assume the responsibilities necessary for the administration of such programs. This appears to be unlikely because many foreign institutions resist performing even the limited functions asked of them under the Guaranteed Student Loan Program. Furthermore, it is clear that it would be difficult to ensure accountability by foreign institutions under the aid programs. The Federal Government would have no power over these institutions to ensure proper administration of program funds. Nevertheless, the matter of assistance for those attending foreign institutions is currently under review by the Department of Health, Education and Welfare as part of a more general review of all higher education programs in preparation for a proposal for the reauthorization of the Higher Education Act.

VETERANS' BENEFITS

Home loans

Chapter 37 of title 38, U.S.C. authorizes veterans home loan benefits. By regulation, the property purchased with a Veterans Administration loan must be located within the United States, its territories or possessions. The VA home loan program is intended to help eligible veterans obtain credit for homes by guaranteeing loans made by private lenders.

To effect a loan guarantee, the VA must perform certain functions in order to minimize any loss to the Federal Government. Some of these functions concern establishing reasonable values, establishing and enforcing minimum property standards, enforcing title and lien requirements, conducting foreclosure and liquidation procedures, collecting debts, and acquiring, managing, repairing, and disposing of foreclosed properties. Substantial resources would be required to develop and maintain in the VA the needed expertise in real estate and commercial law of many foreign countries in order to even minimally carry out these functions and to verify that loans to purchase property in other nations are made properly and that the Government's security in such property would be adequately protected. The use of overseas branches of American banks as loan vehicles has been considered, however, the complications associated with this alternative make it inadvisable. Some of these complications are:

Political risk.—Commercial banks are sometimes unwilling to lend overseas without a "political risk guarantee" from the Federal Government. The cost of providing such a guarantee would be substantial and would require the VA to increase its guarantee far beyond that normal for loans in the United States.

Lending restrictions.—Some countries have absolute prohibitions against U.S. lending institutions holding first liens on property. Additionally, all commercial banks have "country limits" which are set by the bank and regulatory agencies to restrict the loan amount outstanding at any one time in a particular country.

Fluctuating exchange rates.—Since VA's liability is limited by statute to a dollar amount based upon a percentage of the outstanding loan balance, it would be necessary for loans made overseas to be stated in U.S. dollars. Frequent exchange rate fluctuations make it exceedingly difficult to underwrite loans which would be valid on that basis. A veteran's income stated in U.S. dollars will also fluctuate if the veteran is paid in local currency.

Maturity limits—VA loans in the United States normally have a thirty-year term, whereas U.S. commercial banks abroad customarily limit their loan maturities to shorter periods of time. It would be very unlikely that any commercial bank would agree to offer long-term mortgage financing overseas, even with VA guaranty protection.

Direct educational benefits and loans

Educational assistance benefits for eligible veterans are payable under chapters 32 and 34 of title 38, of the United States Code. When the veteran is living abroad these benefits are provided when the program of education is at an educational institution approved as an institution of higher learning. However, the statutory definition of the term institution of higher learning [38 U.S.C. 1652(f)] does not embrace schools located in a foreign country. Rather, it refers to schools empowered by an educational authority under state law to grant a degree or, when no such law exists, schools accredited for degree programs by recognized accrediting agencies. The Veterans Administration has recently proposed to amend the existing provisions of law to allow enrollment only in a foreign school which is recognized to be comparable essentially to a fully recognized degree-granting institution by the appropriate foreign education authority, and is approved by the Administrator.

Eligible veterans training in the United States are entitled under section 1798 of title 38 to receive educational loans from the Veterans Administration in an amount up to $2,500 per ordinary school year provided economic need is demonstrated. This educational loan program has been subject to abuse as is seen in a high default rate. Furthermore, the problems encountered in attempting to collect loans from individuals living abroad are significantly more difficult than for residents in the United States. For this reason, it is not recommended that legislation be enacted to extend the educational loan program to persons training outside of the United States.

EMPLOYMENT

Unemployment compensation

Many Americans living and working abroad are covered by an unemployment compensation program which provides payments to those who become involuntarily unemployed. The Employment Security Amendments of 1970 (Public Law 91–373) provide for coverage of United States citizens who perform work outside the United States for American employers. The applicable law is generally the law of the State in which the employer's principal place of business in the United States is located. Americans employed outside the United States by the Federal Government are covered under the unemployment compensation program for Federal employees. Members of the Armed Forces are also covered by a separate program.

Claimants living in Canada are covered by an executive agreement on unemployment compensation. U.S. law applies to them with respect to covered employment in this country, and they are covered by the Canadian unemployment compensation program with respect to their employment in Canada. They may claim benefits under Canadian or U.S. laws while remaining in Canada or upon their return to the

United States. The program with Canada is unique, because the two countries are contiguous, similar systems are employed, and the volume of cases is sufficient to warrant the program and the expense of its administration.

The only Americans abroad without unemployment compensation coverage are those working for foreign employers. It is not known how many Americans are in this category or how many return to the United States as a result of having their employment terminated, but there is no evidence of a widespread need for a special purpose program to cover them. However, those living abroad who do return to the United States after being employed overseas are eligible for programs based on need, including aid to families with dependent children, supplemental security income, food stamps, etc.

With respect to extending unemployment compensation coverage to Americans working overseas for foreign firms, it must be understood that compliance controls over foreign employers outside of the United States would likely be limited, at best. It would be difficult to obtain necessary data on individuals' wage and employment histories. These data form the basis for determining if the individual had sufficient employment to qualify for benefits and the amount and duration of such benefits. Similarly, it would be difficult to obtain reliable information concerning the reasons for the claimant's separation so that benefits could be limited only to those individuals involuntarily unemployed. In cases where the employer's response differed from the claimant's contention, it would be difficult to convene a proper hearing to resolve the issue. Such problems could weaken the system's financial security. Furthermore, the dangers of adverse selection must be taken into account. Such a voluntary program would attract those who believe they are likely to need such benefits in the future, while those who do not expect to need them would be less likely to apply for coverage. The premiums necessary to keep the fund solvent could, therefore, be quite high.

Department of Defense overseas hiring

There are no restrictions imposed upon the United States by the terms of Status of Forces Agreements (SOFAs) in the hiring of United States civilian personnel to work with and for the Armed Forces (as opposed to civilian personnel to perform general labor). However, under the NATO SOFA, local civilian labor needs of the Defense Department are met through local employment exchanges. (Such civilian workers are not regarded as members of the U.S. military force or its civilian component and are thus subject to different rules.) However, the fact that local labor needs are often met by utilizing local exchanges does not mean there is a restriction on the hiring of U.S. citizens. In fact, attempts by German labor unions to have U.S. Army Europe limit its hiring of U.S. citizens in the "hired abroad" category are resisted by U.S. Army Europe and the U.S. Embassy, Bonn.

The United States has entered into several agreements for labor services at military bases abroad in which we are obligated to give preferential treatment to nationals of the host country. In Belgium, the United States has agreed to favor local nationals for positions where local labor can be utilized. There is usually a provision in these agreements that permits the United States to hire others if the particular trade or skill is not available locally. Countries where such agreements exist are the Philippines, Denmark (for Greenland), and Spain. In England and Japan the U.S. Government relies on indirect hire arrangements whereby those countries' governments recruit and hire personnel for U.S. installations. There is no preferential hire agreement as such, but those countries do control the hiring.

Apart from the Status of Forces Agreements, and where it is not prohibited by them, the Federal Government tries to give employment to dependents of U.S. military personnel and dependents of other U.S. Government personnel overseas. For a number of years, the Civil Service Commission (now the Office of Personnel Management) has granted the Defense Department an excepted hiring authority (Schedule A) for use in hiring dependents of its civilian and military personnel. This policy of giving employment to qualified family members of American employees carries out a congressional mandate and is consistent with the Government's need to recruit and retain competent staff overseas. The policy purposely favors dependents but is not aimed specifically at U.S. citizens who are not dependents.

The State Department and, to some extent, the Department of Defense are encountering increasing employee resistance to overseas assignments, because spouses of Federal employees are finding it difficult to find employment abroad. Job opportunities for foreigners in many countries abroad are limited and work permits are often hard to obtain. Language and social barriers also make it difficult for spouses and other dependents of Federal employees to find employment overseas. This situation has resulted in the Congress enacting legislation in 1977 and 1978 on the subject. In 1977 (Public Law 95–105), the Secretary of State was directed to give consideration to employing qualified family members of Federal employees in filling certain local-hire positions and to provide counselling and placement assistance overseas to spouses desiring to work. In 1978 (Public Law 95–426), Congress directed the President to seek agreements with foreign nations to facilitate employment of family members of U.S. personnel abroad, and to direct any U.S. post overseas to give consideration to converting vacant alien positions for staffing by qualified family members instead.

Restrictions on outside employment of non-appropriated fund personnel

Department of Defense regulations (DOD Directive 5500.7, "Standards of Conduct") contain the following provision:

XII. OUTSIDE EMPLOYMENT OF DOD PERSONNEL

A. DOD personnel shall not engage in outside employment or other outside activity, with or without compensation, that:
1. Interferes with, or is not compatible with, the performance of their government duties;
2. May reasonably be expected to bring discredit on the Government or the DOD Component concerned; or
3. Is otherwise inconsistent with the requirements of this Directive, including the requirements to avoid actions and situations which *reasonably can be expected to create the appearance of conflicts of interests.* [Emphasis added]

*   *   *   *   *   *   *

D. DOD personnel are encouraged to engage in teaching, lecturing and writing. However, DOD personnel shall not, either for or without compensation, engage in activities that are dependent on information obtained as a result of their Government employment, except when (a) the information has been published or is generally available to the public and the agency and gives written authorization for the use of nonpublic information on the basis that the use is in the public interest.

This regulation does not prohibit all outside employment. It applies to all employees whether paid from appropriations or from non-appropriated funds and whether the employee resides abroad or in the United States. As such it sets a reasonable policy that seeks equitably to protect the interest of the United States Government.

Life insurance sales standards

The Secretary of Defense exercises authority to take what he determines to be appropriate action to ensure the health, morale, and welfare of members of the Armed Forces. Providing for the welfare of those personnel includes prescribing appropriate protective measures where neither Federal nor State consumer protection policy govern.

Because of widespread abuses in the selling of life insurance to military personnel overseas, the Department of Defense has established controls regarding the sale of insurance on DOD installations in foreign areas. The Defense Department has determined that agent accreditation for selling insurance on military installations abroad is the responsibility of the major overseas commands. In order for an agent to be accredited for sales abroad he must possess a current state license and have at least one year of successful life insurance underwriting in the United States or its territories. A thorough check of qualifications by the overseas command is required before granting an agent a clearance to solicit for an accredited insurer. This procedure is essential to ensure the quality, training and experience of agents accredited for overseas operations.

SOCIAL SECURITY

Payment of medicare benefits for services provided outside of the United States

The Social Security Act prohibits payment for medical services or items not provided within the United States. Citizens living abroad can enroll in Medicare, but reimbursement is only provided for treatment received in the United States. Thus, care is not provided for U.S. residents or travelers in a foreign country except in a few minor cases. (Americans traveling in Canada are reimbursed for emergency hospital care provided under certain circumstances, and the cost of some foreign hospital care in border situations is reimbursed to U.S. residents. The desirability of an amendment to the Social Security Act to provide reimbursement for emergency services for U.S. citizens traveling to other countries will be reviewed by the Department of Health, Education and Welfare.) The Medicare Handbook, which is sent to all beneficiaries, contains a statement concerning the lack of coverage abroad.

There are two primary difficulties in extending Medicare services abroad: (1) determining reimbursement rates for foreign services;

and (2) ensuring compliance with Medicare standards by foreign medical personnel and facilities. With regard to reciprocal agreements with other countries, the main problem is with differences in eligibility standards between foreign health programs and the Medicare programs. These administrative difficulties are significant, but not insurmountable. A great deal of study would be required before the advisability of these programs is determined. However, the current estimated cost of full coverage for the approximately 226,000 eligibles abroad would be $375 million. In view of the need to limit Federal expenditures, this cost is a major concern.

Insulating the social security earnings test for Americans abroad from exchange date fluctuations

American social security beneficiaries in the United States, and those beneficiaries living abroad whose employment is covered under social security, may have their benefits reduced if their post-retirement annual earnings exceed certain amounts. When these earnings of Americans abroad change in response to local inflationary impact or fluctuation in exchange rates, the workers may suffer by comparison with workers in the United States. It has been suggested that the annual earnings test in foreign countries be allowed to float with reference to a neutral standard or that the original retirement benefit be indexed to the cost-of-living of the particular country.

Only a small percentage of beneficiaries abroad have their benefits reduced as a result of the earnings test. Although currency fluctuations affect the rate of exchange to local currency after the dollars have been earned, their benefits are determined on the same dollar basis as the benefits of retirees in the United States. Those who work in noncovered employment; i.e., those who work for foreign governments or firms, are not subject to an earnings test, but to a test of time worked. This group is not affected by changes in wage rates or exchange rates.

The Social Security Administration has avoided using special indices for social security benefits according to the country of residence of the beneficiary, not only because of the severe administrative problems created by special indices, but also because of the policy to maintain uniform standards within the program to the greatest extent possible. In the United States, in spite of wide variations in wage levels and cost-of-living among different areas, the standards are uniform for all areas.

TAXATION

The question of the appropriate U.S. taxation of citizens abroad was debated intensively in 1977 and 1978 by Congress. Representatives of Americans living abroad were active throughout that debate and had ample opportunity to argue their position. Many did not plead for tax exemption but urged relief for claimed added costs of living abroad.

The numerous provisions of the Internal Revenue Code and regulations pertaining to Americans living overseas do not treat those citizens unfairly compared to citizens living in the United States. The Foreign Earned Income Act enacted November 8, 1978, retains the principle that U.S. citizens have an obligation to pay U.S. income tax wherever they live, but it reduces the tax base of Americans working overseas for extended periods by allowing special deductions for added costs abroad of housing, education and general cost of living differences, plus a deduction for annual travel to the United States for each family member. If a foreign location of a citizen's domicile is a hardship post, a special deduction of up to $5,000 a year is authorized. These deductions are in addition to the standard deduction or other itemized deductions applying to all citizens. Employees required to live in camps in hardship locations may choose a $20,000 income exclusion instead of the special deductions. In addition, higher moving expense deductions are allowed and more generous rules are provided for tax free reinvestment of the capital gain on the sale of a house with respect to foreign moves.

A number of other tax issues which are of concern to Americans abroad are addressed below.

Administrative matters

The Internal Revenue Service does its best to make information and returns available to overseas taxpayers in a timely way and to provide personal assistance to the extent its budget permits.

There are five special publications of relevance to overseas Americans and one comprehensive guide exclusively for them. Widely used specialized forms are mailed to all U.S. taxpayers overseas. If a form is little used, it is too costly to mail to all Americans living abroad; however, this year the foreign bank account form and the new foreign moving expense form have been added to the mailed package. Airmail is used to transmit printed material and correspondence overseas, although, admittedly, there have been occasional instances in which the mailing of IRS material has been unduly delayed. Some Americans abroad have also criticized the short ten-day period allowed to pay income tax assessments. IRS is now reviewing this matter to see whether a longer period is warranted for some or all foreign addresses.

In addition to permanently stationing IRS personnel in key embassies overseas, IRS tax specialists visit a number of principal cities to respond to questions and to provide other assistance. In 1979 there will be more and longer visits due to the change in law in 1978. Complaints of a lack of adequate assistance have probably been due to the uncertain status of the law in the last couple of years; now that new legislation is in place, the tax forms should remain relatively unchanged from year to year.

In 1976 there were only 164,000 tax returns filed from abroad (other than from military post offices), compared to a total of 84.5 million individual income tax returns. From that perspective, the publications and personal assistance provided to overseas Americans are substantial when compared to the assistance given Americans at home.

Foreign postmarks on tax return submissions.—Foreign postmarks are accepted, provided that it is reasonable to believe that the return was filed on time. The IRS may disallow a foreign postmark if it is of doubtful validity; but, in general, it is the policy of the IRS to accept foreign postmarks.

Tax deadlines.—Taxes of U.S. taxpayers payable with the return are due generally no later than April 15 of each year. An extension of time to file the return and to pay taxes due with the return (to June 15) is granted automatically to U.S. citizens and residents living or traveling outside the United States. Taxpayers who are not abroad may receive an extension of time to file their return by submitting the appropriate forms. Taxpayers who utilize an extension of time to file their return are responsible for payment of interest on the tax due from April 15.

Estimated tax returns relating to the current taxable year are due generally on April 15. An extension of time to file the estimated tax return (to June 15) is granted automatically to U.S. citizens and residents living or traveling abroad under proposed regulations which, once final, will be effective for returns due in 1979 and thereafter. Taxpayers who utilize an extension of time to file estimated tax returns are not responsible for payment of interest accruing during the extension period.

Credit for taxes paid abroad

Foreign sales taxes have historically not been deductible for U.S. income tax purposes because of the administrative difficulties of checking on so many different systems. However, under the Foreign Earned Income Act of 1978, qualifying U.S. citizens working abroad are allowed to deduct a cost of living differential for excess living costs abroad. Foreign sales taxes, including the value added taxes (VAT), are reflected in the cost of living index.

Moreover, unlike state and local income taxes, which may only be deducted in computing taxable income for Federal income tax, income taxes imposed by political subdivisions of foreign countries may be credited against Federal income tax, reducing the tax dollar for dollar. This credit provides a significant advantage to Americans abroad who are subject to foreign income taxes. For example, in Switzerland, the total Swiss income tax burden is higher than in the United States, yet the income tax levied by the national government is insignificant. Being allowed to credit income taxes paid to the cantons is therefore a very significant benefit to U.S. citizens living in Switzerland. (In fact, it is not unusual for Swiss taxes to offset all of the U.S. tax liability of an American working in that country.)

Residents of the United Kingdom, whether living in their own home or rented quarters, pay a residency tax called "rates." Since the resident, not the owner, bears this tax, the IRS has ruled that "rates" are not real estate taxes. The Internal Revenue Code permits deducting property taxes, but not occupancy taxes.

Double taxation of U.S. source income

U.S. taxpayers residing overseas, who perform some work in the United States or who remain abroad but are in a partnership which has U.S. source income, must treat their earnings in these situations as U.S. source income. Similarly, U.S. taxpayers residing overseas may have U.S. source investment income. By virtue of residency the foreign country may also tax these earnings, avoiding double taxation either by exempting the US. source income or giving a credit for the U.S. tax on the U.S. income. If the country of residence limits its credits to an amount lower than the U.S. tax liability, double taxation of the U.S. income may result (the U.S. foreign tax credit does not apply against foreign tax on U.S. income). Where such problems of double taxation occur they can be resolved in a tax treaty. Tax treaty negotiations include consideration of this issue along with other aspects of double taxation. When a problem arises under an existing treaty, relief can be provided in a special protocol. The one case that has arisen to date came about as a result of a change in French income tax law, effective in 1979. A protocol to the U.S.-France income tax treaty was negotiated to prevent double taxation; it is now before the U.S. Senate, and once approved will be effective as of the change in French law.

Exchange rate fluctuation and taxation on the basis of U.S. dollars

When income or capital gains are reported for U.S. tax purposes, the value is expressed in U.S. dollars. Due to fluctuating exchange rates, the value of income or an asset which remains constant in foreign currency terms will vary in U.S. currency terms. In countries where the currency has strengthened relative to the dollar, a U.S. taxpayer may report a higher U.S. dollar income or inflated capital gain, even though his foreign currency income or foreign property value has remained constant.

To alleviate situations such as these, a cost of living differential deduction, which reflects variations in exchange rates, is allowed under the Foreign Earned Income Act of 1978. While exchange fluctuations work both ways, the cost of living differential rule operates only when foreign costs are higher in dollar terms and does not increase "income" when foreign costs are lower. Thus, there is no negative deduction in a low cost of living country.

Taxation of U.S. Government employees abroad

The Foreign Earned Income Act of 1978 changed the taxation of Americans employed abroad in the private sector to conform fairly closely to the taxation of Americans employed abroad by the U.S. Government. Government employees may exclude certain allowances from taxable income; private sector employees must in general treat the allowances as income but may then deduct amounts for qualifying excess foreign housing costs, education, other added living costs, home leave travel, and hardship conditions. The tax savings of an exclusion or a deduction from gross income are generally the same.

Tax-free Government allowances are more generous than the private sector deductions in some respects, such as housing costs. In other cases, such as the home leave travel and hardship deductions, the private sector treatment is more generous.

Taxation of income blocked by exchange controls

The rules which American residents abroad must observe with respect to blocked foreign income are the same rules which apply to Americans living in the United States. Blocked income can be taken into income when earned. If taxpayers elect to treat it as income in the year it becomes unblocked, it becomes analogous to receiving a lump-sum payment for services performed in a prior year. The income averaging provisions of U.S. tax law may be used to reduce the tax.

Rules regarding a nonresident alien spouse

The rules concerning joint filing status, where one spouse is a nonresident alien are the same for Americans living in the United States as they are for Americans abroad. Both spouses must be subject to U.S. tax in order to qualify for the benefits of the maximum tax on earned income. Married taxpayers who choose not to file a joint return must file as "married filing separately" rather than as single persons.

This is the so-called "marriage penalty" for which there seems to be no solution satisfactory to all. If these rules, including the prohibition against an annual option on filing a joint or separate return, were changed only for U.S. citizens abroad married to non-resident aliens, such citizens could escape tax on their share of the spouse's community income. This is not possible for U.S. citizens living in the United States who are married to non-resident aliens.

Deduction for attendance at foreign conventions

The present rules limiting deductions for expenses incurred in attending foreign conventions to two such conventions a year were introduced in 1976. The Administration considers those rules inadequate to prevent abuse and burdensome on the taxpayer in terms of reporting requirements. In January 1978, the Administration proposed new legislation in which the deduction would have depended on whether it was reasonable to hold a convention at a foreign location. One test of reasonableness was to have been whether a substantial portion of the members resided in that country. That would have alleviated the problem faced by overseas taxpayers who attend conventions in their country of residence. The Congress did not accept the Administration's proposal; no further initiative on this matter is planned by the Administration at this time in view of the recent congressional consideration.

Deductions for charitable contributions

The rules pertaining to the deductibility of charitable contributions made by a U.S. taxpayer are the same, regardless of where the taxpayer lives. To be deductible, contributions must be to an organization organized and operated exclusively for charitable purposes and the funds must be used for the same charitable purpose. The Internal Revenue Service requires charitable organizations to be acountable; there would be virtually no way it could make a foreign organization accountable and ensure that the funds are used for charitable purposes. Contributions to U.S. charities which are used abroad may be deducted; thus, while a contribution cannot be deducted if made directly to a foreign charity, deductions can be taken for amounts spent on charitable purposes in a foreign country by a U.S. charity whose books and records are available to the Internal Revenue Service.

III. SECOND PRESIDENTIAL REPORT

THE WHITE HOUSE,
Washington, January 24, 1980.

Hon. FRANK CHURCH,
Chairman, Committee on Foreign Relations,
U.S. Senate, Washington, D.C.

DEAR MR. CHAIRMAN : Section 611 of Public Law 95–426, as amended by Section 407 of Public Law 96–60, required that I transmit a report to you on Federal statutes and regulations which "treat United States citizens living abroad differently from United States citizens residing within the United States or which may cause, directly or indirectly, competitive disadvantages for Americans working abroad relative to the treatment by other major trading nations of the world of their nationals who are working outside their territory".

On August 27, 1979, I transmitted to you such a report, addressing many of the legal provisions that affect U.S. citizens residing abroad and comparing those provisions with the treatment accorded U.S. citizens residing in the United States. Modest but useful recommendations were made, and this Administration has taken steps to follow up on them, as noted at the end of the report enclosed with this message.

The additional report I am not transmitting concentrates on the taxation of Americans living abroad. It is clear to me that the phrase "competitive disadvantage" refers primarily to Federal taxation. Therefore, as I noted in my message of August 27, 1979, I asked the Secretary of the Treasury to prepare a report on this complicated subject, which, as you know, has involved the Congress and this Administration in long deliberations in recent years.

The various studies undertaken on the taxation of Americans living abroad do not yet provide clear evidence of competitive disadvantage and its impact on American economic interests. In addition, the Foreign Earned Income Act of 1978 has been in place for only one year. Consequently, the Treasury Department has not yet had a chance to submit to Congress, as required by that Act, a report on the operation of the new provisions for tax year 1979 and on the economic and revenue effects of the new law. Until some assessment is made for at least the first year's operations, I believe it prudent not to recommend changes in the law.

I believe, however, that this report will be helpful to the Congress and to the Administration in understanding the complicated and controversial area of tax policy and law. I fully intend to explore these important matters and to work with the Congress in developing any needed improvements.

Sincerely,

JIMMY CARTER.

(23)

REPORT ON EQUITABLE TAX TREATMENT OF UNITED STATES CITIZENS LIVING ABROAD

(As required by Section 407, Public Law 96–60, amending Section 611, Public Law 95–426)

EQUITABLE TREATMENT OF AMERICANS LIVING ABOARD

EQUITABLE TREATMENT OF U.S. EXPATRIATES

A report submitted to Congress in August 1979, required by section 611 of Public Law 95–426, compared the treatment of Americans living abroad to that of American citizens living in the United States.[1] A detailed review was made in the areas of citizenship, education, veterans' benefits, employment, social security, and taxation. Changes were recommended or have been undertaken to correct discriminatory aspects of the citizenship rights of children of expatriates, the use of the military postal service by certain non-Defense Department schools abroad, vocational rehabilitation benefits to veterans living abroad, and social security qualifications and coverage of Americans abroad.

Section 407 of Public Law 96–60 amended the scope of section 611 to require that the President report to the Congress those Federal statutes and regulations which treat Americans living abroad in a way that may cause them "competitive disadvantage" relative to the treatment accorded by other major trading countries to their citizens abroad. The major area where competitive disadvantages are claimed pertains to taxation, particularly the taxation of income. The United States is the only major industrialized country which taxes on the basis of citizenship. Consequently, income taxation is the focus of this report. The foreign countries whose laws are considered are Canada, France, Germany, Japan, and the United Kingdom.

U.S. EXPATRIATES

Why they live abroad

Many Americans live outside the United States for some period of their lives. The circumstances vary widely. Some U.S. citizens born abroad of American parents may never live in the United States. At the other end of the scale, many students live abroad for short periods. Two large components of the expatriate community (excluding U.S. Government civilian and military personnel) are Americans employed abroad and Americans who retire abroad. Those who work abroad include those who move abroad because that is where their work takes them, and those who choose to live abroad for other reasons and find employment there. The range of occupations is wide, as is the range of

---

[1] Report, Equitable Treatment of United States Citizens Living Abroad, August 1979

(24)

employers. They include exporters, importers, manufacturers, bankers, teachers, researchers, journalists, lawyers, doctors, engineers, storekeepers, consultants, construction workers, office workers, and entertainers, to name a few. They include employees of U.S. corporations, of affiliated foreign subsidiaries, of independent foreign corporations, of international organizations, of charitable organizations. Some are self-employed, including partners in law, accounting and other professional associations.

How many?

There is no accurate count of how many Americans live overseas other than as U.S. Government civilian or military employees. The State Department compiles estimates reported from each consular district abroad, but cautions that its figures are by no means a census. The State Department tabulation includes all U.S. citizens who register with a consular post, without regard to how long they stay in the foreign location. It also includes estimates of resident Americans who may not have registered. The number of those who do not register is estimated using such available evidence as membership in an American club, Chamber of Commerce, or other organizations available to Americans. Fluctuations, up and down, in the yearly estimates for a given country suggest that these are at best "ball park" figures. The State Department estimate as of June 1979 is 1.5 million non-government individuals, including dependents.

The 1970 Census of Population, on the other hand, reports 236,000 U.S. citizens abroad (other than U.S. Government civilians and military personnel) including dependents, but cautions that this reporting was done on a voluntary basis and is probably incomplete.

Tax return data offer a partial source of information, but they are subject to delays and do not include persons not subject to tax or who, though subject to tax, fail to report. For tax year 1976, there were 174,000 income tax returns filed by Americans abroad (including the Panama Canal Zone and Virgin Islands but not including returns filed from military post offices), representing a total of 440,000 individuals including dependents. In that year, about 140,000 taxpayers claimed the exclusion of foreign earned income under section 911 of the Internal Revenue Code. The other 34,000 may have derived various types of other income (dividends, etc.), or they may have planned to remain abroad for a shorter time than necessary to qualify under section 911. For tax year 1977, preliminary figures show a drop in the number of returns filed abroad to about 150,000. This drop presumably reflects, at least in part, the delayed filing of returns claiming section 911 benefits due to the change in law in November 1978 and the extension to February 15, 1979, of the filing deadline for most qualifying taxpayers.

There is also a large number of Americans living abroad who receive social security benefits, many of whom may not be required to file a tax return because they do not have taxable income of $750 or more (for 1979, $1,000 or more) per person for the taxpayer and dependents. It is difficult to estimate how many are in this category. The total number of social security recipients overseas is currently about 312,000, of which 125,000 to 140,000, or 40–45 percent, are estimated to be U.S. citizens. Adding this number to the number of tax returns filed from abroad would double count those social security recipients who file a tax return to report other income. On the other hand, the number of social security recipients does not take into account dependents of those recipients who do not themselves receive social security benefits and who do not file tax returns.

On the expansive assumption that there are 140,000 U.S. citizen social security recipients who have no taxable income and, therefore, should be added to the estimated 440,000 persons accounted for by tax returns from abroad, the total of non-government Americans abroad would be close to 600,000, including dependents. This is less than 40 percent of the State Department estimate. Students and persons living on investment income or inheritances may add 50,000 to 100,000 to this total, but there still is a large gap.

Some Americans abroad may fail to file tax returns. Under the tax rules applicable prior to 1978, Americans eligible to claim the exclusion of foreign earned income were exempt from tax on the first $20,000 or $25,000 of such income. Although legally obliged to file a return if their gross income before the exclusion exceeded the allowable amount of personal exemptions (whether or not there was any tax liability), persons whose income was fully excludable may not have been aware of the requirement. (Under the 1978 Foreign Earned Income Act, the exclusion is for most persons replaced by special deductoins which must be claimed on the return, which should eliminate this cause of failure to file.) Others may have had a high enough local tax that there would be no net U.S. tax after foreign tax credit, and may have concluded that a penalty was unlikely when no tax was owed. And, in general, compliance is more difficult to enforce among persons who live for prolonged periods outside the United States.

In short, it is difficult to explain the discrepancy between the data reported by the State Department and the tax return and social security data.

Where do they live?

As indicated above, there is no precise count of Americans living overseas (excluding U.S. Government civilian and military personnel and their dependents). However, by all available measures, the country with the largest population of such American citizens is Canada, which appears to account for about 15–20 percent of the total. Mexico and the United Kingdom are also major locations. The State Department and social security data show Mexico following Canada with 12–14 percent of the total. Tax return data show a considerably lower percentage of U.S. expatriates in Mexico. The United Kingdom accounts for about 7–8 percent of the total, according to State Department and tax return data. Together, Canada, Mexico and the United Kingdom account for nearly 40 percent of the total, according to State Department data, one-third of the total according to social security data, and one-fourth of the total according to (1975) tax return date. Italy and Germany also have large U.S. populations. Saudi Arabia (and formerly Iran), Australia, France, Belgium, Japan, Israel, Greece, Spain, Switzerland, Brazil and Venezuela are among other relatively large centers of U.S. expatriates, with smaller numbers spread throughout the world.

There is no unanimous view of where taxing jurisdiction should lie when income involves international transactions. The two major views are referred to as source basis taxation and residence basis taxation. Most countries use a combination of both, taxing residents or domiciliaries on their worldwide income and taxing nonresidents and non-domiciliaries on income derived from sources in that country. The United States, as previously indicated, is virtually unique in taxing income not only on the basis of both residence and source, but on the basis of citizenship as well.

Source basis taxation

Pure source basis taxation would assign the right to tax income exclusively to the country where the income arises.

Residents would be exempt from tax on all foreign source income, while nonresidents and residents alike would be taxed on income arising in the country. Pure source basis taxation is rarely practiced, but a number of income tax systems, especially of capital importing countries, do rely heavily on taxing income at the source. Argentina is an example of a country which taxes income almost exclusively on the basis of source. In such a case, source rules are very important. For example, if the country views employment income as having its source where the services are performed, it will only tax income from services performed within its territory; but if it views the source of employment income as where the payment originates, it will also tax income from employment abroad if paid for by a local person or company. The latter view is not uncommon among countries which emphasize source basis taxation.

Residence basis taxation

In contrast, pure residence basis taxation would assign the right to tax exclusively to the country of residence of the recipient. Residents would be subject to tax on their worldwide income; nonresidents would not be taxed. Source rules are important to avoid international double taxation of residents, but in addition, a definition of residence is essential. In practice, pure residence basis taxation is rarely if ever practiced. Perhaps the closest example is the Soviet Union, although it taxes on the basis of citizenship rather than residence. The Soviet Union taxes the income of Soviet citizens, including those who work abroad, and is generally willing to exempt from tax on a reciprocal basis income derived within the Soviet Union by persons who are not Soviet citizens. Most countries use both residence and source basis taxation, taxing residents on their worldwide income, and also taxing nonresidents on income having its source in that country.

Residence vs. domicile vs. citizenship

Few countries have a single precise definition of residence for tax purposes; generally a number of factors are relevant, such as the place of permanent residence or center of economic interests as well as the period of physical presence. A number of countries employ a broader concept of "domicile" to describe persons who retain ties of family or home ownership to the country or show an intent to return there even though they may spend prolonged periods abroad. The United States exercises a still broader jurisdiction in taxing nonresidents and non-domiciliaries who are U.S. citizens (and in special circumstances certain former citizens with U.S. income). It is common in such cases to provide special exemptions or deductions to residents, domiciliaries, or citizens who are employed abroad. These special rules are described in the next section.

On the other hand, some countries provide special tax relief to certain categories of residents. Japan taxes "nonpermanent residents" and the United Kingdom taxes persons "not ordinary resident" on a more limited basis than other residents. Belgium and the Netherlands provide special deductions to foreign nationals. These reliefs are not necessarily limited to persons employed in the country, but may also apply to persons receiving pensions or investment income. Diplomats are generally treated as residents of the sending country by the country to which they are assigned, even if resident in the latter for a long period.

TAXATION OF EXPATRIATES

Canada

Canada taxes nonresidents only on their Canadian source income, while residents are subject to tax on their worldwide income. The criteria for determining residence are not spelled out in the law, but may be found in court cases. The main criteria are:

time spent in the country during the tax year in question and preceding years;
why the individual was in Canada and/or absent from Canada;
whether he has a place of abode in Canada;
origin and background;
way of living;
what other ties he has to Canada.

One court case concerned a man who lived in Canada until he was 51, then left and set up a home in the United States. He subsequently purchased a home in Canada where his wife lived all year round. Although he never spent more than 150 days a year in Canada, the court held him to be a Canadian resident. Another case concerned a student at the University of Toronto who was abroad for 11 months studying languages as part of her course work. When she returned to Canada, she discontinued her studies and took an apartment in Montreal. She was held to have remained a resident of Canada during the period of her studies abroad. Other court cases have held that a person can be resident in two countries at the same time, and that at any given time, an individual has to be resident in some country. The Canadian Income Tax Act also extends the meaning of "resident" for the taxable year to Canadian diplomats, members of the Canadian Armed Forces, and individuals who "sojourned in Canada in the year for a period of, or periods the aggregate of which is, 183 days or more."

When an individual works abroad without sufficiently severing his ties to Canada to be considered a nonresident, he remains subject to Canadian tax in full, with relief from international double taxation but with no special exclusions or deductions related to overseas employment. Moreover, Canada imposes a "departure tax" on certain income, including unrealized capital gain on certain property, when a resident of Canada moves abroad.

The Canadian Government recently proposed to amend its tax treatment of expatriate employees beginning in 1980 to allow an exemption of one half of foreign earnings up to a maximum annual exemption of $50,000 for employees of taxable Canadian employers who worked in prescribed countries for more than six consecutive months on a construction, installation, agricultural, or engineering project; in oil or gas exploration and extraction; or in other prescribed activities. However, this proposal was not acted upon. It was part of the 1980 budget which included controversial fiscal measures and brought about a vote of no confidence, defeating the government.

France

France taxes individuals who are neither resident nor domiciled in France, and who do not have a residence in France, only on their French source income.

In general, France taxes individuals who have their domicile in France on their worldwide income, whether or not they reside there. Individuals are considered domiciled in France if their home or place of principal abode is there; if they perform personal services there, whether as an employee or self-employed, unless it can be shown that those services are of minor importance; or if their center of economic interests is in France.

However, France provides special tax relief to certain domiciliaries who work abroad. French nationals domiciled in France are exempt from French tax on the income for the services performed abroad if they meet one of two conditions: (1) the foreign earned income is taxed by the country of employment in an amount equal to at least two-thirds of what the French tax would be on that amount; or (2) the services are performed abroad during a period of more than 183 days in twelve consecutive months in a qualifying activity. Qualifying activities are construction or assembly projects, installation and operation of industrial plant, planning and engineering services connected with either construction or industrial operations, and exploration for and extraction of natural resources.

Domiciliaries of France working overseas for an employer based in France who do not qualify for exemption under either of these two conditions are taxable in France on the salary that would have been received in France for those services. Special allowances attributable to employment outside the country are not taxed; this same rule applies to French Government employees stationed abroad.

Although these exceptions to worldwide taxation are by statute granted only to French nationals, they are also available to nationals of countries with which France has an income tax treaty requiring nondiscriminatory treatment of foreign nationals. They are not available with respect to business or self-employment income or with respect to employment abroad by a foreign employer.

An individual who is neither resident nor domiciled in France but who has one or more residences in France, whether owned or rented, directly or through a third party, is subject to tax on a minimum French income of three times the rental value of the French residence(s). Where actual French source income is higher, the actual amount is the base for the tax. The tax rate applied is the rate applicable to dividends, currently 25 percent. This tax does not apply if the individual can show that he is subject to tax in another country on his worldwide income in an amount equal to at least two-thirds of the French tax on that amount. Nor does it apply to U.S. residents, under the terms of the U.S.-France income tax treaty.

Federal Republic of Germany

Germany taxes nonresidents only on their income from German sources, with the exception that, beginning in 1975, German citizens (and relatives belonging to their households) who are employed abroad by a German public (governmental) entity are subject to tax on their worldwide income if the country in which they reside taxes them only on income arising in that country.

German nationals who emigrate to a low tax country but retain significant commercial interests in Germany may be taxed more heavily than other nonresidents on their German source income for ten years. (The United States has a similar provision applicable to former citizens.)

In general, Germany taxes residents on their worldwide income. An individual is considered to be a resident if he has his domicile or his principal place of abode in Germany, whether or not he is physically present in Germany. Domicile is defined as the place an individual resides under circumstances leading to the conclusion that he will continue to use his residence there. A principal place of abode is where a person is located under circumstances that show more than a temporary presence. Any individual who is physically present in Germany for more than six months of the tax year is generally considered to be a resident from the beginning of the tax year.

However, a resident who is employed abroad for more than three months but not more than two years in the construction, operation or repair of plant or equipment or in exploring for or extracting natural resources is exempt from tax on the foreign earnings for those services.

Where exemption does not apply, an allowance for the overall added cost of living abroad may be excluded from the tax base. The amount excludable is fixed by the government and based on the cost of living differential allowed to government employees at the foreign location.

Japan

Japan taxes individuals who are neither resident nor domiciled in Japan only on their Japanese source income.

In general, Japan taxes individuals who maintain their domilice ("jusho") in Japan on their worldwide income, whether or not they reside in Japan. Domicile is determined on the basis of facts and circumstances which indicate that the individual intends and has taken actions to make his habitual home in Japan.

However, Japan provides special tax relief to certain residents who work abroad. When a Japanese domiciliary works outside the country as an employee, he is not taxed on special allowances paid him to compensate for higher price levels abroad or to compensate for extra costs incurred to maintain his living standard, allowances which do not put him in a more beneficial position than he would have enjoyed in Japan. This exclusion is only available where such allowances are received: it would not, for example, be applicable in the case of self-employed persons.

United Kingdom

The United Kingdom taxes nonresidents only on their U.K. source income, which includes income derived on the U.K. continental shelf.

In general, the United Kingdom taxes individuals who are domiciled or resident in the United Kingdom on their worldwide income. However, individuals who are resident but "not ordinarily resident" are only taxable on remuneration for services performed abroad for a foreign employer to the extent that the earnings are remitted to the United Kingdom. Remuneration for services performed in the United Kingdom for a foreign employer are taxed on one half of the amount net of expenses or on three-fourths if the recipient was a resident of the United Kingdom for nine of the ten preceding years. Individuals who are "ordinarily resident" are in principle taxed at the normal rates on their worldwide income, with the exceptions noted below.

"Ordinary residence" is not defined in the Tax Acts, but as interpreted by the Courts it involves the intention and evidence of habitual residence in the United Kingdom. A person can be ordinarily resident in the United Kingdom while physically absent for the entire year. Persons moving to the United Kingdom are treated as ordinarily resident as of the third year of their arrival or from the date of arrival if there is a clear intent to take up permanent residence or to remain at least three years.

An individual who is ordinarily resident in the United Kingdom and who performs personal services outside the United Kingdom as an officer or employee is exempt from U.K. tax on the remuneration for such services if the individual remains outside the United Kingdom for at least 365 days, including return visits for not more than 1/6 of the number of days from the first departure from the United Kingdom, and in any event, for not more than 62 continuous days in the 365 day period. Thus, when the individual has been absent from the United Kingdom for 60 days, he may return for 10 days, and on returning abroad may count his period of absence as 70 days. After another 20 days abroad, he would be allowed to return for 5 more days (1/6×90=15−10=5) without interrupting his period of qualification toward the 365 days. Where a person qualifying for the exemption also performs some services within the United Kingdom, the portion of compensation qualifying for the exemption as earned abroad is defined as reasonable compensation for the duties performed abroad.

Employees who do not qualify for the full exemption may deduct 25 percent of their foreign earned income if they spend at least 30 days working outside the United Kingdom during the tax year (including days off in a full work week) or have a separate employment with a nonresident firm for which they perform services wholly outside the United Kingdom (with no minimum time period).

The deduction is also available to persons ordinarily resident in the United Kingdom who carry on a trade or business abroad or who are self-employed. Such persons may deduct 25 percent of their foreign earnings if they derive income from a trade or profession carried on wholly outside the United Kingdom, or if they perform services through a nonresident partnership. Losses from a foreign business or profession (reduced by 25 percent if the 25 percent deduction applies to profits) may be offset against other foreign earned income of the same or the following year or subsequent profits of the same business or profession. Foreign losses may not reduce income from U.K. sources.

The 25 percent deduction is computed by taking 25 percent of a reasonable amount for the foreign services gross of any special overseas allowances and tax equalization payments but after other allowable business expense deductions. For persons who work both in the United Kingdom and abroad for the same employer or for related companies, the "reasonable amount" of foreign earnings is initially presumed to be that portion of the annual earnings which the days worked overseas bears to the total days worked.

United States

The United States taxes individuals who are neither residents nor citizens only on their U.S. source income. Like Germany, the United States continues for a period of 10 years to tax certain nonresident former citizens (in Germany it is former residents) on U.S. source income, defined more expansively than for other nonresidents, at the rates applicable to citizens.

In general, the United States taxes residents and nonresident citizens on their worldwide income. Residence depends on the intent and actions of the individual with respect to making his home in the United States. Relevant factors include the terms of his visa, length of stay, and ties in the community.

However, the United States provides special tax relief to certain residents and citizens who work abroad. Citizens who are bona fide residents of a foreign country for at least a full taxable year and citizens or resident aliens who are physically present outside the United States for at least 510 days in an 18 month period may deduct from the tax base certain added expenses incurred abroad for housing, education, general cost of living differentials, and home leave travel. Those in hardship areas may deduct an additional $5,000 per year. Employees living in camps in hardship areas may elect, instead of the special deductions for excess costs and hardship conditions, to exclude $20,000 of foreign earned income plus the value of the meals and lodging furnished by the employer. To qualify as a camp, the housing must be substandard and in a remote area where satisfactory housing is not available on the local market.

The deductions or exclusion are not limited to cases where the employer pays allowances. The deductions are also available to self-employed persons and persons engaged in business, on the portion of profit attributed to their labor.

SUMMARY

Bona fide foreign residents

The United States provides tax relief to Americans employed abroad who qualify under either of two categories: as bona fide foreign residents or as physically present in one or more foreign countries for a prescribed time period. Under current law, the relief is generally the same for both groups, but in the other countries reviewed here, a similar distinction results in different tax treatment.

An individual who permanently leaves his home in Canada, France, Germany, Japan or the United Kingdom, moves with his family to another country and takes up permanent residence there will not be subject to tax by his country of former residence on income derived outside its territory. The exemption is a result of abandoning residence or domicile. In contrast, for an American, comparable exemption from U.S. tax on foreign income requires giving up U.S. citizenship.

Physical presence abroad

An individual who moves from one of the above-mentioned countries but leaves his family there, retains a home there, or otherwise indicates an intention to resume residence there in the future generally does remain subject to the tax jurisdiction of his country of former residence. However, the tax imposed is typically lower than the tax applicable to residents.

The degree of relief varies. An individual who works abroad but continues to be a Canadian resident for Canadian tax purposes is taxed on the same basis as residents who are physically present in Canada. On the other hand, an individual who is "ordinarily resident" in the United Kingdom and works abroad is fully exempt from United Kingdom tax on his foreign earnings in some cases and is allowed a 25 percent deduction in other cases. France and Germany exempt from tax the foreign earnings of individuals who work abroad in selected activities, such as construction and oil exploration and extraction.

In other cases, France taxes the salary which would have been received if the individual were working in France, exempting special allowances received for overseas employment. Germany and Japan exclude from the tax base certain overseas allowances which compensate for added living costs abroad.

The United States allows special deductions for certain added living costs abroad, applicable to both bona fide foreign residents and those physically present in one or more foreign countries the requisite time. Employees living in camps in hardship areas may elect instead to exclude $20,000 of foreign earned income and the value of lodging and meals furnished by the employer. Given that such individuals typically earn more than $20,000 a year, the U.S. approach is almost always less generous than exemption; depending on the foreign living costs, it may be comparable to the approaches which exclude certain allowances or provide a flat deduction.

The different national provisions are summarized in the following chart.

CONDITIONS UNDER WHICH FOREIGN INCOME IS EXEMPT FROM TAX OR RECEIVES SPECIAL RELIEF

		Special relief limited to foreign employment income	
Country	All foreign income, complete exemption of foreign source income	Exemption of foreign employment income	Reduced taxation of foreign employment income
Canada	Nonresidents	No	No.
France	Nondomiciliaries	Sent abroad by a French employer for more than 183 days in 12 consecutive months and engaging in selected activities, or if foreign tax equals ⅔ of French tax.	Base salary only.
Germany	Nonresidents (not domiciled or usually resident).	Abroad more than 3 mo but less than 2 yr and engaging in selected activities.	A specified cost-of-living allowance is exempt.
Japan	Nondomiciliaries	No	Net of cost-of-living allowances.
United Kingdom	Nonresidents and non-domiciliaries.	If work abroad more than 365 days	Taxed on ¾ if abroad more than 30 days.
United States	Nonresident aliens	No	Deductions for certain added foreign living costs; $20,000 alternative exclusion in certain camps.

Fairness

One major goal of an income tax is equity, or fairness, in the sense of equal treatment of persons with equal incomes and in equal circumstances. But the perception of equity depends on who is being compared.

For many countries, the relevant comparison is among residents. Such countries do not tax the foreign income of nonresidents. Thus, individuals residing in the same country face the same tax rules, regardless of their nationality or domicile. Canada and the United Kingdom follow the residence criterion; but, as noted above, both extend the meaning of residence to include certain persons living abroad who maintain significant ties to the home country, and Canada imposes a tax on departing residents.

For other countries, the relevant comparison is among domiciliaries, a somewhat broader concept than residence. Japan, France, and Germany use this approach, although France and Germany exempt nonresident domiciliaries who are employed abroad in certain activities.

For the United States the relevant comparison is among citizens. Thus, a U.S. citizen residing abroad is, like a U.S. resident, subject to U.S. income tax on his worldwide income (with certain adjustments in the case of foreign earned income), rather than being taxed like a nonresident alien only on income from U.S. sources. Income taxes paid to foreign countries on foreign income may be credited against the U.S. tax on that income. As a result, a U.S. citizen whose foreign income tax liability is as high as or higher than the U.S. tax will have no net U.S. tax liability and will be in the same position as other nationals in that country. But U.S. citizens whose foreign income tax is lower than the U.S. tax will have to pay an additional tax to the United States beyond the income tax liability of other nationals in that foreign country. For Americans living abroad who tend to compare their tax burden with that of their immediate neighbors and colleagues, this situation is not perceived as equitable.

Is it fair to ask Americans living abroad where the local income tax is less than the U.S. tax to pay more than other nationals living there? The defense of citizenship basis taxation rests on the belief that U.S. citizenship confers benefits independently of residence. It is not necessary that the amount of benefit received be reflected precisely in the amount of tax charged. Income tax liability is measured by ability to pay, not, like a user charge, by the amount of services used during the tax year. But benefit is an important consideration in the scope of an income tax. Taxing the income of nonresident citizens is justifiable only if they derive significant benefit from their U.S. citizenship.

The infrequency with which U.S. citizenship is renounced suggests that it does have value even for permanent residents of other countries. At a minimum it assures the right to re-enter and remain in the United States. Many, probably most, Americans abroad are there temporarily; i.e., they retain a U.S. domicile. For them, the benefits of U.S. citizenship are more extensive. Typically, they grew up and attended school in the United States, their children may attend U.S. colleges, and they expect to return to the United States eventually. They derived benefits from U.S. Government expenditures while in the United States at a time when their income, and therefore their income tax, was generally relatively low, and they will derive benefits as residents again when they return. Moreover, even during the period of nonresidence, there is no fixed pattern of distribution of benefits. For example, the benefits of government spending on education and police and fire protection, which are derived largely by residents, are financed largely by state and local governments, which tax on a residence basis and not on the basis of citizenship; while the principal Federal expenditures, for defense and social security programs, benefit nonresident citizens as well.

It may be worth noting that changing to residence basis taxation would not be an unmitigated blessing to Americans abroad. If the practice of other countries were followed in defining residence or domicile in terms of permanent home rather than present location, most Americans employed abroad would continue to be treated as residents or domiciliaries. Special rules would be needed to exempt their foreign income. Alternatively, if residence were defined more narrowly, for example, by treating Americans absent from the United States for 17 out of 18 months as nonresidents for tax purposes, their tax on U.S. income could increase. Nonresidents are subject to U.S. tax at 30 percent of the gross amount of certain U.S. source income such as dividends, interest, and royalties. Income tax treaties generally reduce this rate reciprocally, and are in effect with most industrial countries. But there would be cases where U.S. nonresident citizens, if taxed like nonresident aliens, would incur a heavier tax than at present on their U.S. investment income.

Competition

Income tax systems frequently depart from the equity objective in specific instances to achieve other desirable goals. An income tax which provides incentives to expatriate employees, relative to other expatriates and to residents, is generally justified on the grounds of export promotion.

One consequence of taxing the foreign income of nonresident citizens is that, when those individuals live in a country where the income tax is lower than in the home country, they will have a higher tax burden than their neighbors, who are subject only to the lower host country income tax. Thus, they will either be more costly to employ or less willing to work abroad. In either case, it is argued, exports will suffer. Firms which hire the more expensive employees will lose contracts to firms using the cheaper labor, which can, accordingly, submit lower bids. Firms which hire the cheaper foreign nationals will find themselves using more foreign materials as well, as their employees will turn to suppliers in their own countries with which they are more familiar. For these reasons, some take the position that the United States should give up citizenship basis taxation, at least in the case of Americans employed abroad, in the interests of promoting U.S. exports.

Subsidiary reasons advanced for providing incentives to Americans to work abroad are that overseas employment increases the total volume of employment available to Americans and generates greater international understanding and good will. Sending Americans to work abroad expands the total employment of Americans only if there is a domestic surplus of the skills of those who go abroad to work so that they would otherwise be unemployed or would replace other domestic employees, making the latter unemployed. From time to time this may be the case in certain employments, teaching for example, but Americans working abroad have a variety of skills. Many Americans employed abroad by U.S. multinationals have supervisory skills which are not in excess supply at home. Employment of Americans abroad may or may not generate good will. It would be inaccurate to generalize. In some environments, the presence of Americans abroad has a favorable impact; in other environments, the impact may be negative. In any event, there is no evidence that American employees abroad have an advantage in this respect over Americans abroad in other capacities, as permanent residents, invited visitors, or travellers.

Thus, the principal argument for tax exemption of Americans employed abroad is export promotion. Given that objective, exempting from tax the foreign earnings of Americans employed abroad is one possible policy tool, which should be evaluated and compared with other possible alternative measures.

A case where the impact of present U.S. tax policy on exports could be significant is in labor intensive industries operating in low tax jurisdictions. One such example is the construction industry in Saudi Arabia (where foreign employees are not subject to any local income tax). In such cases, the added U.S. tax cost could increase the total cost of the project by an important margin. If equally competent foreign nationals can be hired without the added tax cost, they will tend to replace Americans in such situations. And if foreign suppliers can produce goods of equal quality at no higher price than U.S. firms, the employment of foreign nationals will reduce U.S. exports as the foreign nations direct orders to the firms they know best. This type of situation gave rise to a special relief provision in the U.S. Foreign Earned Income Act of 1978. The provision of section 911, as amended, which allows employees living in camps in hardship areas to exclude $20,000 of foreign earnings, plus the value of lodging and meals furnished by the employer, was intended to benefit the construction industry abroad, especially in the high cost, low tax Middle East. Unusual hardship was also an important factor in enacting this provision. Similar concern is reflected in the provisions of French and German law exempting employees engaged in construction work abroad.

But it is not clear how prevalent this type of situation is, or what its impact is in terms of overall exports (even assuming no offsetting changes such as exchange rate adjustments). Americans employed abroad engage in many activities, some of which may be entirely export related and others of which may have no connection with exports. For those in export activities, the added U.S. tax cost may cause a significant increase in the export price or it may have an insignificant effect. And the employment of foreign nationals rather than Americans will divert demand to foreign rather than U.S. suppliers (and conversely, the employment of Americans will result in orders to U.S. suppliers) only if the foreign and U.S. equipment are very good substitutes in terms of both quality and price. A competent engineer or purchasing agent will not write specifications or place orders for inferior supplies or be ignorant of differences in quality.

One approach to evaluating tax exemption of some or all expatriate American employees as an export incentive would be to gather more information on the export impact of Americans employed abroad; for example: precisely how many Americans are employed abroad; what they do; in which countries their local income tax is below their U.S. tax; how much the added U.S. tax increases the export price; and how much exports would be likely to increase if there were no U.S. tax. A related consideration is the significance of the non-tax costs of hiring Americans; how would the cost of hiring Americans compare to the cost of hiring third country nationals if there were no U.S. tax on foreign earnings? Other aspects to be considered include the effects of such other U.S. rules as the anti-boycott and anti-bribery regulations. Is the availability of credit and insurance a constraint on U.S. exports? How effective are the marketing efforts of the U.S. firms themselves? Gathering the necessary data and disentangling these various strands would be a complicated assignment. It is further complicated by the fact that the new rules of income tax treatment of Americans working abroad introduced by the Foreign Earned Income Act of 1978 were fully effective for the first time in 1979.

A more limited approach would be to identify activities which can be shown to be export sensitive and to devise selective incentives for the targeted areas. As indicated earlier, construction appears to be the primary area of concern. Even in such cases, however, further tax relief should be compared with direct spending alternatives. (One obvious drawback to the use of tax relief is that it entrusts to the Internal Revenue Service decisions which are outside its area of expertise. For example, the special "camp" provision of section 911 of the Internal Revenue Code as amended by the Foreign Earned Income Act of 1978, requires the Internal Revenue Service to administer a program of aid to the overseas construction industry, a field in which the Commerce Department, not the IRS, has expertise.)

The studies done to date on the issue of Americans employed abroad do not permit conclusive policy judgments on what changes, if any, would most effectively encourage exports.[1] Moreover, they all predate

---

[1] In February 1978, the Treasury Department published a report "Taxation of Americans Working Overseas: Revenue Aspects of Recent Legislative Changes and Proposals" which analyzed the 1975 tax returns filed by Americans claiming the foreign earned income exclusion under section 911 and compared the effect by income level and geographic area of various alternative tax rules.

Also in February 1978, the General Accounting Office published "The Impact on Trade of Changes in Taxation of U.S. Citizens Employed Overseas," which included both the results of interviews with affected taxpayers and employers and of an econometric study using a model of Data Resources, Inc. (DRI). The DRI model indicated that repeal of the relief for Americans employed abroad would increase the value of U.S. exports because the drop in demand would fail to offset the increase in price. The methodology of this model has been widely criticized.

In April 1978, the Congressional Research Service of the Library of Congress issued "U.S. Taxation of Citizens Working in Other Countries; An Economic Analysis" by Jane G. Gravelle and Donald W Kiefer (Report 78-91E) which evaluated section 911 and various alternative proposals on the basis of tax neutrality, equity and national economic goals. The study found that tax incentives to Americans to work abroad appear to occur at the expense of other Americans and that the impact on exports is indirect, temporary and small.

In August 1978, the Commerce Department issued, "U.S Policy Toward the Taxation of Foreign Earnings of U.S. Citizens," by Dr. Roy Blough, which reviews the various policy considerations and concludes that incentives to meet competition by third country nationals can be justified as analogous to "anti-dumping" measures, but that relief for hardship conditions is not justified on competitive grounds and too difficult to measure to adjust for on equity grounds.

In October 1978, the Treasury Department issued "The American Presence Abroad and U.S. Exports" by Professor John Mutti, which attempts to quantify the "buy American" factor of the presence of U.S. nationals abroad and tentatively concludes that such presence does have a significant impact on exports. The author cautions that his results are preliminary, and do not directly address the tax factor.

the Foreign Earned Income Act of 1978. That law requires the Treasury Department to report to Congress on the operation of the new provisions, beginning with the tax returns filed for 1979 and at two year intervals thereafter. The report will seek to identify, to the extent the data permit, the economic effects as well as the revenue cost of the new provisions.

A Task Force of the Subcommittee on Export Expansion of The President's Export Council issued a report on December 5, 1979, which makes three recommendations on the taxation of expatriate Americans:

(1) Regulations and interpretations in force under the current tax law concerning Americans living in camps in hardship areas (Section 911) should be simplified and made less restrictive, in keeping with the intent of Congress.

(2) The current tax law concerning allowances to employees for excess living costs incurred while working abroad (Section 913) should be interpreted in the least restrictive and simplest manner.

(3) Work should begin immediately to encourage enactment of a new tax law to put Americans working overseas on the same tax footing as citizens from competing industrial nations.

The first recommendation is well taken. The proposed regulations were too restrictive. The temporary regulations issued on December 31, 1979, are substantially less restrictive and are believed to accurately reflect the intent of Congress in directing special relief to this situation.

The second recommendation is also being followed. The law is complex and highly detailed in this area, so the regulations have little flexibility. But the comments received are being carefully considered in preparing the revised regulations. And improvements have already been made in the cost of living calculations.

The third recommendation, that Americans working overseas be taxed more lightly, if at all, is expressed in general terms. It assumes that tax exemption would reduce U.S. export prices, prompting an increase in demand sufficient to make a significant increase in the value of U.S. exports. As noted above, the evidence to date does not support this assumption. Any such proposal should be compared with other tax or non-tax measures in terms of likely effectiveness and relative simplicity. Most U.S. export activity takes place in the United States, so measures to reduce domestic taxes or costs of production may be more effective and preferred by exporters. Non-tax measures have administrative advantages. Selective tax exemption for certain overseas earnings may be beneficial to exports if targeted to be cost effective, but the impact may not be large enough to appreciably improve the overall U.S. export position.

SOME RELEVANT DOCUMENTS

Canada: Income Tax Act, Sections 114 and 212, and Regulation Section 105. *Canadian Tax Reporter*, published in the United States by Commerce Clearing House; A. B. McKie, "Canadian Tax Commentary: A Question of Residence," *The Tax Executive* Vol. XXVII, No. 3, April 1975, pp. 263–274. (Published in Washington, D.C. by the Tax Executive Institute).

France: Law 76–1234 of December 29, 1976 (Journal Officiel of December 30, 1976).

Germany: Income Tax Law, Section 6, paragraphs 34 and 50; U.K. Board of Inland Revenue, "Taxes Outside the United Kingdom," published in the United States by Commerce Clearing House.

Japan: Income Tax Law, Article 9(1)(vii); "An outline of Japanese Taxes, 1979."

United Kingdom: Finance Act of 1977, Schedule 7; Inland Revenue publications 20 and 25.

United States: Internal Revenue Code sections 911 and 913; Internal Revenue Service publication 54.

See also the studies cited in footnote 1, pp. 20 and 21.

ACTIONS UNDERTAKEN ON RECOMMENDATIONS SET OUT IN THE PRESIDENT'S REPORT TO THE CONGRESS OF AUGUST 27, 1979—EQUITABLE TREATMENT OF UNITED STATES CITIZENS LIVING ABROAD

1. Loss of citizenship guarantees by children when parents file for foreign citizenship abroad

The August 1979 report recommended a change in Section 349 of the Immigration and Nationality Act which now provides that a citizen, who, while under the age of 21, acquires foreign nationality upon an application of a parent or through naturalization, will lose United States citizenship if he or she fails to enter the United States to establish a permanent residence prior to age 25.

The Justice Department will reiterate its support of a change in Section 349 which would provide that loss of nationality shall occur only when a citizen applies for naturalization in a foreign nation on his own behalf after the age of 21. The Department will work with the Congress toward enactment of this provision in the current session of the Congress.

2. Transmission of citizenship to children born abroad

The August 1979 report recommended a change in Section 301 of the Immigration and Nationality Act which now limits the ability of citizens to transmit citizenship to children born abroad by, among other things, stipulating that a citizen parent must have been physically present in the United States for ten years for his or her child to receive United States citizenship.

The Justice Department will reiterate to the Congress its support of legislation reducing the requirement for the parent of physical presence in the United States to two years. The Department will work with the Congress toward enactment of this provision during the current session of Congress.

3. Military Postal Service (MPS) privileges for certain schools sponsored by Americans abroad

The August report recommended the services of the MPS be provided American sponsored schools having dependents of military and civilian employees of the United States.

The Departments of State and Defense have notified all United States diplomatic missions that American sponsored schools having dependents of United States Government employees enrolled are authorized to use the MPS for first class mail weighing less than sixteen ounces and containing official school correspondence, test materials, student records, etc. In addition, such schools can seek full MPS service upon exceptional circumstances.

4. Vocational rehabilitation benefits to veterans living abroad

The August 1979 report pointed out that the Administration had proposed legislation to remove certain limiting provisions of current law which inhibit veterans from obtaining vocational rehabilitation traning abroad. The House of Representatives has favorably acted on the matter in H.R. 5288 and the Senate will soon consider the Administration's proposal in S. 1188.

The Veterans Administration intends to work with the Congress toward enactment of these bills during the current session of the Congress.

5. Seven-day earnings tests for social security beneficiaries abroad

The August 1979 report pointed out that the Administration had proposed legislation to change the seven-day a month post-retirement work test to a 45-hour work test is being sought from the Congress as part of the Administration's proposed Social Security Amendments of 1979. The change in law would permit beneficiaries engaged in non-covered employment outside the United States to work up to 45 hours a month without having their benefits reduced.

The Department of Health and Human Services will actively seek enactment of this change in law during the current session of the Congress.

6. Social security protection for Americans abroad

The August 1979 report recommended that international bilateral agreements (called "totalization agreements") be entered into with foreign countries so that gaps in U.S. social security protection for American citizens working outside the United States may be remedied. Under these agreements, coverage and earnings of nationals of both countries may be combined to establish benefit eligibility, and increase benefit amounts, while dual coverage and taxation of the same work (which now occurs frequently) is eliminated.

Agreements with Italy and the Federal Republic of Germany are in effect and an agreement with Switzerland will be submitted to Congress in early 1980. Discussions with Canada, Belgium, Denmark, Finland, France, Iceland, Israel, Japan, Spain, Sweden and the United Kingdom are underway, and initiation of discussions with other countries is being considered.

APPENDIX A

THE
PRESIDENT'S EXPORT COUNCIL

SUBCOMMITTEE ON
EXPORT EXPANSION

DECEMBER 5, 1979

REPORT OF THE TASK FORCE TO STUDY
THE TAX TREATMENT OF AMERICANS WORKING OVERSEAS

THE PRESIDENT'S EXPORT COUNCIL
WASHINGTON D C 20230

December 10, 1979

The President
The White House
Washington, D. C.

Dear Mr. President:

The Executive Committee of the President's Export Council has
asked me to express to you its strong concern over the adverse effects
on exports of the present rules (Sections 911 and 913) concerning taxation of foreign earned income of Americans living overseas.

The Foreign Earned Income Act of 1978 has done little to alleviate
the problems of differences in tax treatment between American citizens
working overseas and their counterparts from competing industrial nations.
The result has been that third-country nationals, who generally do not
have the burden of paying taxes in their home countries on their foreign
earned income, are employed instead of American citizens. This has
brought about a sharp loss in the U. S. share of overseas business volume
in vital economic sectors, largely because third party nationals tend to
specify equipment manufactured in their home country, whereas American
citizens would specify and order U. S. equipment with which they are
most familiar.

A particularly disturbing example is the decline in the position of
American contractors on projects in the Mid-East. According to McGraw-
Hill, U. S. companies had contracted for $8.9 billion or 10.3% of the total
contracts let in the Mid-East from June 1975 through April 1978. During the
13 months ending in June 1979, U. S. contractors received only $346 million
or 1.6% of the total contracts awarded. The loss of U. S. jobs both overseas
and at home to foreign competitors, and the accompanying loss of U. S. exports
comes at a time when it is crucial to maintain U. S. prestige and presence
overseas and a firm emphasis on increasing our share of the world market.

43

The President   - 2 -   December 10, 1979

The President's Export Council appointed a task force to study this problem. The following administrative recommendations, aimed at putting Americans who work in the private sector overseas on a more comparable tax footing with citizens of competing industrial nations, are adapted from this report.

- Regulations and interpretations in force under the current tax law concerning Americans living in camps in hardship areas (Section 911) should be simplified and made less restrictive, in keeping with the intent of Congress.

- The current tax law concerning allowances to employees for excess living costs incurred while working abroad (Section 913) should be interpreted in the least restrictive and simplest manner.

We have discussed these recommendations with Secretary Miller and would appreciate your endorsement of them.

The final task force recommendation is that work begin immediately to encourage enactment of new tax provisions directed to this problem. We have called upon a broad spectrum of the American export sector for comments on specific legislative points which would relieve the burden under which they now operate, and would be in the national interest.

I am sure it was not the Administration's intent, or that of Congress to discourage the employment of Americans by U. S. business overseas. The tax law must be one that enables Americans to face the uncertainties of life abroad and serve as the leading edge of the export growth that is necessary if we are to maintain the leading economic role for the U. S. in today's world that is so essential to our welfare.

Respectfully yours,

Reginald H. Jones
Chairman

THE PRESIDENT'S EXPORT COUNCIL
SUBCOMMITTEE ON EXPORT EXPANSION

Task Force to Study the Tax Treatment
of Americans Working Overseas

I. THE SITUATION

Despite the enactment of the Foreign Earned Income Act of 1978, Americans are still being taxed out of competition in overseas markets The result is a sharp loss in the United States' share of overseas business volume in vital economic sectors The current situation contributes to our negative balance of payments, a loss of U S jobs to our competitors, and the decline in U S presence and prestige abroad

II. TASK FORCE RECOMMENDATIONS

Americans working overseas are essential to a viable export program An increase in the number of Americans assigned abroad can increase our exports, reduce the negative balance of payments, enhance our country's image, and raise employment in the U S

Recognizing that it is in the best interest of our nation to encourage Americans to work overseas, the Task Force recommends the adoption of tax policies that are comparable to those of major competing industrial nations, none of which now tax citizens who meet overseas residency tests We urge the development and enactment of new legislation to put Americans who work in the private sector overseas on the same tax footing as citizens of competing industrial nations In the interim, the following remedial actions should be taken

1 Regulations and interpretations in force under the current tax law concerning Americans living in camps in hardship areas (Section 911) should be simplified and made less restrictive, in keeping with the intent of Congress.

2 The current tax law concerning allowances to employees for excess living costs incurred while working abroad (Section 913) should be interpreted in the least restrictive and simplest manner

3 Work should begin immediately to encourage enactment of a new tax law to put Americans working overseas on the same tax footing as citizens from competing industrial nations

III. BACKGROUND

Foreign Trade Encouraged

Beginning in the 1920's, after the U S emerged from World War I as a major exporting nation, the income earned by Americans at work in foreign countries was virtually exempt or excluded from U S taxes, as a matter of public policy and by specific acts of Congress The purpose was to encourage foreign trade It was recognized that the export of U S goods and services depended, in large measure, on the presence of Americans in overseas markets.

The U.S tax policy was not unique. All of our trading partners, and certainly all of the world's major producing nations, had long excluded income earned by citizens at work overseas from taxation

In the early 1950's some revisions were made in the tax treatment of U S. citizens working overseas The principal aim was to halt abuses by highly paid movie stars These revisions altered foreign residency tests and placed a ceiling on the amount of foreign-earned income that could be excluded The income and allowances of most Americans working overseas was below the $20,000 limit, so they were not affected They were not meant to be

Additional technical adjustments were made during the 1960's in foreign residency tests and in the sums that could be excluded By the mid-1970's, the effects of inflation — rising living costs and rising salaries and benefits for overseas American workers — had overtaken the amount of foreign-earned income that could be excluded from U S taxes

Policy Shifts in 1976

Responding to misguided arguments that Americans overseas were being granted preferential tax treatment, Congress in 1976 reduced the exclusion to $15,000 and changed the manner in which it was computed so its maximum practical effect became about $3,000 The philosophy behind these provisions was directly contrary to the principles which had guided the United States' tax treatment of overseas Americans for more than 50 years Instead of encouraging Americans to work overseas, the 1976 amendments actually discouraged such employment In fact, even before the 1976 amendments, it was becoming less attractive to work overseas Inflation was running at between 50 percent and 300 percent higher than domestic inflation, a fact that should have been recognized by increasing the $20,000 exclusion rather than decreasing it

Further, the Tax Court ruled in 1976 that employer furnished housing was taxable to employees at full local rental value, rather than the value of similar housing in the United States These rulings were interpreted as a strong indication that employer contributions to offset extraordinary overseas living expenses — or so-called "keep whole" contributions — were taxable to overseas employees, whereas such amounts often may have gone unreported up to that time

These rulings, when combined with the 1976 tax code revisions, produced effects that Congress and the Tax Court did not foresee For example, in the oil-rich Middle East, the costs to an employer of maintaining an American worker at something approximating the standard of living he or she would have enjoyed at home could exceed the actual salary paid to that worker by three or four times As a result, some Americans overseas became liable for more taxes than they received in real income

The 1976 tax policy shifts on foreign-earned income actually amounted to a substantial tariff on our own goods and services by our own government

Foreign Earned Income Act of 1978

After belatedly postponing the effective date of the tax code revisions, Congress moved in 1978 to remedy the devastating mistakes of 1976 with the Foreign Earned Income Act Unfortunately, the 1978 Act is inadequate The House of Representatives had passed a realistic bill, but the law that was eventually enacted represents a compromise with a more restrictive Senate version Section 911 of the Act provides a $20,000 exclusion for overseas Americans living in qualified camps in remote hardship areas Section 913 provides deductions for certain allowances for extraordinary overseas living expenses under fairly strict qualifications Both Sections 911 and 913 are very complex Moreover, regulations drafted by the Internal Revenue Service under the new law effectively reverse the intent of Congress by compounding the complexities beyond reason

Even if the Foreign Earned Income Act of 1978 is interpreted in the least restrictive way possible, it is clear that overseas Americans are not currently competitive with citizens of other nations in terms of taxes

IV. RATIONALE FOR RECOMMENDATIONS

Americans at work overseas direct business to our domestic economy If we are to increase exports in order to bring our trade accounts into balance, we must encourage more U S citizens to accept assignments with American business overseas Concurrently, we must continue to be sensitive to the geo-political ramifications of having more Americans working abroad Overseas employees of American business are seen as representatives of our country Through their participation and visibility in international business affairs, they can function as goodwill ambassadors whose work exemplifies America's ideals and values

To achieve these benefits will require, among other things, that current tax laws bearing on foreign-earned income be changed At present, our nation's tax policies discourage the employment of Americans overseas Many American companies doing business overseas, especially in the manpower-intensive service industries, are sending American employees home in order to keep some vestige of market share For example

- Recruiting firms in France, Germany, Italy and the United Kingdom report they are swamped with requests for qualified citizens of their respective countries to replace Americans who are being forced home by U S tax policies

- Several leading U S contractors in the Middle East have reduced their American staffs by more than half, and adopted hiring policies overseas that specifically exclude Americans on future work

- The University of Petroleum and Minerals in Saudi Arabia says Americans now make up less than 30 percent of its teaching staff, compared to more than 80 percent several years ago

Replacing American employees with citizens of other countries is the only way American companies can remain competitive This means that as U S companies operating overseas ''de-Americanize,'' sales of goods and services move away from this country and toward the competing industrial nations

- A report by the Government Accounting Office suggested that the impact of current U S tax policies for overseas Americans might be very significant — with a reduction of 5% or more of total exports or a loss in overseas sales of at least $6 to $7 billion, based on available data And the GAO report cautioned that its projections might well prove conservative [1]

---

[1] Impact on Trade of Changes in Taxation of U S Citizens Employed Overseas, Report to the Congress, Comptroller General, February 21, 1978, page 10

- The Commercial Counselor of the Embassy of Saudi Arabia recently observed

"U S tax treatment of American companies doing business in foreign countries makes them less competitive *vis a vis* European and Japanese (and other) companies, which receive better tax treatment from their governments In the case of Saudi Arabia, it is noticed that American companies, in order to overcome the higher costs resulting from the unfavorable tax treatment, have tended to hire non-American engineers and other skilled personnel Naturally, these prefer equipment and specifications originating in their countries (European or Japanese, etc), which represent a loss in American exports to Saudi Arabia Thus, the end result of U S tax treatment of American personnel working abroad has been a net loss of American sales abroad ''

That means a loss of jobs in our economy Estimates vary Using the low end of the Department of Commerce estimate that for every $1 billion in new economic activity between 40,000 and 70,000 jobs are created, a loss of 5% of our current overseas export volume — or about $7 billion in economic activity — would produce a job loss of 280,000 Using the same Department of Commerce figures, if the U S decided on policies to increase exports by at least $30 billion annually as a means of bringing the trade accounts into balance, at least 1 2 million new jobs would result

If we increase our nation's exports we will increase job opportunities for Americans at home and abroad In order to achieve such improvement, we must re-assess our tax policies We also must write new tax laws directed at placing Americans on a competitive footing with other nationals in overseas markets (See Chart Below)

V. CONCLUSION

The principle underlying the taxation of Americans working in other countries should be to encourage, rather than discourage, employment with U S business overseas The implementation of this principle through changes to the Internal Revenue Code will increase the number of U S. citizens who are willing to work overseas, resulting in an increase in American exports.

Respectfully submitted,

Robert Dickey III
John Wood Brooks
D.L Commons
Maurice Sonnenberg

Comparison of Tax Policies for Overseas Employees

	Tax on Salary	Tax on Incentives, Bonuses	Tax on Benefits (Retirement, Health, Insurance Etc.)	Tax on Cost of Living Allowances	Tax on Additional Income Earned Out of Home Country	Notes	Government Subsidies (to Individuals)
United States	Yes[1]	Yes	Yes	Yes[2]	Yes	[1]20,000 exclusion under Section 911 for those in qualified camps [2]Certain deductions permitted under complex Section 913 tests	No
Japan	No	No	No	No	No[1]	[1]Rental, interest, etc. on off-shore investments totally exempt from taxation during non-residence status only	Yes
Italy	No[1]	No	No	No[2]	Complex formulas to discourage foreign investments	[1]Complex non-residency requirements [2]Limitation placed on daily expenses for home leave and R&R	Government owned companies
France	No[1,2]	No	No	No	Complex formulas	[1]Assumes accompanied tour rules for dual residency—unaccompanied—very complex [2]Recent government policy aimed to encourage more French engineers to accept overseas work	Government owned companies
Korea	No	No	No	No	No	[1]Most liberal policies with respect to individuals — Korea committed to exports of domestic unemployment	Yes
Germany	No[1]	No[2]	No	No[3]	Some limitations Generally liberal	[1]Complex non-residency requirements aimed at tours of less than 6 months [2]Complex definitions [3]Some limitations designed to reduce excesses	Few
Canada	No[1]	No	No	No	No	[1]Accompanied tour only. If family of head of household remains in Canada all worldwide earnings subject to full taxation	No
	No	No	No	No	No	[1]Recently liberalized tax policies in order to encourage acceptance of overseas assignments	Few
United Kingdom	No	No[1]	No[2]	No	Complex requirements	[1]U.K. recently liberalized tax policies in order to encourage. [2]Some limitations.	Few

Compiled from data provided by Worldwide Consultants S.A., a multiple-source firm, 1979.

49

PRESIDENT'S EXPORT COUNCIL
EXECUTIVE COMMITTEE

CHAIRMAN

Reginald H Jones
Board Chairman and Chief
   Executive Officer
General Electric Company

VICE CHAIRMAN

Paul Hall
President of Seafarers Internation
   Union of North America

MEMBERS

Honorable Bill Alexander
Member of Congress

Morris M Bryan, Jr
President
Jefferson Mills

George D Busbee
Governor of Georgia

Harry E Gould, Jr
Board Chairman and Chief
   Executive Officer
Gould Paper Company

Honorable Jacob Javits
Member of Congress

J Paul Lyet
Board Chairman
Sperry Rand Corporation

Ms Herta Lande Seidman
Deputy Commissioner
New York State Department of
   Commerce

Honorable Adlai E Stevenson
Member of Congress

C William Verity, Jr
Board Chairman and Chief Exect
   Officer
Armco, Inc

PRESIDENT'S EXPORT COUNCIL
SUBCOMMITTEE ON EXPORT EXPANSION

CHAIRMAN

Mr Harry E Gould, Jr
Chairman of the Board
Gould Paper Corporation

MEMBERS

Honorable Bill Alexander
Member of Congress

Honorable C Fred Bergsten
Assistant Secretary for
International Affairs
U S Department of Treasury

John Wood Brooks
Board Chairman
Celanese Corporation

D L Commons
Chief Executive Officer
Natomas Company

Robert Dickey III
Chairman and President
Dravo Corporation

Honorable Thomas S Foley
Member of Congress

Honorable Kenneth Allen Gibson
Mayor of the City of Newark

Honorable John D Greenwald
Deputy General Counsel
Office of the Special Representative
for Trade Negotiations

Dr Kelly N Harrison
General Sales Manager
Office of GSM
U S Department of Agriculture

Ernest B Johnston, Jr
Deputy Assistant Secretary
for International Trade Policy
U S Department of State

Honorable Stanley Marcus
Acting Assistant Secretary for
Industry and Trade
U S Department of Commerce

Ms Joyce Dannen Miller
Vice President
Amalgamated Clothing and
Textile Workers Union

Honorable John L Moore, Jr
President and Chairman
Export-Import Bank of the
United States

Honorable Howard D Samuel
Deputy Under Secretary for
International Affairs
U S Department of Labor

Ms Ruth Schueler
President
Schueler and Company, Inc

Ms Herta Lande Seidman
Deputy Commissioner
New York State Department of
Commerce

Maurice Sonnenberg
Investment Consultant

Honorable Adlai E Stevenson
U S Senator

EX OFFICIO MEMBERS

Mr Reginald H Jones
Chairman of the President's Export
Council
Chairman of the Board
General Electric Company

Mr Paul Hall
Vice Chairman of the PEC
President, Seafarers Internationa
Union of North America

APPENDIX B

REPORT SUBMITTED BY AMERICAN CITIZENS ABROAD: "LAWS AND REGULATIONS OF THE UNITED STATES THAT DISCRIMINATE AGAINST AMERICAN CITIZENS LIVING ABROAD, OR THAT MAKE OVERSEAS AMERICANS NONCOMPETITIVE IN THE MARKETS OF THE WORLD"

AMERICAN CITIZENS ABROAD,
Switzerland, December 3, 1979.

Mr. JIMMY CARTER,
President of the United States,
The White House,
Washington, D.C.

DEAR MR. PRESIDENT: Nearly a year ago, on December 18th, 1978, ACA prepared and sent to you a report identifying fifty issues that we felt needed to be addressed in your report to the Congress on discriminatory American laws and regulations that affect Americans living overseas. We were most pleased that your staff found our report of use, and that you took the trouble to acknowledge ACA's role in helping you prepare the report that you submitted to the Congress on August 27th, 1979.

Earlier this year the Congress asked that you prepare an expanded version of the same report. This time the Congress asked that you address not only how our laws may be discriminating against our citizens abroad, but also the equally vital question of how our laws may be impeding the ability of American citizens to compete in the major markets of the world.

ACA has prepared a new report covering both of these perspectives on the overseas American situation. We are most pleased to send this new report to you with this letter, and we hope that you and your staff will find this report as useful as the first one.

We earnestly hope that in your new report you will not only address the specific issues that are raised, but that you will also lead us and the Congress toward more felicitous treatment of overseas Americans so that all Americans can better prosper. This will very much depend upon your willingness to address two fundamental questions. First, what basic guarantees do overseas Americans have concerning their retention of obligations, rights and benefits when they are resident outside of the United States. Secondly, what guarantees do overseas Americans have that American laws and regulations will not put them at a competitive disadvantage, with respect to citizens of other nationalities living outside of their country of citizenship.

We thank you for being willing to address these two critical questions of basic American policy because we are convinced that once they are addressed good speed will be evidenced in bringing the myriad individual issues into a proper conformity with these basic policy positions.

We wish to renew our offer to serve you and your staff in any appropriate manner to help in the preparation of your new report. We await your call.

Our kindest regards and thanks for your most kind consideration.

Most sincerely,

JOHN IGLEHART.
DON V. W. PERSON.
FRANCIS PRIBULA.
LARRY R. KOHLER.
ANDY SUNDBERG.

INDEX OF ISSUES IN THE ACA REPORT TO THE PRESIDENT AND OF THE RESPONSE OF THE PRESIDENT IN HIS REPORT TO THE CONGRESS

¹ Not addressed

² Not addressed yet.

Annex ACA's first report of Dec. 18, 1978, as reprinted in the Congressional Record of the Senate, Jan. 23, 1979.

PREFACE

The oil crisis of 1974 was a major turning point in the history of the Free World. The sudden, brutal, increase in the price of petroleum which began then has been followed by successive price increases whose end is nowhere in sight.

Overnight, the international economic order was abruptly changed. Countries whose individual national economies had been structured so as to give general foreign trade equilibriums balancing imports with exports began, sooner or later, to understand that these old structures would no longer suffice. Much greater emphasis would henceforth need to be given to building exports at a very rapid and sustained rate to compensate for the huge new requirements to pay for the much more expensive fuel imports.

Different nations reacted differently to this new challenge. Take, for example, France. Soon after the oil crisis, leading French companies began to apply pressure to the French Government to evolve new policies for stimulating exports. In the summer of 1976, then Prime Minister Jacques Chirac created a special commission to study the problems confronting Frenchmen while they lived away from France. It was asked to identify programs that could be tried to encourage more French citizens to be willing to move abroad to strengthen the role of France around the world. This commission was headed by a former Government Minister, Andre Bettancourt.

After a year's work, the Bettancourt Commission issued a series of recommendations, many of which were subsequently enacted. The overseas Frenchman was already being rather well protected abroad. He already had some subsidized French schools at his disposition, already had no taxation of his earned or unearned income, already had the right to elect six Members of the French Senate to represent uniquely his interests. But more was felt to be needed. And more was given. Social Security benefits were increased. The taxation of Frenchmen who retained their domicile in France and were only temporarily abroad was lessened. More subsidies were granted to overseas French schools. The list was impressive.

In West Germany similar studies were undertaken. The overseas German is not as well taken care of as the overseas Frenchman, but he still has some significant encouragements. While abroad the overseas German has subsidized schools for his children, no taxation of his earned or unearned income, the right to remain voluntarily in the Social Security system at home, the right to unimpeded transmission of German citizenship to his children born abroad, etc.

In Japan, the Government recognized its responsibility toward overseas Japanese citizens. There was, of course, no taxation of Japanese citizens abroad. But there were new programs to subsidize Japanese schools abroad. Other concerns were studied and other incentives proposed.

In the post-1974 crisis environment, the United States took a most curious tack in a very different direction. It was decided that the overseas American was the recipient of too many special favors and these had to be reduced. Despite the fact that the overseas American was the only individual in the international marketplace carrying the full burden of his home country taxation on both his earned and unearned income this was felt to be not enough. Historically some exclusions from overseas earned income had been granted by more indulgent Congresses. Indeed, in 1926, the Congress decided that it would help the foreign trade interests of the United States to exclude from U.S. taxation all income earned overseas by Americans resident abroad. This principle prevailed until 1962 when with the excuse that a few movie stars were abusing this exclusion it was decided to place a ceiling on the amount that could be excluded from U.S. taxation. Since 1962, the existence of this exclusion in any form came to be looked upon as an unjustified loophole in American tax law.

Thus, in 1976, when the full force of the new international economic order was coming to be realized by our major competitors abroad, the United States chose to strike a blow at the big loophole enjoyed by Americans abroad. Suddenly, overnight, the average amount of tax that had to be paid by overseas Americans to the United States was tripled! No such augmentation in tax liability had ever been seen at home since the introduction of the progressive income tax system.

Naturally enough, the overseas American community was stunned and thrown into a turmoil. A number of major American companies realized that they could no longer remain competitive overseas if they employed Americans abroad. Many senior American executives went home. At the same time a tremendous amount of pressure was applied to the Executive Branch of the Government in Washington and to the Congress to reverse this astonishingly inappropriate policy. It was not easy to convince the Congress that action needed to be taken. For one thing, the Congress had been convinced by the Department of the Treasury that the impact of the closing of the loophole would be small. To the general surprise of everyone, the actual impact of the change that was made was nearly ten times the estimate that the Treasury had given to the Congress.

No one likes to admit having made a mistake. And, as is so inevitable with ferreting out loopholes and closing them, there is a certain amount of temporary euphoria and gratuitous demagoguery which commits proud legislators and senior civil servants to positions which it is later very hard to abandon.

To the great dismay of the overseas American community, the newly-elected President Carter chose for his principal tax advisor the same person who had been the architect of the loophole closing fiasco of 1976. True to form, when the necessity of amending the 1976 changes became universally apparent, the Treasury Department came forward with very few positive suggestions. Eventually the Congress adopted a more generous new law, but for many Americans abroad this still left them in a situation that was less favorable than the one that they had enjoyed in 1976, And, it was readily apparent that overeas Americans were in a class by themselves as the only individuals who faced the problems of ubiquitous double taxation and at the same time had fewer home country benefits than anyone among their competitors abroad.

In 1978, a few of the wiser leaders of the Congress began to suspect that what the United States was doing to the overseas American might be very dangerous to the United States. After some reflections, the Congress decided that a close look should be taken at the present practices of the United States toward its overseas citizens to see if these were not some systematic manifestations of discrimination in American laws against those living abroad.

In 1979, the Congress began to realize that the treatment being given to overseas Americans might not only be discriminatory, but might also be creating economic harm to the United States in making Americans non-competitive against citizens from other countries in the great markets of the world.

CONGRESSIONALLY MANDATED STUDIES

In 1978, Congress passed and the President enacted Public Law 95–426. Section 611 of this act was a request by the Congress to the President that he carry out a study to determine to what extent American laws and regulations were discriminatory against Americans living abroad. This mandate was prefaced by a Congressional expression of concern for the "fair and equitable treatment by the United States Government" of overseas Americans in the areas of taxation, citizenship of progeny, veterans' benefits, voting rights, social security, and other obligations, rights and benefits.

In 1979, Congress passed and the President enacted Public Law 96–60. Section 407 of this act is an amendment to the previously mandated study. The Congress stated in the preamble to the new section that: "American Statutes and Regulations should be designed so as not to create competitive disadvantage for individual American citizens living abroad or working in international markets."

The record shows that the Congress is concerned not only with analyzing individual laws and regulations and their affect on fair and equitable treatment of Americans abroad, or their affect on the ability of Americans to compete abroad, but also with the more fundamental questions of the basic policy of the United States towards its citizens abroad. Indeed it is generally recognized that such a policy clarification is a prerequisite to the analysis of how individual issues of laws and regulations can be determined to be non-discriminatory or competitively helpful or harmful.

AMERICAN CITIZENS ABROAD

In the summer of 1978, a group of overseas Americans created a new organization, American Citizens Abroad, for the express purpose of helping the President carry out the study that had been mandated by the Congress. ACA gathered information from hundreds of overseas citizens. ACA studied the myriad statutes and regulations that affect Americans abroad. And, ACA prepared a report identifying fifty issues that needed to be addressed by the President in his report to the Congress. ACA's first report was submitted to the President of the United States on December 18th, 1978.

THE PRESIDENT'S FIRST REPORT TO THE CONGRESS

On August 27th, 1979, the President sent to the Congress a Report on Equitable Treatment of United States Citizens Overseas. The submission of this report came as a surprise to many as just two weeks previously, on August 15th, 1979, the President had signed Public Law 96–60, whose Section 401 extended until January 20th, 1980, the deadline for the new report, of expanded scope, that the Congress had requested on overseas Americans.

It came as an even bigger surprise, and as a profound disappointment, to those who read this report to discover that the President had chosen not to address any of the basic policy questions as to how Americans should be treated while abroad. All that he had offered the Congress was a list of issues that had already been identified by ACA with little of substance in suggesting redress or even accepting that redress in the name of equity was called for.

CONGRESSIONAL REACTION TO THE PRESIDENT'S REPORT

A number of Members of the Congress were disturbed by the President's approach to the study on overseas Americans as it was presented in his August 27th Report. Some took the trouble to write individually to the President to clarify the intent of the Congress in asking for such reports from the Executive Branch. Some specifically asked the President to address the basic policy questions of how overseas Americans fit into the social, political, economic and ideological objectives of the United States, and how far American obligations, rights and benefits are supposed to extend to, or be denied to, our citizens while they are away from home.

ACA'S NEW REPORT

ACA has carried out another review of the problems confronting Americans living away from home. This new review covers not only the issues that were addressed in the first ACA report, and the answers to some of these issues as given in the President's report to the Congress, but also attempts to place these and other issues into the context of how American practices enhance or hinder the ability of American citizens to compete in the world marketplace.

This new ACA report follows below. It is structured to be useful to those who have been asked by the President to carry out the new research effort. The issues that were identified in the first ACA report follow in the same numerical sequence. New issues that are raised in this Second ACA report follow the numbering sequence starting at issue fifty-one. A cross-reference of the ACA issues to the responses to some of the issues in the President's report is shown in the index at the beginning of this report.

To avoid redundancy, the ACA issues previously identified will be addressed anew only in summary form. The President's analysis will also be mentioned only in summary form. The new ACA comments on these issues, both to reply to the President's report and to add new commentary on their international competitive import will be kept as brief as possible.

The original ACA report, and the President's report to the Congress will be appended to this new ACA report for ready reference. The issues that were addressed in the President's report have been numbered for cross-reference purposes in the order in which they appeared in his report.

INTRODUCTION TO THE SECOND ACA REPORT

It is beyond dispute that the overseas American has greater burdens and fewer benefits while he is away from home than almost all of his competitors from other Free World countries. The explanation for this unfortunate competitive situation comes from myriad factors related to the origins of the United States as a country, its generally insular mentality, its traditional disdain for involvement in overseas markets, and its curious xenophobia which spills over onto its attitude toward its own citizens who have gone abroad, for whatever purpose.

The luxury of such prejudices, which may have had only nominal cost in the past, may be beyond the resources of the United States today. For this reason, the new international economic realities make a reassessment of the American treatment of its overseas citizens imperative.

The overseas American community has no natural constituency representation in the Government. There is no Department of the Cabinet which is designed to look out for the rights, and problems of overseas Americans. There is no Committee of the Congress which has jurisdiction over the entire spectrum of issues that concern Americans living away from home. And, unfortunately, there are no individual representatives of the overseas American community sitting in Washington as the elected representatives in the Congress, or as the appointed delegates of their interests anywhere in the Administration.

It is not surprising, therefore, that all eyes turn toward the White House for resolution of this complicated problem. Nowhere else in the Federal Government can all of the disparate threads of this Gordian knot be drawn together and cleaved asunder.

If the President refuses to address the basic questions that plead for clarification, there is no other place that these questions can be addressed.

ACA, therefore, adds its voice to those of the Members of the Congress who have asked the President to lead us toward more felicitious policy. The questions that the President is invited to address are simple yet quite profound in their domestic and international import. They are:

1. What basic policy does the United States have toward the overseas American in terms of the obligations, rights and benefits that should be retained by or denied to the overseas American? And, what justification is there for any differences in the treatment of the American abroad from the treatment he would have had if he had remained at home?

2. What basic policy does the United States have toward the overseas American in terms of guaranteeing him the ability to compete on an equal basis with individuals of other nationalities in the international markets of the world? What justification is there for U.S. policies that impede the ability of individual Americans to compete abroad?

ACA hopes that the President will accept to confront these questions. And, subsequent to this long-overdue clarification of basic American policy, ACA hopes that the President's new report to the Congress as requested by Public Law 96-60, Section 407, will once again analyze all of the issues that affect Americans living overseas to bring all U.S. laws and regulations into harmony with the new policy guidelines for defining equity and international competitive ability.

ACA, once again, renews its offer to assist the President, members of his Administration, and the Members of the Congress, in the identification of problems facing overseas Americans, in the analysis of the harm that these problems are causing for all Americans, and in the elaboration of successful methods of redress.

ISSUE No. 1

Short title

Constitutional right of children born abroad.

Summary of the problem.—In 1971, in *Rogers* vs *Bellei*, the Supreme Court by a narrow majority of five-to-four ruled that American children born abroad have diminished Constitutional Rights as citizens of the United States. While the Congress can do nothing to arbitrarily deprive U.S. citizens born in the United States of their citizenship, no such prohibition impedes the actions of the Congress in dealing with Americans who were born abroad.

ACA's question.—ACA asked that the President address the issue of whether there should be two classes of citizens in the United States, those with full Constitution rights, and those with only some of the Constitutional protections.

The President's reply.—The President chose not to directly address the problem of second-class citizenship rights as defined by the Court in the *Bellei* case. The President merely restated the general findings of the Court.

ACA's renewed question.—The unanswered question remains. Should there be two classes of citizenship in the United States? Should some citizens have fewer Constitutional protections than others? We invite the President and the Congress to both reflect on the implications of this present situation.

ACA would like to also mention that taking umbrage in a decision of the Supreme Court to justify maintaining such discrimination against a certain class of American citizens has hisstorically not been well justified. In the late 1800's the Supreme Court found it Constitutional to discriminate against some citizens on the grounds of race. In the early 1900's the Supreme Court found it Constitutional to discriminate against some citizens on the grounds of their sex. It is not surprising, therefore, that the Court may have found that the geographical location of a citizen's birth gives sufficient justification for diminishing an American's rights. What is needed is a clear recognition by the American people that such a tortured interpretation of our Constitution is not worthy of our great country.

We appeal for redress on this fundamental issue.

ISSUE No. 2

Short title

Presidential eligibility of children born abroad.

Summary of the problem.—The Constitution states that for a person to be eligible to run for the office of President of the United States he must be a natural born American citizen.

ACA's question.—Is a child born abroad to an American citizen parent a "natural born American citizen"?

The President's reply.—The President stated that "the meaning of the term 'natural born citizen' has never been definitely determined. Its meaning has been argued for years and legal authorities are divided on the issue. Because of the legal complexities inherent in this issue and the skills and judgment required to interpret relevant provisions of law, it is appropriate and advisable to look to the courts for its resolution."

ACA's renewed question.—The question remains, what is the presidential eligibility status of a child born abroad to American parents?

The President suggests that the appropriate forum for resolution of this definitional problem is in the Courts. We doubt that he seriously means what he says. Let us take a quick look at what such an action by the Courts would involve.

In the United States one cannot ask the Supreme Court for an advisory opinion on a basic Constitutional issue. There must be a case. And the case must be appropriate to raise the question that needs resolution. In the situation at hand, the President is suggesting a monumental institutional crisis.

To bring this question to the Supreme Court for ultimate resolution an American born abroad would have to have been nominated by one of the major political parties and been elected to the office of President. Only then could a suit be brought challenging his Constitutional eligibility to fill this office. Thus a President-elect, and a tense nation, who had just elected him, would have to await the judgment of the Court as to whether he was Constitutionally entitled to fill his office. We doubt that the President seriously intended to suggest that this is how this question should be resolved. We doubt that there is any other way for the Courts to make a definitive finding.

We ask once again, therefore, for the President to consider recommending to the Congress an appropriate form of legislation to resolve this definitional problem. We recommend to the President that heed be taken of the action of the First Congress in 1791 when the first immigration legislation specifically used the terms "natural born citizens" to describe the status of some children born abroad to an American parent.

This issue is a Constitutional time-bomb that would be much better addressed prophylactically than left to create a situation of dire institutional crisis some day in the future. Failure to address the problem will also further complicate the political aspirations of the forty-thousand plus children born abroad with American citizenship each year.

We appeal for redress on this important issue.

ISSUE No. 3

Short title

Congressional representation for Americans abroad.

Summary of the problem.—Nearly two million American citizens live outside of the United States. While recent legislation has finally granted overseas Americans the right to participate in Federal elections, many of those abroad feel cut off from their local communities at home and do not exercise their franchise. Further, while problems of major concern to overseas Americans, including taxation of those abroad, are frequently addressed by the Congress, there is no representation from the overseas community to protect their interests.

ACA's question.—Why are overseas Americans not given their own representation in the Congress?

The President's reply.—The President stated that "A nonvoting representative in the Congress for all Americans living in foreign countries has been suggested by some. The constitutional basis for representation in the Congress for the District of Columbia, Guam and the Virgin Islands are those clauses of the Constitution granting to Congress power over the District of Columbia and the territories of the United States. To create a representative in the national legislature of individuals in areas of the world over which the United States has no sovereignty would alter the basic scheme of national representation as it presently exists."

Beyond stating what was already obvious to nearly everyone, the President did not have any further recommendation as to whether or not such representation for overseas Americans was desirable.

ACA's renewed question.—ACA asks once again, why do overseas Americans not have their own representative in the Congress?

During the last few years, representation in the Congress in the form of non-voting delegates has been granted to inhabitants of:

Area	Population	Delegate
American Samoa	32,000	1
Virgin Islands	110,000	1
Guam	115,000	1

Those living in Puerto Rico are granted a Resident Commissioner with similar statute in the Congress to the non-voting Delegates.

The overseas American community has a total population over fifty time larger than that of the residents of American Samoa. The problems faced by overseas Americans involve the clash of sovereignties between the United States and more than 150 other nations.

The Constitutional niceties of justifying creation of a representative for those living abroad could be met creatively by any number of artifices. An uninhabited island belonging to the United States could be defined as the territorial attachment of those abroad. Some other form of justification could equally easily be found.

What needs to be answered is the very simple query: Do overseas Americans deserve their own voice in the Federal legislature, or not?

We ask the President to address this question.

ISSUE No. 4

Short title:

Transmission of citizenship to children born abroad.

Summary of the problem.—Some children born abroad to an American citizen parent automatically acquire American citizenship at birth. Some children do not. The deciding criteria is whether or not both parents are Americans, or whether in the case where only one parent is American this parent has previously lived in the United States for a requisite period of time.

If both parents of a child born abroad are American citizens, the child will be American at birth if either of the parents has ever "had a residence" in the United States prior to the child being born abroad. If only one parent is American, this parent must have previously lived for ten years in the United States, five of which after the age of fourteen. Failing this previous residency test, the parent cannot transmit citizenship to his child and the child may well be born with no nationality at all. It is much easier for an illegitimate child to have American citizenship. When the father does not recognize the child, he will automatically be American if his American citizen mother has previously lived for one year in the United States.

ACA's question.—ACA asked why there are different categories of rights for American citizens living overseas in terms of when children born overseas can have American citizenship at birth. Why do not all Americans abroad, as individuals, have the same rights to give their children their most precious human right, their nationality?

The President's reply.—"Section 301 of the Immigration and Nationality Act imposes limitations on the ability of United States citizen parents to transit citizenship to children born abroad. This is particularly true in cases involving one citizen parent and an alien spouse. In such an instance, the citizen parent must have been physically present in the United States for ten years, at least five of which were after the age of fourteen. The Congressional purpose in enacting these restrictions was to prevent the perpetuation of successive generations of absentee United States citizens whose ties and loyalty to the United States might be questionable. That underlying goal of the transmission of citizenship requirement is reasonable and the means chosen to attain the goal are rational."

Nevertheless, the President did support some redress for those abroad. Under "Recommended Acting," the President stated: "In the last session of Congress, a bill (S. 2314) was introduced which would reduce to two years the period of residence in the United States necessary to transmit United States citizenship to a child born abroad. That bill was supported by the Administration. The Administration will support a slightly revised version which is expected to be introduced in the current session of Congress."

ACA's renewed question.—Americans living overseas have a number of questions concerning U.S. laws governing transmission of citizenship to children born abroad.

First, we are not sure where the President, or the various branches of his Administration, really stand on what is the appropriate amount of prior residence that should be required of an overseas American parent with an alien spouse. Last year, in addition to commenting favorably on S. 2314 which would reduce prior residency to only two years, the Carter Administration also commented favorably on a different bill that would have done away with any prior residency requirement for citizenship transmission abroad. Has the President or his various Departments now taken a new position, or is this just an invitation to the Congress to propose new legislation that the President feels would have the greatest chance of success in the present Congress?

Second, an even more basic question needs to be asked: Why does the location of a child's birth make so much difference under American law? In many cases it could be possible for the mother to be flown at great expense and great inconvenience and possible danger to the unborn child, to the United States for the birth. In such circumstances the child would be an American citizen. No matter what the loyalty of the parents might be, the fact that he was born within the specially defined latitudes and longitudes would suffice for him to be American. Is there some metaphysical force that provides special loyalty guarantees when the birth takes place within the United States? The question might sound absurd, but the law leads to such a conclusion.

Third, a child born abroad with one American parent surely has greater chances of being a loyal American citizen than one born with no American citizen parents. Our law gives full citizenship rights to children of casual tourists visiting the United States even for only one day. If this child goes abroad he remains an American all his life time And, if he should ever meet a similar one-day visitor child abroad and marry his children will also be American citizens This seems bizarre

Fourth, the United States has signed the Universal Declaration of Human Rights, Article 15 of this Declaration states: "(1) Everyone has the right to a nationality." Since signing this Declaration, the United States has not adapted its legislation to bring itself into conformity with this promise. It would be humiliating to the United States if one of its citizens were forced to appeal to the International Court of Justice to force the United States to recognize the nationality of a child born to an American abroad.

Fifth, the present law creates obstacles to American citizens being willing to move abroad to promote American goods and services in the export markets. Recently ACA was contacted by a naturalized American citizen who was sent to Europe by his American company employer. This company helps medium-sized American corporations develop markets abroad for their products and services. Because the naturalized American employee has not lived for ten years in the United States and because he has an alien spouse his soon-to-be-born child will have no rights to American citizenship. Yet the only reason that he is abroad, rather than in the United States, is to build U.S. trade.

Sixth, it is unbecoming to the United States to have its citizens abroad suffer the anguish of having children born abroad who are "Displaced Persons". An American citizen, born in New York, asked ACA for help in a case involving his young son. The child was born in Belgium of an American father and a British mother. Because of the unfortunate laws of the three countries involved, the child was born stateless. He is a refugee. How this protects the United States is unclear.

Defining the right to a nationality as one of the most precious of all Human Rights because it brings with it the protections of a sovereign state, ACA asks the President to indicate why some Americans should be denied the right to transmit their American citizenship to their children when they are born abroad? We take small comfort in the President's assurances that the present law is reasonable and rational. It is also the cause of intolerable Human Rights tragedies.

We ask for redress. And, we ask that the President consider recommending legislation to the Congress that would give to each individual American citizen, without regard to his choice of a spouse, the same right to transmit American citizenship to his children no matter what latitude or longitude the child may be in when he breathes his first breath.

We justify this request also for the international competitive consequences that it would have for Americans abroad. A number of other countries, notably France and West Germany, already have such enlightened laws. Curiously, the United States, from 1791 to 1940, also permitted its overseas male citizens to transmit citizenship to children at birth without a prior residency requirement. U.S. law has grown much more harsh in the last few decades. Does anyone know why? Can we afford the luxury of this discrimination any longer? Will this unfortunate legislation prevent talented Americans from being willing to move abroad to help their country? Many questions need to be answered.

ISSUE No. 5

Short title

Discriminatory preference in citizenship transmission qualifications of parents.

Summary of the problem —American laws setting the requirements which must be met by citizens having children abroad so that the child can be an American citizen at birth make a distinction between those who are abroad as employees of the U.S. Government, or of Inernational Organizations, and those who are not attached to the Government in any way. The distinction gives significant benefits to the first group, and denies these benefits to the second.

ACA's question.—When it comes to qualifying to transmit citizenship to children born abroad, why are some Americans given greater privileges than others? What makes a Government employee more valuable and more deserving of human rights guarantees for his children than a citizen who is not working for the Government?

The President's reply —"Section 301(g) of the Immigration and Nationality Act gives benefits with respect to the transmission of citizenship requirements to certain individuals, such as military personnel and government employees who may be abroad involuntarily at the direction of the United States Government, and those working for an international organization. These persons can count time spent abroad in the service of the United States Government or an international organization as a period of physical presence in the United States for purposes of transmission of citizenship. In making a distinction between persons residing abroad voluntarily and those serving abroad with the Government or an international organization, Congress was carrying out a legitimate purpose and had sound basis for its distinctions."

The President, thus, justifies the existence of two different classes of Americans abroad, one with more rights than another. However, he further states: "The enactment of the legislation liberalizing the general requirements for transmission of citizenship, as cited in Section I of this report (see Issue 4 above), would significantly lessen the difference in treatment between those abroad who are in the service of the U.S. Government or international organizations and other Americans living abroad." Subsequent to such recommended action the distinction wold remain, but would be of lesser import.

ACA's renewed question.—Does the President really feel that there is a need to make a distinction between Americans living overseas in terms of their ability to transmit basic Human Rights to their children simply because of different kinds of employers of Americans abroad?

The President stated that the Congress, in making such a legislative distinction, was carrying out a legitimate purpose on a sound basis. Doubtless good reasons can always be found for almost any action taken by the Congress. But that is not the point. The point is whether such a distinction is necessary, and whether it is right.

A clue to the President's thinking is given in the use of the word "voluntary" in justifying the distinction made between Government employees and those not working for the Government. Presumably this implies that only Government employees are sent abroad by their employers without choice. This would come as a surprise to many employees of major corporations who have also been sent overseas. Of course these private sector Americans could always refuse to go abroad. They could quit their jobs. But, then again so could most of the Government employees. The issue of voluntariness as a justification for this distinction would not seem a valid example

It might be argued that employees of the Government are working for the good of the country while the private sector Americans are only out for their own selfish interests. This, in most cases, would also be hard to justify. Indeed, it is often not clear who is making the most important contribution to the health and welfare of the United States, the clerk at an Embassy or a prominent American professor, lawyer, doctor, engineer, consultant, poet or architect. The point really is that the United States should not be in the business of making such curious value judgments of the worth or contributions being made by its overseas citizens. Yet, any other basis for making distinctions between how different classes of overseas Americans should be treated is hard to find.

ACA would like to ask the President to address the question of whether some overseas Americans should have more privileges than others? If so, how is such differential treatment to be justified? Explanations given to date are quite evidently inadequate. All Americans should be equal before the law. Or have we missed something?

<h2 style="text-align:center">ISSUE No. 6</h2>

Short title

Retroactivity of the revocation of citizenship retention requirements.

Summary of the problem —In 1978, the Congress finally abolished the requirement that children born abroad with American citizenship in families where only one parent was an American citizen had to return to the United States for a specified period of subsequent residence failing which the child automatically lost his American citizenship on a given birthday.

When this change was made, the Congress failed to make the change retroactive. Hence some children who were born abroad have been stripped of their American citizenship for failure to comply with requirements that no longer exist.

ACA's question —Why, if the Congress recognizes that conditions subsequent for the retention of citizenship acquired at birth abroad are wrong, should not the revocation of this abandoned principle apply equally to those previously struck by its inequity as to those fortunate enough to still be too young to have been assaulted by it?

The President's reply.—"There are no longer any provisions of law which discriminate against citizens born abroad with respect to retention or loss of citizenship. During the hearings on the bill, Congress considered arguments for and against retroactive repeal of Section 301 (b) (which had previously required the subsequent residency as a condition of retaining citizenship if acquired at birth abroad), and found sufficient reasons for repealing the statute prospectively only. The arguments against retroactive repeal were grounded on difficulties, legal and administrative, inherent in restoring citizenship status to persons who have previously lost it, and in the "ripple effect" that such action would have on derivative citizenship claims, tax obligations, and social security benefits. Reconsideration of this matter has resulted in the conclusion that the Administration should not seek a revision in the recent legislation enacted by the Congress."

When the changes to Section 301 (b) were being discussed by the Administration and the relevant Members of the Congress, the Administration took a strong position in favor of making the revocation of the retention requirements retroactive. There were good reasons for doing this First, there was a relevant historical precedent. Earlier, when the subsequent residency requirements had been made less draconian in 1952, the Government initially opposed retroactivity and then reversed itself and argued in the Federal Courts that retroactivity should be used. Children that had been stripped of their failure to comply with previous requirements were restored to their citizenship status, problems of administration, and ripples, notwithstanding.

Second, the Administration had a strong argument to the effect that the size of the potential complications issue was small. After all, only a modest number of children had been abused by the old law and most of these were not necessarily old enough to have had large families for derived citizenship complications, and surely none was yet old enough to have social security retirement problems. Indeed, according to the State Department, we were only talking about 2,000 people.

Additionally, while there would be a need to adopt new administrative procedures to handle the retroactivity processing, State had just been relieved from the large burden of having to chase after children born abroad to take their citizenship away from them and thus there was a net freeing of administrative capacity in any case.

ACA's renewed question.—ACA is most disappointed by the change in the Administration's stand on this issue From being a strong defender of overseas Americans in 1978, the Administration has abandoned the disinherited children abroad. Now the Administration cites the very arguments to justify this new policy that it had so effectively shown to be without substance only one year earlier.

ACA asks once again, why is the Administration abandoning the 2,000 citizens who have been stripped of their American citizenship under provisions of a law that is now recognized to have been unjust? Surely, if justice has any meaning, it must be worth some small administrative inconvenience to be rendered.

We ask the President to reconsider his new policy and not abandon the 2,000 disinherited innocents abroad

ISSUE NO. 7

Short title

Loss of citizenship by American children abroad due to actions of their parents.

Summary of the problem—U.S law calls for the loss of American citizenship for anyone who obtains naturalization in a foreign country even if this naturalization results from the actions of a parent, guardian, agent or by the naturalization of a parent having legal custody of such an individual.

Children can lose their American citizenship even though they could do nothing to defend themselves against this loss.

The law provides that a child can retain his American citizenship, despite the provisions of the law calling for such loss, if he returns to the United States to commence permanent residence before the age of twenty-five.

At issue here is involuntary expatriation and whether it is really Constitutional, especially in light of the Supreme Court's ruling in *Afroyim* v *Rusk*

ACA's question—Should children born with American citizenship be forced to lose this precious possession through actions taken when they were minors, or taken on their behalf by a parent or custodian?

The President's reply.—"The Act specifies that a United States citizen, who, while under age twenty-one acquires foreign nationality upon application of a parent or through naturalization of the parent, will lose United States citizenship if such person fails to enter the United States to establish a permanent residence prior to his twenty-fifth birthday. Loss of citizenship, however, does not occur automatically; it can occur only when it is clear that the subject willfully failed to comply with the requirement for the express purpose of transferring or abandoning allegiance. Evidentiary requirements to support a finding of intent to transfer or abandon allegiance are very high. As a result, few findings of loss of citizenship are made under this section, and these provisions no longer serve to revoke a person's citizenship unless the citizen wishes to lose citizenship."

Nevertheless, the President further recommended: "Although this provision of law is no longer viable, it still remains in force and, when applicable, must be administered. To avoid the difficulties and inequalities that the law imposes on young American citizens by requiring their return to the United States before the age of twenty-five and in view of the fact that Congress has repealed a similar proviso in Section 301 of the Act, the Justice Department will propose legislation to amend Section 349(a)(1) to provide that loss of nationality shall occur only when a citizen applies for naturalization in a foreign state on his own behalf after age twenty-one."

ACA applauds the initiative of the President in seeking to nullify this unfortunate law. ACA calls upon the Congress to act swiftly to bring about this proposed change.

ISSUE NO. 8

Short title

Citizenship loss by naturalized Americans going abroad within 5 years of naturalization.

Summary of the problem.—Present U.S. law requires not only that an immigrant be lawfully admitted for permanent residence, and must reside subsequently for 5 years in the United States as conditions precedent to being eligible for acquiring American citizenship. The law further requires that such naturalized citizens must subsequently reside for a further five years in the United States. If during the first five years after acquiring U.S. citizenship the newly naturalized American chooses to reside abroad, he is presumed by law, although with the possibility of submitting countervailing evidence, to have obtained his naturalization by concealing a material fact or by willful misrepresentation when he did not reveal his true intentions with respect to residence.

ACA's question.—The basic issue involved here is what constitutes the essence of the acquisition of U.S. citizenship? Does it simply consist of an immigrant's wanting to reside within the geographical confines of the United States? Or does it rather constitute an allegiance by an individual to a unique way of life with all of the material and ideological implications that this entails? Further, is a naturalized American a real American when he obtains his new citizenship, or does he have a further condition to fulfill before being the equal of other citizens? He can be sent to war. He must pay taxes. But he cannot choose where he will live.

One finds once again in the present law an overwhelming emphasis on the physical location of the individual, much akin to the other sections of the Immigration Act of 1952, most of which have now been successively abandoned.

The President's reply.—The President's reply to this issue was lengthy. Only the concluding paragraph is quoted here. The full text is found in the annex to this report.

Said the President: "It is clear that Congress did not intend to extend naturalization benefits to those whose intention was to reside permanently abroad rather than in the United States. Limiting naturalization to those who intend to reside in the United States permanently is not discriminatory simply on the basis that a natural-born citizen does not have to have such an intent. Naturalized citizens are required to meet other requirements that are not imposed on natural born citizens, such as literacy in the English language, good moral character, and certain periods of residence and physical presence in the United States. It seems reasonable, in conferring the benefit of citizenship through naturalization, to take account of whether or not the individual seeking citizenship intends to maintain a permanent residence in this country. The five-year residence obligation is designed to gauge this intent."

The President defends the present law and does not propose any change.

ACA's renewed question.—There have been some major innovations in U.S. law concerning immigration and naturalization in the 20th Century. Two very different concepts have been developed in parallel. One concerns the elaboration of conditions precedent to the acquisition of citizenship. The other concerns conditions subsequent to the acquisition of U.S. citizenship.

The elaboration of conditions precedent to granting U.S. citizenship to an immigrant are the most fundamental and incontestable right of the Government. They merely define the conditions of entry for any newcomer to our privileged society.

The elaboration of conditions subsequent, however, is a most unfortunate innovation because it de facto, and de jure, creates automatically two classes of citizenship.

The 1952 Immigration and Nationality Act was replete with condition subsequent requirements. Naturalized citizens could never live more than five years in the country from which they originally came (ruled Unconstitutional by the Supreme Court in the *Schneider* case) ; children born with more than one nationality at birth risked losing their citizenship later in life if they ever lived more than three years in the country of their other nationality (struck from the Statute books in 1978) : children born abroad with only one American parent risked losing their citizenship if they did not return to live for a specified period in the United States later in their lives (also struck from the Statute books in 1978).

The conditions subsequent still applying to the naturalized citizen are the last significant vestige of this innovative and multi-class of citizenship mentality.

What is most offensive in this requirement is the automatic assumption that fraud or deceit was the "intent" of the naturalized citizen if he goes abroad within five years of naturalization. The Government needs to offer no proof of such fraud or deceit. This is a most distressful contradiction of the usual legal principle that an individual is considered to be innocent until "proven" guilty.

ACA asks the President to reconsider his support for this unfortunate legal principle. If ten years' residence is felt to be necessary to establish that one really wants to be an American citizen, the law should be changed to recognize this real intent. Once a person has become an American citizen he should be the equal to all of the others without any restriction or presumption of moral turpitude because of some innocent act.

ACA asks the President to work toward the elimination of any such laws that set up different classes of citizenship. All Americans should be equal before the law in all respects. We seek redress.

Issue No. 9

Short title

Naturalization of alien spouses.

Summary of the problem.—U.S. law establishes that an alien spouse can be naturalized as an American citizen by two different methods. Either the spouse comes to reside for three years in the United States, or the spouse can acquire U.S. nationality without any residence in the United States if the American citizen marriage partner is one of a privileged group of citizens.

The law states that special privileges for the immediate naturalization of an alien spouse accrue to U.S Government Employees, employees of American institutions of research, employees of an American firm or corporation engaged in promoting foreign trade, employees of international organizations, priests and ministers, and missionaries.

ACA's question.—Why has the Government found it necessary to separate overseas Americans into two classes of citizens? Why is a Government filing clerk deserving of a privilege that is withheld from a university professor, a doctor, lawyer, poet, consultant or architect? Why are not all Americans equal before the law?

The President's reply.—"In recognition of the fact that many United States citizen spouses are regularly assigned abroad in the course of their employment, and that these assignments are for extended periods of time, Congress enacted section 319(b) which waives the three-year residence requirement in those cases where the citizen spouse is directed abroad on a regular (as opposed to temporary) assignment of the type set forth in the statute. Under the statute, many military spouses and those married to employees of organizations or firms defined in the subsection have been naturalized early to accompany or join the employed person abroad. The statute requires such persons to declare their intention to resume permanent residence in the United States upon termination of the tour of duty abroad."

"Section 319(b) attempts to define certain types of obligatory employment abroad which furthers the interests of the United States Government. It was not the intention of Congress to benefit those who choose to go abroad to run their own businesses, work for foreign employers, or for leisure purposes. If all spouses of United States citizens living abroad were entitled to immediate naturalization, discrimination would be effected against those United States citizens who choose to live in this country and whose spouses have to fulfill the three-year residence requirement provided in section 319."

The President's answer is extraordinary. The law gives privileges to those who further the interests of the United States Government. That premise is in itself doubtful given the heterogeneous categories of privileged Americans identified by the statute Even more basic, again, is the notion that selections should be made among Americans who live abroad in terms of some a priori judgment of the merit and contribution being made by classes of American citizens.

The will to create privileged and deprived groups of U.S. citizens, and to justify privileges for those who are bureaucrats rather than entrepreneurs is a determined and pervasive one.

ACA's renewed question.—We wonder how the President will explain why overseas missionaries, ministers and priests serve the "interests of the United States Government". It was our understanding that the Government was supposed to stay out of religious activities at home and abroad.

Secondly, even accepting that the citizens of the cloth are somehow doing the Government's work abroad, is it really true that they are contributing more to the United States than American doctors, lawyers, engineers, professors, poets or architects also working abroad? It would rather severely strain credulity to make such a claim.

Thirdly, why is the criteria that of furthering the interests of the Government and not that of the "people" of the United States?

Fourthly, why have any such value judgments at all?

The President seeks to justify the present discrimination in the law by saying to make the immediate naturalization of a spouse abroad a privilege available to all overseas Americans would be an injustice to alien spouses in the United States who would still have to fulfill their three year residency requirements for naturalization. It is not clear why discrimination needs to take umbrage in an equally questionable legal requirement. The President surely doesn't wish to suggest that there must be at least one group that must sit at the back of the bus abroad to avoid having to reconsider a related law back home.

We ask the President to work with us to continue to rid U.S. law of all attempts to make value judgments among Americans living away from home. All Americans abroad should be equal before the law. We seek redress.

ISSUE NO. 10

Short title

Education of American children abroad.

Summary of the problem.—While considerable amounts of Federal revenues are returned to the individual States of the United States each year to help provide for the education of American children, there is almost no comparable support given to Americans living overseas to educate American children abroad.

ACA's question —Why does the United States not take better care of the overseas American child in terms of providing more adequate educational assistance :

The President's reply.—"Some have proposed that the Federal Government contribute in some direct way to the education of children of all Americans living abroad, pointing out that some other governments make substantial budget expenditures for this purpose. The United States Government, under the authority of the Fulbright-Hays and Foreign Assistance Acts has for some time provided support to many American-sponsored primary and secondary schools abroad. This program is administered by the Department of State. The Congress annually appropriates funds to the State Department, the Agency for International Development and the International Communication Agency to finance this support. As in the United States, no Federal funds (except for special cases of compensatory education for disadvantaged children) are provided for tuition grants to private schools. Such grants would raise a serious constitutional question in many cases."

ACA's renewed question —One of the major objectives of the Carter Administration has been the creation of a Cabinet-level Department of Education. That there was felt to be such a need for a Department at the highest level of government is eloquent testimony to the role that the Federal Government is expected to play in education matters in the United States. To then claim that it would be improper for the U.S. Government to be more greatly concerned with the educational problems of overseas children does not seem consistent.

The U.S. Government should be concerned with helping educate the American child abroad for two basic reasons. First, it is in the interest of the United States for all of its citizens to have an education which will best prepare them to fulfill their full obligations of citizenship and participation in our nation, whether this is by being physically present at home, or abroad. Secondly, it is important that help for the education of our children abroad be given in a way that will insure that overseas Americans are competitive with the nationals of other countries.

Each year the Government of France spends more than $90 million to provide educational facilities and services abroad to their overseas citizens. The Government of France has publicly stated that there is an obligation to spend as much, if not more, to insure the proper education of a French child abroad as is spent for the same child in France. By subsidizing overseas French schools in a major way, the French Government helps overseas Frenchmen compete in markets around the world.

Each year the West German Government spends over $100 million to build, staff and service overseas German schools for its citizens abroad. This direct educational subsidy also helps make the overseas German competitive in many markets around the world.

Japan and a number of other countries also have important programs of subsidizing education facilities abroad.

Compared to these other countries, the schooling aid given by the United States to American children abroad is woefully inadequate. While some programs have been developed for supporting schools abroad, much of this money goes to educate foreigners in "American type" educational establishments rather than to help American children abroad. Also, the selection of locations where much of this aid is to be given reveals the fact that much of this expenditure is a disguised form of foreign aid for political purposes rather than for educational aims.

It is a simple fact that the present policy of the United States to essentially ignore the overseas American child's educational needs not only harms the individual children but also handicaps the parents in their ability to compete in many markets around the world.

ACA calls upon the President to address two basic questions. Would it not be in the best interest of the United States to help provide for the education of American children abroad? Secondly, why should American parents have to suffer the competitive handicap of not having educational institutions subsidized abroad when rivals of other nationalities have such support from their own governments?

We appeal for a basic policy statement on this issue from these two fundamental perspectives.

ISSUE NO. 11

Short title

APO privileges for American schools abroad.

Summary of the problem.—Unlike many other countries, the United States provides almost no assistance at all for educating the children of private citizen Americans abroad. One practice had been permitted to evolve, however, through the generosity of the Department of Defense. With DOD indulgence, a number of overseas American schools were allowed to enjoy the usage of the Military Postal Service (MPS) whereby educational materials could be sent at low cost from the United States to the overseas school locations

In March, 1978, in an economy move, DOD abruptly terminated this indulgence and forced a number of overseas schools to undergo severe hardship in their operations through extra cost in obtaining educational materials, and extra time due to the frequent inefficiencies of the foreign postal systems that were henceforth used.

ACA's question—Why, in the name of small scale economies, should it be the children who have to suffer abroad?

The President's reply.—"Because the MPS was established for the purpose of supporting the active U S. Armed Forces deployed abroad, the Defense Department decided to delete from the list of eligible users of the system all individuals and organizations not operating in direct support of the Defense mission. The non-Defense Department tuition fee schools were only one group among the several organizations eliminated from the list of eligible users The Defense Department's action also reflected the views of the House Committee on Post Office and Civil Service, which had recommended "that the Department of Defense in concert with the Postal Service take the necessary action to insure that each user of the MPS will pay a fair share of the cost of maintaining the system." A significant consideration affecting the Defense decision in this matter was the fact that dependent children of military personnel and Defense Department employees in these schools frequently represent less than one percent of the total enrollment."

Having justified the DOD policy, the President nevertheless convinced DOD to modify its stand. The President further reported: "Although the curtailment of MPS service applied to all non-Defense tuition fee schools, the Department of Defense has agreed that these schools, having Defense Department and other U.S. Government dependents enrolled, are authorized to use the MPS for first class letter mail weighing less than sixteen ounces and containing official school correspondence, test materials, student records, etc. In addition, the Defense Department has agreed to continue to review individual requests for reinstatement of full service based upon exceptional circumstances."

Subsequent to ACA's request for redress the situation has improved. But, there are a number of further considerations that need to be addressed.

ACA's renewal question.—The new DOD policy consists of a willingness to extend limited MPS services to tuition fee schools abroad if such schools have among their enrolled students dependents of the U.S. Armed Forces or of other employees of the Government. Why is the United States continuing to make a distinction between bureaucrats and those in the private sector?

It might be suggested that DOD is not the relevant department of the Government to provide services to all Americans abroad. But that would not coincide with recent Congressional action making DOD the principal responsible body for administering the overseas election provisions whereby all U.S. citizens abroad can vote in U.S. Federal Elections.

Further, if DOD is not the relevant body, why is not some similar form of postal assistance offered to help facilitate the education of American children abroad? Large sums of Federal money are given to individual States each year to supplement local revenues for educational purposes. Why could not some modest sums be allocated to help children abroad?

Finally, it should be recalled that the President used the necessity for all of those enjoying the MPS services to pay their fair share of the costs of this system as a justification for eliminating overseas schools from among the MPS beneficiaries. It does not seem to follow that using the MPS under the same conditions as other eligible organizations implied in any way that the schools were not willing to pay their fair share. We wonder why this particular comment was appended to the President's statement?

ACA asks why the United States favors some children and discriminates against others overseas for this assistance to their education? Why are not all American children equally deserving of assistance abroad?

ISSUE No. 12

Short title

Educational allowances for U.S. Government employees abroad.

Summary of the problem.—Government employees must send their children to Department of Defense schools where they exist abroad. Only in cases where no such schools are available can government dependents have their tuitions and fees reimbursed for attending private educational institutions.

Some government employees feel that this does not allow their children a free choice of educational opportunity.

ACA's question.—Why does the U.S. Government not allow a greater freedom of choice for dependent children in their schooling abroad?

The President's reply.—"The choice afforded employees abroad where Defense schools exist is the same as the choice they would face at home, namely, either to utilize a publicly-supported school at no direct cost or a reimbursed cost or to pay for attendance at a private or other school not supported by the U.S. taxpayers. Education allowances are provided only in cases where there is no such choice."

ACA's renewed question.—Why does the Government not consider giving greater leeway to dependents of Government employees abroad in the selection of the school most appropriate for their children?

In this regard it is instructive to observe that a number of other countries have found a method for subsidizing, at least in part, the education of many children of private sector citizens by sending the government dependents to private schools that have been organized abroad.

We wonder whether it would not be more equitable in terms of the disbursements of taxpayers dollars to have as few DOD schools as possible, and only in the case of situations where there is no possible local American school that could be created. Getting DOD out of the education business would permit much greater flexibility in having the Government help all Americans educate their children abroad. The United States could then follow the lead of such countries as France and West Germany whereby the Government would offer subsidies to help construct private schools abroad, help operate them and help find staff for them.

ACA would like to think that some way could be found to make the educational facilities abroad available on an equitable basis for all American children. It might also improve the impression of choice and control that Government families feel they exercise over their children's schooling also.

ISSUE No. 13

Short title

Government aid for U.S. students abroad.

Summary of the problem.—American students attending foreign higher education institutions are ineligible for almost all Federal Student Aid programs except the Guaranteed Student Loan Program (GSLP). Almost all of the aid programs what are not available to Americans abroad predicate their benefits on the location of the institution where the aid will be used.

With a generally recognized need for more Americans with a foreign language capability, and a better understanding of other countries, the absence of Federal assistance to American students abroad is a great misfortune to all Americans.

ACA's question.—What definition of equity requires benefits for students to be denied to those abroad?

The President's reply.—"Federal aid for higher education is intended to ensure equal educational opportunity for all students. Under current law, assistance for study at foreign institutions is available only under the GSLP. It has been suggested that Americans studying at foreign institutions should be made eligible for all HEW student financial assistance programs. If this were the case, foreign institutions would have to be willing to assume the responsibilities necessary for the administration of such programs. This appears to be unlikely because many foreign institutions resist performing even the limited functions asked of them under the GSLP. Furthermore, it is clear that it would be difficult to ensure accountability by foreign institutions under the aid programs. The Federal Government would have no power over these institutions to ensure proper administration of program funds. Nevertheless, the matter of assistance for those attending foreign institutions is currently under review by the Department of Health, Education and Welfare as part of a more general review of all higher education programs in preparation for a proposal for a reauthorization of the Higher Education Act."

Having given a list of possible obstacles that would have to be overcome in giving more equitable treatment to overseas American students, the President did not choose to make any recommendation for an appropriate form of redress.

ACA's renewed question.—Why is it equitable to withhold educational assistance from American citizens abroad if the same assistance is available to students in the United States? If given programs prove to be difficult to administer abroad, why cannot new programs of comparable benefit, but more amenable to administration abroad be conceived and carried out?

We hope that the President will address this issue again and give us his recommendation of the most appropriate form of equity for Americans abroad.

ISSUE No. 14

Short title

CHAMPUS expiration for veterans abroad with no medicare at age 65.

Summary of the problem.—One of the major benefits that retired military personnel enjoy both in the United States and abroad is a program of civilian health and medical care subsidized by the U.S. Government, called CHAMPUS.

CHAMPUS protects the retired serviceman up to the age of 65. At this time CHAMPUS benefits cease because retired servicemen are automatically eligible for medicare coverage which is similar in nature and scope.

The Congress has chosen not to offer medicare benefits to any Americans living overseas despite the fact that many have contributed to the Social Security system for many years to obtain such benefits. As a result, the retired veteran loses his CHAMPUS benefits and has nothing to replace them abroad at an age when health and medical care protection is most needed.

ACA's question.—If a retired serviceman deserves CHAMPUS protection before the age of 65, why is this protection not guaranteed to those over age 65? Why has CHAMPUS not been amended to cover the overseas retiree until such time as medicare benefits become available overseas?

The President's reply.—The President chose not to address this issue.

ACA's renewed question.—Why are elderly retirees of the Armed Forces being treated this way?

ISSUE No. 15

Short title

VHA benefits for veterans abroad.

Summary of the problem.—Veterans living in the United States have a significant benefit, that of a veteran home loan to assist in acquiring a residence, which is denied to those living abroad.

ACA's question.—Why are VHA benefits denied to Veterans abroad?

The President's reply.—The President listed a number of problems that would be encountered in trying to extend this benefit to Veterans living overseas. Cost is one problem. Complicated administrative burdens is another difficulty.

The President mentioned that using the overseas branches of U.S. banks had been suggested but this would still leave great difficulties such as finding banks willing to underwrite loans abroad because of political risks, lending restrictions, fluctuating exchange rates and incompatible maturity limits.

ACA's renewed question.—No one suggested that giving the VHA benefit abroad would be as easy as giving the same benefit in the United States. The President rightly identified the major obstacles involved. But, he did not address the basic question that still remains: Should Veterans abroad be denied one of their most basic benefits?

We do not feel that the difficulties that have been enumerated are in any way insurmountable. Indeed similar difficulties confront the U.S. Government in trade and foreign investment areas. And difficulty with fluctuating exchange rates and placing valuations on foreign transactions has never impeded the zeal of the U.S. Government in extracting taxes from U.S. Veterans abroad.

The question remains, why discriminate against the veteran abroad? VHA loans surely could be given, despite the extra difficulties of the overseas environment. The President must first answer the really fundamental question: should they be given? An even better question is: what definition of equitable treatment justifies denying overseas Veterans this benefit?

It is perhaps worth mentioning also that many veterans serve overseas, and many were wounded overseas. Why is there the reticence to give them benefits overseas?

ISSUE No. 16

Short title

Vocational rehabilitation benefits for veterans abroad.

Summary of the problem.—Disabled veterans, many of whom have been disabled abroad, cannot receive vocational rehabilitation benefits abroad. VA regulations limit the availability of such training in a foreign country, other than the Philippines, by specifying that such training may be authorized only if adequate training for the selected objective is not available in the United States or its possessions and, if training is pursued under the direct supervision of a representative of the VA.

ACA's question.—Why are these restrictions being applied to the rehabilitation training of Veterans?

The President's reply.—The President indicated that there was some improvement pending on this issue. Said the President: "The Veterans Administration has recently proposed legislation which will remove the restrictions noted above and give the Administrator greater flexibility in meeting the veteran's legitimate rehabilitation needs. In those cases where vocational rehabilitation is provided outside the United States, the VA will make arrangements through contract or otherwise for necessary training assistance and supervision."

ACA's response—ACA applauds the President and the Veterans Administration for proposing this needed change. We hope that the Administration will work forcefully to see that this legislation is enacted.

70

Issue No. 17

Short title

DOD overseas hiring practices.

Summary of the problem.—Over the last several decades the United States Government has made a series of agreements with foreign governments which control access to civilian jobs associated with the U.S. Government as an employer abroad.

Some of these agreements provide for the preferential hiring of foreign workers. Some provide for such foreign labor to be selected by foreign governments.

The net result is that the U.S. Government is not an equal opportunity employer abroad. To further exacerbate the difficulties faced by some Americans seeking to work for the U.S. Government abroad, there have been several laws enacted by the United States during the last few years, (Public Law 95–105 and Public Law 95–426) which have authorized the preferential hiring of dependents of U.S. Government employees for certain positions abroad.

ACA's question.—Why is the U.S. Government not an equal opportunity employer abroad?

The President's reply.—The President cited a number of different types of agreements entered into by the U.S. Government abroad either under bi-lateral Status of Forces conditions, or in the more general NATO SOFA context. These agreements explain how the discrimination has come about, but do not explain why we accept this discrimination against the employment opportunities of our own citizens.

The President further justified discrimination against the employment opportunities of some U.S. citizens abroad as follows: "The State Department and, to some extent, the Department of Defense are encountering increasing employee resistance to overseas assignments, because spouses of Federal employees are finding it difficult to find employment abroad. Job opportunities for foreigners in many countries abroad are limited and work permits are often hard to obtain."

ACA's renewed question.—We sympathize with the dependents of U.S. Government employees abroad in terms of their desiring to be able to work when they accompany their spouses abroad. We doubt the wisdom of creating preferential job hirings for these people as the most appropriate answer. And we doubt that anyone would want to maintain that such discriminatory hiring is in any way an equitable manner of treating other Americans living overseas who might also wish to compete for the same employment.

Recruitment for overseas assignments is a major problem. But should the answer lie in creating classes of overseas American citizenship, one with special privileges and one without?

ACA would like to ask that the Congress and the President take a consistent stand on equity and work to insure that the United States Government becomes and remains an equal opportunity employer as much abroad as at home, at least as far as U.S. citizen job applicants are concerned.

Issue No. 18

Short title

DOD outside employment rules.

Summary of the problem.—The Department of Defense has issued a number of regulations which control the opportunity for DOD personnel to earn outside income. DOD has also issued regulations which control the opportunities of non-DOD personnel to sell life-insurance to DOD personnel abroad.

ACA's question.—Why has the DOD resticted the rights of its own personnel to seek outside supplementary income, and why has it set barriers to the ability of retired servicemen to be able to sell life insurance to servicemen on duty abroad.

The President's reply.—The President indicated that outside supplementary income opportunities for service personnel are controlled by several regulations to insure that such outside employment does not conflict with the serviceman's job or with the needs to keep information obtained in the line of duty secure from unauthorized release. Said the President: "This regulation does not prohibit all outside employment. It applies to all employees whether paid from appropriations or from non-appropriated funds and whether the employee resides abroad or in the United States. As such it sets a reasonable policy that seeks equitably to protect the interests of the United States Government."

This policy statement sounds reasonable. That was never brought into question. But, what was asked by ACA in its first report was the more important question of why the interpretation of this policy has been so draconian as to preclude much of the available outside employment opportunities that occur abroad, for example all employment with civilian firms dealing with U.S. military personnel abroad.

With regard to the standards set for the sale of life insurance to military personnel abroad, we wonder why the U.S. Government has here again taken such a draconian stand. A number of U.S. military personnel choose to retire abroad, especially those with a foreign spouse. The present U.S. DOD rules preclude such retirees from ever being able to sell U.S. life insurance to DOD personnel abroad unless the retiree goes back to the United States for a significant period of time.

This life insurance policy seems, again, to be a rather draconian one designed more for the tranquility of the DOD than for equitable treatment of Americans abroad.

ACA's renewed questions.—ACA would like to ask the DOD to once again examine its policies on the outside employment of DOD personnel to see if the severity in the interpretation of benign sounding regulations is really necessary. ACA believes that a softening of some of this interpretation would still protect DOD yet give greater supplementary income opportunities to DOD personnel assigned abroad.

ACA also wonders why retirees abroad cannot acquire the needed training to sell life insurance to DOD personnel abroad without having to spend time in the USA. Why is no apprenticeship program or correspondence course qualification accepted?

The meagre fare meted out to many of our service people abroad today, both active duty and retired, impels us to be as indulgent as possible in allowing for supplementary income to be earned abroad.

We appeal to the DOD to ease up and give the overseas service personnel a better chance to economically survive abroad.

ISSUE No. 19

Short title

Social security participation by Americans abroad.

Summary of the problem.—Many American citizens living abroad have not accumulated the minimum forty-quarters of coverage in the U.S. Social Security system before leaving the United States. As such they are not vested and covered by this system.

Unlike many foreign countries, the United States has not made any provision for voluntary participation in the U.S. Social Security program for Americans living away from home. Because of this lacuna, many overseas Americans, coming home upon retirement, find that they lose benefits from foreign Social Security programs to which they have been contributing and have no U.S. Social Security benefits to replace these.

But, in addition to this problem, there are others, particularly confronting Americans living in overseas countries where there is no effective local social security program at all.

Finally, a number of Americans, working abroad for foreign subsidiaries of U.S. companies find that they must participate in U.S. Social Security even if they are already part of a foreign plan. This leads to double coverage and extra expense not only for the individual, but also for his employer.

ACA's question.—Why is the U.S. Social Security program predicated so much on institutions and not on serving the individual? Why cannot individual Americans living abroad choose to voluntarily remain participants to Social Security?

The President's reply.—"A basic problem with any voluntary participation scheme is adverse selection. Those persons who would volunteer to participate in social security would tend to be those who would receive the largest returns on their contributions, thereby unduly increasing the cost of the program. It would be unfair to burden those who are compulsorily covered with the increases in cost resulting from a special provision permitting voluntary coverage for Americans residing abroad. It would also be unfair to those in the United States who wish to be exempt from social security coverage.

"If coverage were extended to American employees of foreign corporations, foreign governments, international organizations and foreign subsidiaries on an individual voluntary basis, there would be a question of establishing an appropriate contribution rate for most of them in order to avoid distorting costs to the social security trust funds. . . .

"The inability to compel compliance by foreign employers and international organizations also means that reliance would have to be placed on the employee to comply with social security reporting requirements. Although individuals electing voluntary coverage would presumably report their earnings, there is potential for abuse."

The President then made his recommendation. "The Social Security Administration believes that the problem of gaps in U.S. social security protection for American citizens working outside the United States can be remedied by totalization agreements. The 1977 amendments to the Social Security Act authorized the President to enter into these bilateral agreements to provide for limited coordination between the social security systems of the United States and other countries. Under an agreement, coverage and earnings from both countries may be combined to establish eligibility for, and entitlement to, benefits; furthermore, dual coverage and taxation for the same work is eliminated and the problem of adverse selection is avoided. A totalization agreement is already in effect between the United States and Italy; negotiations for similar agreements have been completed with West Germany, and are underway with Switzerland, Canada, Israel and the United Kingdom. Additional agreements are contemplated; however, they do require substantial time to develop and ratify."

What is striking about the President's answer to the question of why coverage of Americans abroad is not allowed on a voluntary basis, is the fact that the protecction of the individual nowhere appears to be a concern of the United States.

The President's reply was drafted by the Social Security Administration and the perspective of this reply was entirely that of a large bureaucracy trying to defend itself against having to confront a new problem that might be complicated to resolve.

ACA's renewed question.—ACA would like to ask the President once again why the primary concern is with keeping the social security bureaucracy happy, and not with endeavoring to insure that the overseas American citizen has as much protection as possible?

What is the policy of the United States in terms of wanting to insure that social security coverage is guaranteed, without undue burden, to all Americans no matter where they might live on this earth? Or does the United States care at all about the problems of overseas Americans other than whether their entry to the social security program might make this system more expensive, and more difficult to administer?

The President's recommended solution, the establishment of bilateral totalization agreements does not solve the social security problems for many Americans abroad. What happens to Americans living in developing countries where there is no local social security program of any merit, and where it is unlikely that any totalization agreement will be possible during the next several decades? Why are these Americans abroad not as important to the United States as those who happen to be living in more advanced socially protective areas?

Mr. President, we ask that you address the basic issue in this question. We suggest that the Social Security Administration is not the appropriate venue for carrying out your policy review. No bureaucracy voluntarily seeks to increase its own burdens, but it does inevitably defend whatever the present policy may be. We don't need defense of the status quo. This is all too painfully evident to those of us abroad. We need a new look at what we are doing to overseas Americans, and why. This must be done by a politician, not a bureaucrat.

There is a further, internationally competitive dimension to this problem also. Why are Americans expected to compete abroad in many areas without any social security protection while they confront in the same markets foreigners whose home countries offer much greater social security protection to them while they are away from home? Many of our strongest competitors have gone far ahead of us in reducing the problems of double social security contributions and in guaranteeing coverage for everyone that needs, or wants, it. Mr. President we urgently appeal to you to address this question once again.

Issue No. 20

Short title

Social security coverage for Americans in international organizations abroad.

Summary of the problem.—U.S. Social Security regulations will not allow U.S. citizens working abroad for International Organizations to participate in the U.S. social security system.

ACA's question.—Why are American international civil servants being mistreated this way?

The President's reply—The President's reply to this question is encompassed in his reply to Issue No. 19. Essentially the problem is two-fold. First, if such participation were to be voluntary only those Americans likely to receive useful benefits from the program would participate, and even then they would be tempted to abuse the system because they would have to report their overseas earnings themselves for their contribution calculations.

Second, it would be a burden for the U.S. Social Security system to try to determine what rate to use to calculate the payments to be made by these U.S. citizens. These two obstacles are so overwhelming that there is no recommendation that the present practice be changed.

ACA's renewed question.—Once again the President has refused to address directly the question of equitable treatment of Americans abroad. Instead he has chosen to take umbrage in the bureaucratic explanation that resolving this problem for the American abroad would require some changes at the Social Security Administration.

Mr. President, once again we appeal to you to address the basic question of equitable treatment of Americans abroad not irrelevant subsidiary questions such as bureaucratic comity. We have no doubt that if you were to direct the Social Security Administration to come up with a new program of coverage that would embrace the overseas American civil servant, they would do a fine job.

The question remains, what should we be doing to protect Americans abroad? We appeal to you for a direct answer.

ISSUE No. 21

Short title

Compulsory social security participation for self-employed Americans abroad.

Summary of the problems.—Americans who are self-employed abroad must, under present U.S. Social Security regulations, contribute to the U.S. Social Security system.

This mandatory participation for the self-employed abroad creates a severe competitive handicap for Americans abroad in countries where there is a local social security system that is also compulsory for the same individuals.

ACA's question.—Why is Social Security participation by self-employed overseas Americans compulsory?

A subsidiary question involves changes that were made in 1978 to the U.S. Income tax laws whereby the former Section 911 Foreign Earned Income exclusion was eliminated. This exclusion had previously sheltered the foreign earned income of overseas self-employed Americans from compulsory Social Security payments. With the extinguishing of the 911 exclusion, many overseas Americans had a sudden massive increase in their social security premiums. ACA's second question was why nothing was done to extend this sheltering of the first part of the self-employed individuals overseas income from U.S. Social Security taxation?

The President's reply.—The President chose not to specifically address this problem. His answer was encompassed in his reply to Issue No. 19 (see above). The general tenor of this reply was that problems with double taxation for social security were most appropriately handled by bilateral totalization agreements with individual foreign countries.

ACA's renewed question.—ACA asks the President once again to explain to overseas Americans why the self-employed abroad must contribute to the Social Security program in the United States?

From the point of view of the individual overseas American the U.S. rules for social security appear capricious. The concern is not at all for the protection of the individual abroad. It is rather one of making the system simple to administer. Overseas Americans are segregated into a few basic classes and treated differently by class without regard for problems that the individual in one class might have which are not faced by those in another.

ACA asks, therefore, that the President take the trouble to address the question of whether the United States has any obligation to try to help protect overseas Americans as individuals? Further, does the United States care whether our policies create competitive difficulties for some Americans who have to make double contributions for social security? Finally, is it really optimum to try to alleviate such double contribution problems through bilateral treaties? Such an approach will guarantee that these problems will remain for many thousands of overseas Americans for many more decades.

Why cannot overseas Americans be given the right to voluntarily participate in U.S. Social Security?

As a subsidiary question, why did the U.S. Government not make some accommodation in the Social Security regulations to grant a new form of relief to the self-employed abroad for sheltering overseas earned income when the 911 exclusion was lost. We suspect that no one thought of this downstream effect of the tax law change. Will someone be willing to make appropriate relief now that this situation has been identified?

Mr. President we call upon you to address these basic questions. We hope that you will not reply again by merely restating present policy and its defense. What we need to know is whether or not you feel we really deserve equitable treatment as individuals? And, do we deserve attention to insure that as individuals we are not handicapped unnecessarily in our competitive ability against individuals of other nationalities abroad?

ISSUE No. 22

Short title

Seven-day work test discrimination for retired Americans abroad.

Summary of the problem.—The U.S. Social Security regulations set a dollar limit on the amount of outside earned income a person drawing social security retirement benefits can earn before losing his social security benefits.

For retired Americans abroad, working for an employer that is not contributing to the U.S. Social Security Trust Fund, dollar limits do not apply. Instead, an individual is only allowed to work for six days per month, no matter how much income might be earned during these six days. If so much as a minute is worked on the seventh day, ALL benefits are lost for the entire month.

ACA's question.—ACA asked the President to explain why overseas retired Americans were singled out for this discrimination? What justification is there for this work test rather than the dollar limit test used in the United States?

The President's reply.—"This seven-day foreign work test was adopted to avoid the variation in benefit reduction in different countries resulting from prevailing wage rates and foreign exchange rates. Relating the benefit reduction to a test, either of time worked or of wages earned, is a difficult problem because the retirement benefit is geared to a standard of living and a prevailing wage rate in the U.S. Thus, compared to a graduated, dollar-denominated benefit reduction, the worker under the seven-day test will gain in some countries and lose in others, depending upon how much he is able to earn during that period and the current cost of living in those countries."

The President thus implicitly accepts that there is a different method of controlling earnings abroad than that used in the United States, and also that this is not neutral in its impact abroad since retirees in some countries are favored and those in other countries are hurt by this practice.

Further, the President tells us nothing about why a seven-day period was chosen, and why when the limit is reached all benefits for the month in question are lost. In the United States, once the dollar limit is reached the retiree loses half of his benefit dollar for each dollar in excess of this limit. Abroad it is all or nothing. Again more questions are raised than are answered for those abroad.

Finally, it is very obvious that Americans in the liberal professions that usually bring the highest remuneration are those that can most easily arrange their work to fit within the six day limit. Thus, the poorer and most needy American abroad is the one that is the most disadvantaged by the U.S. practice.

To alleviate some of the problem, the President recommended action. It goes in the wrong direction! Said the President. "A provision in the Administration's proposed 1979 amendments to the Social Security Act would change the seven-day work test to a forty-five hour work test. The purpose of the proposed change is to allow a greater flexibility in the allocation of work during the month, so that a retiree engaged in noncovered employment abroad could work up to forty-five-hours per month and still receive full benefits. The Proposed change would not alter the problem of dollar-denominated vs. time-denominated benefit reductions."

We wonder how many overseas Americans will be better off following the President's proposed change. Those who are now working six full days abroad and still qualifying for their benefits will no longer be able to do so. Few if any overseas countries have a workday with less than eight hours of work. The new rules will effectively reduce the number of days of work allowed for these individuals to even less than the six now allowed. The new rule may appear to be more flexible, but in practice it will be even more inequitable than the old rules

But, once again the President has not told us why we have this discrimination at all. Questions of exchange rate problems occur in any case, and often do in the same country where some retirees work for participating companies (hence are subject to the dollar limits) while some others work for non-participating companies (and have the time tests).

ACA's renewed question.—Mr. President, please take another look at what we are now confronting abroad and what you have proposed to "help" us. Please tell us why we have this peculiar time test? Why at the limit all of our benefits are lost rather than only part of them as in the case of the dollar limits? And, if we must have a time test, why has seven days been chosen and under what system of new math is forty-five hours even the equivalent to six working days let alone any improvement over this amount?

We urgently seek redress. Our least fortunate overseas retirees are the ones that suffer the most today and many of these will suffer even more if your proposals come to fruition.

ISSUE No. 23

Short title

Denial of medicare to Americans abroad.

Summary of the problem.—American citizens living outside of the United States are denied medicare benefits even though they may have contributed to Social Security to earn these benefits.

ACA's question.—Why does the United States make this discrimination against Americans living abroad?

The President's reply.—"The Social Security Act prohibits payment for medical services or items not provided within the United States. Citizens living abroad can enroll in Medicare, but reimbursement is only provided for treatment received in the United States."

The President further stated that: "The desirability of an amendment to the Social Security Act to provide reimbursement for emergency services for U.S. citizens traveling to other countries will be reviewed by the Department of Health, Education and Welfare."

Finally, the President explained the problems with offering medicare abroad. "There are two primary difficulties in extending Medicare services abroad: (1) determining reimbursement rates for foreign services; and (2) ensuring compliance with Medicare standards by foreign medical personnel and facilities. With regard to reciprocal agreements with other countries, the main problem is with differences in eligibility standards between foreign health programs and the Medicare programs. These administrative difficulties are significant, but not insurmountable. A great deal of study would be required before the advisability of these programs is determined. However, the current estimated cost of full coverage for the approximately 226,000 eligibles abroad would be $375 million. In view of the need to limit Federal expenditures, this cost is a major concern."

It is hard to know what to make of the President's reply to this question. He lists a number of obstacles which would need to be confronted to give Medicare to Americans abroad, but then admits that these are not insurmountable. Next he admits that there are 226,000 Americans abroad who are eligible for Medicare, which means that they have contributed to the Social Security program. Yet he then tells us that to give them the benefits that they have earned would cost a considerable amount of money and since the U.S. Government needs to be frugal this granting of benefits to those who have paid for them must not be a precipitous act!

The President has consistently refused to give us a definition of equitable treatment whereby to judge the individual problems that are faced by Americans abroad. However, judging from the response given above it is rather clear that equitable treatment does not mean giving those abroad the fruits of their previous contributions as they are given to those who are at home. A most curious form of equity.

There are even more troubling questions to be raised by the President's answer. He indicated that two major problems that would need to be overcome concern reimbursement rates abroad and compliance by medical personnel abroad with Medicare standards. "A great deal of study would be required before the advisability of these programs is determined" concluded the President.

Even those with the barest knowledge of programs already underway and operating efficiently for many years abroad are fully aware that all of the difficulties have been successfully met by a U S. Government program offering medical benefits to retired military personnel abroad, CHAMPUS. No "great deal of study" is really needed other than a telephone call from the Department of HEW to the Department of Defense.

ACA's renewed question.—Mr President, we regret that your answer to our question about the justification for denying medicare to those who have earned it abroad came in such a transparently inadequate form. You have not explained to us how equitable treatment of overseas Americans implies denying benefits to one American and giving them to another simply because of this location of residence. And, it is clearly inadequate to maintain that great problems would have to be resolved before such care could be given abroad because the U.S. Government has long since resolved all of these problems under a different, but very similar, program.

Finally, we doubt that you seriously meant to imply that frugality in Government expenditure is a good reason to deny elderly Americans abroad a benefit that they have paid to obtain. We suspect that trying such an argument on Americans living in Alaska on the same grounds would be considered politically suicidal. The fact that this can be attempted for those abroad with such temerity is sad proof of your estimate of our political merit.

Mr. President, we hope that you will agree with us that your answer is still urgently needed on this question of such great concern to Americans in their last few years of life. It is an affront to those who live abroad and a direct contradiction to all of the generous encomiums you have offered to the elderly American to associate your name with the response you gave in your August 27th report.

Please take another look at this question. And, please address the basic question of what treatment of overseas Americans on the medicare question would conform with any minimum standard of equity.

We urgently appeal for redress.

ISSUE No. 24

Short title

Unemployment insurance for Americans abroad.

Summary of the problem.—While some Americans working overseas are covered by compulsory unemployment compensation programs in the United States. many others are not. Draconian new U.S. tax laws have forced many overseas Americans to return home. Many of these find it difficult to obtain new employment and suffer greatly from not having unemployment insurance while looking for a new job.

ACA's question.—Why does the U S Government not provide an unemployment insurance plan in which overseas Americans can voluntarily participate to protect themselves upon return to the United States?

The President's reply.—We quote from the President's reply at length because it is most instructive. "The only Americans abroad without unemployment compensation coverage are those working for foreign employers It is not known how many Americans are in this category or how many return to the United States as a result of having their employment terminated. but there is no evidence of a widespread need for a special purpose program to cover them."

The President then recited the familiar litany of difficulties that would be faced if such a special program of coverage would be offered. "With respect to extending unemployment compensation coverage to Americans working overseas for foreign firms. it must be understood that compliance controls over foreign employers outside of the United States would likely be limited at best. It would be difficult to obtain necessary data on individuals' wage and employment histories. These data form the basis for determining if the individual had sufficient employment to qualify for benefits and the amount and duration of such benefits. Similarly, it would be difficult to obtain reliable information concerning the reasons for the claimant's separation so that benefits could be limited only to those individuals involuntarily unemployed. In cases where the employer's response differed from the claimant's contention. it would be difficult to convene a proper hearing to resolve the issue. Such problems could weaken the system's financial security (sic). Furthermore. the dangers of adverse selection must be taken into account Such a voluntary program would attract those who believe they are likely to need such benefits in the future, while those who do not expect to need them would be less likely to apply for coverage. The premiums necessary to keep the fund solvent could, therefore, be quite high."

Mr. President, we doubt very seriously that you ever had a chance to review this portion of your report to the Congress. It so demonstrably resonates to the vibrations of a bureaucracy that decided to obfuscate a very simple question. The question that was raised was only: should there be discrimination against some Americans living overseas in terms of their coverage for unemployment? Your advisors chose instead to answer a different sort of query: how many good reasons can we find for not giving unemployment coverage to Americans abroad?

Mr. President, even in answering this very different question you were badly served by your staff. They claim that a justification for not having a "voluntary" program of such unemployment insurance abroad is due to the difficulty of obtaining information about employment and the salaries earned abroad. Surely they need not be reminded that the same information requirement has never been suggested as a justification for not forcing overseas Americans to declare their overseas incomes for U.S. tax purposes. How evident it is, once again, that there is such an imbedded double standard whereby obligations are maintained for Americans abroad and benefits denied using both sides of the same argument as a justification.

ACA's renewed question.—Mr. President, we would like to ask that you once again address this question in its proper form Is there a definition of equity that necessitates making a distinction among Americans abroad in terms of those who can be covered by unemployment insurance and those who cannot? There is a very different question also of why the United States does not consider making such a voluntary insurance program part of a package of inducements to Americans to be willing to work overseas. It is precisely U.S. employees of foreign companies that in many instances are the key individuals who can specify American source goods and services for their overseas procurement needs.

We ask for redress. And we hope that you will counsel your staff members to spare us the tedium of repetitions of the adverse selection argument. We doubt seriously that you support the idea that programs are bad if they only appeal to individuals who might someday have a need for the benefits that they are asked to contribute for. Unless there is a deceptive form of involuntary subsidization of some form or other in every one of the present U.S. Government programs we suspect that everyone should hope someday to derive some benefit from programs in which they are enrolled.

Mr. President, please take another look at this important issue.

ISSUE NO. 25

Short title

Problems for social security earnings limits from fluctuating exchange rates abroad.

Summary of the problem.—Some overseas Americans receiving Social Security Retirement Pensions work for employers who contribute to the Social Security Trust Fund. As such, their outside earnings are restricted to a given dollar amount above which they will lose their Social Security Benefits. Many of these retired Americans are paid in a foreign currency which is not fixed at a given value against the dollar but fluctuates daily against the dollar.

These retired Americans suffer from not being able to predict how much their overseas dollar incomes will be, hence are subjected to unexpected and most unfortunate losses of Social Security Benefits when the overseas currency appreciates.

The difficulty comes from the fact that these Americans are living in a foreign currency environment in which almost all of their expenditures are also in the foreign currency. The use of a dollar standard for them creates difficulties.

ACA's question.—Why cannot some method be found to protect the Social Security Pensioner from loss of U.S. benefits through phantom (dollar apparent) changes in his overseas income due solely to changes in currency exchange rates?

The President's reply.—"When these earnings of Americans abroad change in response to local inflationary impact or fluctuation in exchange rates, the workers may suffer by comparison with workers in the U.S. Only a small percentage of beneficiaries abroad have their benefits reduced as a result of the earnings test. The Social Security Administration has avoided using special indices for social security benefits according to the country of residence of the beneficiary, not only because of the severe administrative problems created by special indices, but also because of the policy to maintain uniform standards within the program to the greatest extent possible. In the United States, in spite of wide variations in wage levels and cost-of-living among different areas, the standards are uniform for all areas."

Unfortunately, the problem of the impact of moving exchange rates was not addressed specifically. The great problem with this new international phenomenon (triggered a few years ago by the United States) is that no one wants to examine the myriad implications of living with systems that function on fixed values in one currency while qualifying in moving values in another system. This difficulty of economic value relativity must be addressed.

ACA's renewed question.—Despite the assurance that "only a small percentage of beneficiaries abroad" suffer from this problem, we feel that some further study of how to help our overseas pensioners is urgently needed. The problem occurs for the needy abroad whose circumstances are such that they "must" work to survive. That they have become the victims of international monetary capriciousness whereby they are the ones who pay for every gyration in exchange rates no matter what force may be behind such monetary changes seems highly unfair. We appeal to the President once again for further study and positive redress to this problem for senior citizen Americans abroad.

ISSUE No. 26

Short title

Cost of living problems for retired Americans abroad.

Summary of the problem.—Related to the issue raised in Issue 25, is the prob lem of the irrelevance of fixing outside earning limits in dollars for retired Americans receiving Social Security Benefits in countries which have much higher costs-of-living than anywhere in the United States.

ACA's question.—Why cannot some allowance be made for either paying benefits, or adjusting the outside earnings limits for those receiving Social Security Benefits abroad to take account of extraordinary costs-of-living in some overseas countries?

The President's reply.—"The Social Security Administration has avoided using special indices for social security benefits according to the country of residence of the beneficiary, not only because of the severe administrative problems created by special indices, but also because of the policy to maintain uniform standards within the program to the greatest extent possible. In the United States, in spite of wide variations in wage levels and cost-of-living among different areas, the standards are uniform for all areas."

This reply once again raises the spectre of "severe administrative problems" to justify not giving further thought to the problems of the retired senior citizen abroad. However the U.S. Government makes generous provision for cost-of-living adjustments in the compensation of Government employees abroad. And, the Congress recently provided for cost-of-living tables to apply to overseas Americans for deductions from overseas earned income. It would appear that both of these precedents accept the necessity for taking account of differences in conditions abroad, and both offer indices that could easily be adapted to the Social Security benefit calculations.

ACA's renewed question.—Why is the United States not more concerned with the plight of its overseas senior citizens? With several overseas cost-of-living indices already in use for Americans abroad, both in the Government employee sector and in the private citizen sector, why not adapt the Social Security benefits to reflect this already accepted reality? We appeal for a new consideration of this problem and for greater compassion for overseas senior citizens.

ISSUE No. 27

Short title

U.S. taxation of overseas Americans creates competitive problems.

Summary of the problem.—The United States tax policy is that all American citizens, no matter where they may live, have the same obligation to pay U.S. taxes on their earned and unearned income.

No other major country of the Free World has this tax approach. All of the rivals to the United States tax their citizens on the basis of their residence. This applies to taxation of earned income and foreign unearned income as well.

Obviously, therefore, whenever an American confronts a non-American abroad, the American will be competing with an extra burden: his tax liability to the United States.

A number of observations can be made about this U.S. policy. First, as a basic principle it is a paradigm example of a situation where equity with

Americans at home conflicts with equity in competition against individuals of other nationalities abroad.

Second, it is most curious that the stoutly maintained necessity for Americans to carry their obligations on the basis of citizenship no matter where they reside is so obviously at variance with the U.S. practice of not giving rights or benefits on the basis of citizenship but rather defining many of these on the basis of residency.

Third, the United States has just expended a considerable amount of time and labor to negotiate a new multilateral trade agreement to insure a freer movement of U.S. goods and services into the major markets of the world. Yet, in parallel with this negotiating effort, the United States has twice expended considerable effort elaborating new tax practices that impede the ability of its citizens to compete in these same markets!

Fourth, the United States maintains that it wants to promote fair competition around the world. One of the basic principles of economics is that factor inputs to a production process are used in proportion to their relative costs. We have chosen to make the input costs of using American labor abroad more costly than the use of labor of any other nationality. In other words, we have unilaterally distorted the world labor market by imposing a unique burden on workers of one nationality, our own.

Fifth, our tax policy hurts the ability of Americans to compete in markets abroad to the extent that these overseas markets do not have a local income tax that is similar to our own. Paradoxically, the overseas markets where we have the most vital interest in strengthening our presence, i.e., those of OPEC countries, are the very markets where our unilateral economic disarmament tactics hurt the most.

Sixth, the cost burden imposed upon Americans abroad not only causes direct competitive disadvantage to individual Americans abroad, it also creates direct and indirect problems for employers abroad, for the U.S. Government abroad, and for all American citizens at home.

ACA was recently told by a senior officer of a large international executive recruitment company that a number of important Middle Eastern, and other developing country, clients have expressed a preference for hiring an American citizen for sensitive jobs that involve large scale corporate and national planning. Many of these clients, however, have reluctantly been forced to hire individuals of other nationalities because the American, who insists on being protected from the IRS, is just too much more expensive than everyone else. These jobs often lead to the specification of goods and services for large-scale projects overseas. Not having an American in these jobs means that there is much less likelihood that American inputs will be given any priority consideration for these projects.

Embarrassment for large American companies abroad occurs as the practice grows of major foreign governments objecting to fees in contracts that cover the costs American companies incur to tax protect their employees abroad. One senior corporate executive told ACA that a major developing country government instructed them to delete such fees from their bids. The government objected to making transfer payments to the U.S. Treasury for work performed in their own countries abroad. This conflict of sovereignty is most unfortunate and can lead to further difficulties on a diplomatic level, and it also can be used to inflame local populations abroad. The extra cost burden assumed by the American company employer in such cases also implies that they must live with lower profit margins in these markets than companies with fewer American employees, or else they must cover these lost revenues with profit from other parts of the world.

It has been estimated that every additional billion dollars of exports of manufactured products provides at least 40,000 new jobs in the United States. Each time our taxation of overseas Americans leads directly, or indirectly, to a loss of exports abroad this means that the U.S. economy suffers. And, of course, this means not only fewer jobs but also lost revenues for the Federal and State Governments from fewer tax generators, and also higher budget deficits for the Federal and State Governments through the need to provide additional unemployment benefits at home. Lest it be thought that this is not a real problem, reputable American industrial sources confirm that the United States has lost billions of dollars in projects in the Middle East alone in the last three years due in large part to the unfortunate tax practices of the United States.

Seventh, a different form of disadvantage can occur to the United States from its policies on taxation. It has often been maintained that since taxes abroad in many cases equal or exceed the amount of tax that is due to the United States, there is really no problem for Americans in many countries abroad This is incorrect. Large American companies, because they need to have personnel policies that appear to be equitable to all of their employees abroad, and because they alone have to worry about sheltering their employees from double tax burdens wherever they might be assigned abroad, have alone among all of the major corporations of the world been forced to adopt a tax-equalization practice This functions basically as follows : the employee is assigned a base reference salary for work abroad that is comparable to what would be earned in the United States for a similar job. The employer then withholds from this salary the amount of U S. tax that would normally be paid in the United States All of the other incentives needed to induce the American abroad are then added to this base (after-tax) salary as well as the cost-of-living allowances, housing, travel, home-leave. R&R and schooling allowances. The corporation then agrees to pay all of the overseas tax that the individual would have to pay on this aggregate income, and to pay the additional U.S. tax, if any, that would be due since the aggregate income abroad is far higher than the base upon which the U.S. equivalent tax is withheld This leads to a very rapidly spiraling of costs abroad, because the tax payments to the foreign government for the salary of the first year must then be added to the taxable salary the following year. Each year the burden gets larger.

A different tax compensation problem arises because of the need to make allowance for the way the individual's unearned income is taxed at home. If the individual has unearned income, and if he would be in a less than 50 percent tax bracket at home, but because of inflated dollar values of the overseas salary his income now is in the 50 percent bracket, many companies will give some indulgence to the extra tax that has to be paid on the unearned income Others will not, and in this case the individual will suffer The case is far worse when the American is married to an alien and the alien spouse has a considerable amount of overseas income, either earned or unearned For, not only does the United States want to tax its overseas citizens, it also tries to tax citizens of other countries living abroad if they have married an American citizen If the alien does not file a joint tax return with the American spouse, the American will have a marginal earned income tax rate that reaches 70 percent!

Thus, overseas American companies, alone among all of the companies competing around the world, cannot structure their overseas salary practices on the basis of the going wages in the overseas markets. They must build and administer these tax protection schemes.

Eighth, the loss of an American employee abroad can have a very dire consequence on the economic health of the United States even within an American company abroad. It has been maintained by some that it really makes no difference whether an American company employs an American citizen abroad or a foreigner to do the same job ACA was recently told that one American company that has manufacturing subsidiaries in a number of countries overseas has an ongoing battle to keep products flowing from the United States when these are in competition with the production of the same products abroad. One senior American in this company reported that he spends considerable amounts of time keeping the foreign subsidiaries run by foreigners from refusing orders that will mean exports from the United States rather than sales from their subsidiaries abroad. If this American is replaced abroad the defense of the interests of the American production facilities will be severely diminished. This same company has been forced to reduce its overseas American staff during the last several years and the problems today can in part be attributed to the decreased presence of Americans abroad in this company.

Ninth, U.S. practice of subjecting all income whether earned or unearned to U.S. taxes means that in cases of conflicts of tax sovereignties it is always the individual American who loses Some overseas countries are starting to tax their residents on their worldwide incomes Tax incentives that may be enjoyed by Americans at home, such as municipal bonds that are exempt from Federal tax, will be liable to taxation by the foreign government Taxes abroad that have a name that differs from the one used in the United States, although the function is very similar, will be simply defined as not a tax for allowable credit purposes by the United States Deductions that are allowed abroad are rarely congruent with those that are allowed at home. In each such case, it is the American citizen who suffers from the sovereignty incompatibility.

ACA's question.—Having identified the myriad unfortunate consequences of having a uniquely heavy burden of double taxation for Americans who live and work abroad, ACA asked the President why it was in the interest of the United States to be treating its overseas citizens this way?

The President's reply.—The President chose not to address this question. He replied . "Many correspondents objected to the tax revisions in the Foreign Earned Income Act, enacted last year (1978). It is frequently alleged that those revisions, especially in the income exclusion provision, will have detrimental effects on the ability of American business to hire American citizens to work abroad, which in turn may result in reduced American exports or reduced profits earned abroad by American business. This report does not address this matter because its purpose is to focus on the issue of discrimination ; because the Commerce Department and the Senate Committee on Banking, Housing and Urban Affairs have recently studied U.S. export policy in depth ; and because, after protracted consideration by Congress and the Administration, the new tax law was enacted just months ago "

The President failed to add a few supplementary facts. First, when the Commerce Department carried out its study on promoting exports it wanted to address the question of tax treatment of overseas American citizens. It was blocked from considering this question by another Department of the Cabinet.

Second, the President failed to mention that he had urged the Congress to resolve outstanding tax issues involving Americans abroad and then when the 1978 Tax Reform Act was passed he found their provisions too generous ! Indeed, we have been told that the President instructed the Secretary of the Treasury to interpret the overseas tax changes "as strictly as possible" and only on that basis was he approving them. This was the incentive to the Treasury Department to give definitions to camps that would qualify abroad for the special income exclusion provisions of the 1978 law in such a manner than almost no camp anywhere in the world could qualify.

Third, the President's premise that the present law needs no further analysis because the Congress and the Administration have just spent considerable time on this question is of dubious historical value for dismissing its importance. The Congress has not been able to deal definitively with this problem since taxation of income first was instituted. Indeed, in 1926 the Congress decided that to promote foreign trade overseas Americans should not have to pay any U.S. tax on any of their overseas earned income. While modifications of this basic policy were made over the following decades in terms of defining what qualified as a foreign residence in terms of location or time abroad, the basic idea of a full income exclusion remained U.S. policy for thirty-six years. It was not until 1962 when in a zeal to stop the abuse of these provisions by a few movie stars that the Congress placed a ceiling on excludable foreign earned income. Two years later the ceiling was lowered. Finally, in 1976. the exclusion was for many overseas Americans effectively abolished.

Thus, when the international economic order was undergoing a profound change after which every Western country would have great new oil import costs to balance with much greater export efforts, the United States chose not to address the problem of how to increase its exports, but rather chose to carry out a major attack on an alleged unjustified tax advantage being enjoyed by Americans abroad. Congress closed this "loophole" in 1976 thereby overnight tripling the average amount of U.S. tax that had to be paid by the U.S. taxpayer trying to compete abroad. It is not difficult to understand why our export performance was even less enthusiastic after this blow than before.

The President did not tell us either that while we were on this loophole closing crusade at home our major competitors were carrying out major studies of how they could induce more of their own citizens to live and work abroad. Nor did he tell us that these other countries expected their overseas citizens to be able to compete from as favorable a position as possible and thus required no tax from them on either their overseas earned or unearned incomes. In addition many countries gave new subsidies to overseas education. expanded social services abroad. gave new human rights guarantees, etc.

The President chose not to tell us that one of the reasons that the Congress and the Administration had to spend so much time in 1978 on the taxation of overseas Americans issue was to undue the damage that had been caused in 1976. Nor did he tell us that part of the reason for this damage was that the Treasury Department misled the Congress in 1976 into thinking that the impact of the loophole closing would be small whereas in actual fact the impact was ten times what Treasury had predicted!

Finally, the President did not tell us how the enormously complicated tax reform provisions of 1978 are supposed to help make overseas Americans more competitive around the world. In actual fact, some Americans abroad are less competitive today than they were under the disasterous provisions of the 1976 Act. Many are not even as well off as they were under the provisions of the pre-1976 Act. We are most alarmed by the complacency manifested by the reply that was given to this crucial question in the President's first report.

ACA's Renewed question.—There are a number of very basic questions that need to be addressed as a matter of great urgency by the President

What competitive position should overseas Americans have when faced with individuals of other nationalities in the major markets of the world? Should Americans, as individual citizens, have to carry unique extra cost burdens, and if so why? If they should not have to carry such economically disqualifying burdens, what recommendations does the President have for new legislation from the Congress on the taxation of Americans abroad?

Finally, there is the intriguing, and unanswered, question of why obligations of Americans are based upon citizenship but rights and benefits are defined by residence? What definition of equitable treatment implies such a double-standard for U.S. policy?

We appeal for redress, and do so in the name of the economic health and welfare of all Americans.

ISSUE No. 28

Short title

Inadequate U.S. tax credit for taxes paid abroad.

Summary of the problem.—In its first report, ACA gave a detailed explanation of how many foreign countries choose to raise their government revenues from a different mix of direct and indirect taxation from that used in the United States. Since the United States will only give credit against U.S. tax liabilities for taxes paid abroad that are fully congruent with U.S. income taxes, many overseas Americans are being doubly taxed and denied credit for taxes that have in economic reality been paid.

ACA's question.—If the United States must insist on being the only major country to subject its overseas citizens to double tax liability, why does the United States not give a more generous treatment to the different forms of taxes that are paid abroad in terms of credit against taxes deemed due to the U.S. Government?

The President's reply.—"Foreign sales taxes have historically not been deductible for U.S. income tax purposes because of the administrative difficulties of checking on so many different systems. However, under the Foreign Earned Income Act of 1978, qualifying U.S. citizens working abroad are allowed to deduct a cost of living differential for excess living costs abroad. Foreign sales taxes, including the value added taxes (VAT), are reflected in the cost of living index. Moreover, unlike state and local income taxes, which may only be deducted in computing taxable income for Federal income tax, income taxes imposed by political subdivisions of foreign countries may be credited against Federal income tax, reducing the tax dollar for dollar. This credit provides significant advantage to Americans abroad who are subject to foreign income taxes. For example, in Switzerland, the total Swiss income tax burden is higher than in the United States, yet the income tax levied by the national government is insignificant (sic). Being allowed to credit income taxes paid to the cantons is therefore a very significant benefit to U.S. citizens living in Switzerland."

The President justifies the disallowance of credit, or even a deduction, for sales taxes or VAT abroad on the grounds that it would create an administrative burden to give this deduction or credit. The President has not told us whether this failure conforms to a basic standard of equitable treatment, or not.

Secondly, the President informs us that the cost-of-living deduction covers the VAT payments that are made abroad. This would be a surprise to Americans living in the United Kingdom paying a 10 percent VAT on most of their purchases because the cost-of-living deduction they are granted comes to a total of $300 per year. It would also come as a surprise to an American living in France because someone buying a new car there pays a VAT of 33 percent on the purchase price of the car, and given the high cost of cars abroad the full cost-of-living deduction for a single person in France of $4.500 could go in great part for a car purchase alone not counting any of the other expenditures during the year on which a 17 percent VAT must be paid.

Third, the President implies that the U.S. Government is being generous in giving a significant "benefit" to Americans living in countries such as Switzerland by allowing a credit against U.S. tax for income taxes paid to Cantonal authorities. We wonder compared to whom this is meant to be a benefit? Compared to Americans living in other countries abroad? No. Compared to citizens of other nationalities living in Switzerland? No. Compared to Americans living in the United States who enjoy having only one tax obligation rather than two? We doubt it.

ACA's renewed question.—If the United States must insist on maintaining its unique form of citizenship based taxation for Americans abroad, it would seem imperative that some basic definition of what is equitable treatment must be given. If the United States chooses to give deductions at home for State sales taxes and denies the same deductions abroad because of "administrative burdens" for implementation of the same deductions this seems hardly fair. If the United States wants to pretend that its cost-of-living deductions abroad are meant to compensate for every case in which a similar form of denial of U.S. comparable deduction or credit is inflicted on those abroad, a much better analysis should be made of what is going on abroad.

It should be recalled that in the case of sales tax at home not only is there a general tax deduction for different revenue classes, but there is also provision for special deductions for special purchases such as cars, boats, trailers, etc. Neither the general deductions nor the special case deductions are given abroad, yet the VAT paid on these items abroad is almost always much higher overseas than in the United States.

We ask the President to restudy this important issue and propose a more equitable method of allowing deductions abroad for the same items that are covered at home. We would prefer to have the President accept to suggest that the United States conform with the overseas tax practices of the rest of the Free World.

ISSUE No. 29

Short title

American tax practices impede the purchase of U.S. goods abroad.

Summary of the problem.—In its first report, ACA showed how the present method of taxing Americans living overseas can impede the purchase by overseas Americans of U.S. made goods. The argument was based upon the fact that U.S. goods, after import duties and transportation have been paid, usually cost more abroad than locally produced goods. If the American needs to earn more marginal income to purchase an American source good he will already have a disincentive to purchase this good If, in addition, he incurs an additional U.S. tax liability because of his extra income, he is even less motivated to make a purchase of American goods.

ACA's question.—ACA asked why, if the United States persists in its misguided policy of taxing overseas Americans, it doesn't do something within the confines of this misguided policy to encourage more purchase overseas of American source goods. ACA proposed that a credit against U.S. income taxes be given for foreign duty and sales tax that must be paid for the purchase abroad of a U S. source good. ACA reasoned that an American at home would not have to pay either for this duty or heavy sales tax, and would in any case be given a deduction for the sales tax paid to his State.

The President's reply—The President chose not to reply to this question.

ACA's renewed question—Since promoting U.S. exports is such a high priority issue, and since the use of U.S. products abroad by American citizens is a good way to demonstrate these goods to foreigners, why does the United States not give a tax incentive to Americans abroad to purchase U.S. goods?

ISSUE No 30

Short title

Taxation of phantom income generated by exchange rate movements abroad.

Summary of the problem.—During the last few years, the international economic order has been profoundly changed. One of the most significant new facts of life is the daily fluctuation of exchange rates between one currency and another. Some Americans working abroad, whose local currency incomes do not vary, find that they have greatly increased U.S. tax liabilities because exchange rate movements give the appearance of dollar value salary increases. Thus, while the actual ability to pay U.S taxes has not increased because there is no extra income abroad in a economically real sense, the American must nevertheless be prepared to find extra resources to meet an inflated U.S tax bill

ACA's question.—Why should the tax liability of an overseas American increase from one year to the next when his overseas income does not move in the local currency in which it is denominated

The President's reply.—"When income or capital gains are reported for U S tax purposes, the value is expressed in U S. dollars. Due to fluctuating exchange rates, the value of income or an asset which remains constant in foreign currency terms will vary in U S. currency terms. In countries where the currency has strengthened relative to the dollar, a U.S taxpayer may report a higher U.S. dollar income or inflated capital gain, even though his foreign currency income or foreign property value has remained constant. To alleviate situations such as these, a cost of living differential deduction, which reflects variations in exchange rates, is allowed under the Foreign Earned Income Act of 1978 While exchange fluctuations work both ways, the cost of living differential rule operates only when the foreign costs are higher in dollar terms and does not increase "income" when foreign costs are lower. Thus, there is no negative deduction in the low cost of living country."

We don't know whether the President meant this response to be serious or whether he was having fun. We were already told that the cost-of-living deduction was supposed to cover sales taxes and VAT that we are denied abroad. Apparently this deduction also is meant to cover phantom income inflation as well, and no doubt it has a triple function of recognizing that there are real cost of living factors also which are not due to either of these other issues !

There are a number of problems in trying to make the COL deduction function as an effective deflator for the phantom income problem First, the COL is calculated once each year based upon costs at a given moment in time. The phantom income generator, however, operates throughout the entire year Given the right currency fluctuation cycle, the phantom income rise could reach its peak six months after the COL has been calculated and fall again to the previous currency equivalent a year after the COL calculation date In this case the new COL would have no cognizance at all of what had happened during the intervening twelve months. This also shows that any reflection of phantom income generation of a cyclical nature rather than a trend nature is fortuitous.

ACA's renewed question.—ACA would like to ask that the President address the phantom income generation problem once again. COL deductions are not an effective remedy and are already overworked from other causes anyway Phantom income taxation is a fact of life. Its most appropriate remedy would be for the United States to conform to the overseas tax practices of other countries.

Issue No. 31

Short title

Taxation of phantom capital gains created by exchange rate fluctuations abroad.

Summary of the problem.—Capital gains for U S. tax purposes are calculated in dollars Most overseas capital investments are made in foreign currencies. Because of foreign currency fluctuations, a dollar capital gain might appear when the economic reality might even be a real capital loss in a foreign currency.

ACA gave an example in its first report of a man who borrowed the entire sum needed to purchase a home overseas Several years later he sold this home for the same amount of foreign currency he had paid to purchase the house. He used the proceeds of the sale to pay off the loan. However, because of changes in the exchange rates during the intervening period, he appeared to have a large capital gain in dollars The fact that he had a comparable loss in his loan account was not germane because such losses are considered "personal items" by the IRS and cannot be offset against capital gains. The American in this example would have to borrow a large sum of money to pay U.S. taxes on a capital gain that only occurred on his tax form

ACA's question.—Why does the United States not make provision in that tax laws to avoid taxation of such transparently inequitable phantom capital gains?

The President's reply.—The President replied that to alleviate such problems overseas Americans are granted a cost of living differential deduction. He did not indicate how this deduction is supposed to shelter phantom capital gains. Nor could he since the COL is not designed to function to this effect.

ACA's renewed question.—ACA would like to ask the President to address several questions. First, what definition of equity requires the IRS to tax phantom capital gains that do not reflect economic reality as in the case mentioned above?

Second, how does the COL give any relief from such taxation as was claimed in his first report?

Third, why is it that only the United States taxes the overseas capital gains of its citizens and what are the international competitive implications of this unique form of overseas taxation?

ISSUE No. 32

Short title

Preferential tax treatment for Government Employees abroad.

Summary of the problem —All allowances and benefits earned by private citizens abroad must be counted as income for U.S. tax purposes. U.S. Government employees are not taxed on their allowances and benefits.

ACA's question.—Why are U.S. Government employees taxed differently abroad than private U.S. citizens?

The President's reply.—"The Foreign Earned Income Act of 1978 changed the taxation of Americans employed abroad in the private sector to conform fairly closely to the taxation of Americans employed abroad by the U.S. Government. Government employees may exclude certain allowances from taxable income; private sector employees must in general treat the allowances as income but may then deduct amounts for qualifying excess foreign housing costs, education, other added living costs, home leave travel, and hardship conditions. The tax savings of an exclusion or a deduction from gross income are generally the same. Tax free government allowances are more generous than the private sector deductions in some respects, such as housing costs. In other cases, such as the home leave travel and hardship deductions, the private sector treatment is more generous."

The President chose not to answer the basic question of why there is a distinction in the way overseas citizens are being treated for tax purposes.

We wish he had. Because it would be interesting to learn why government employees have more generous treatment in most instances even though they are subject to taxation only by the U.S. Government, not to income taxation by any foreign government, hence to no double direct income taxation as are private American citizens abroad.

The President admitted that housing deductions for government employees are more generous than for private citizens abroad. Indeed they are. U.S. private citizens are only allowed a deduction for housing that exceeds a certain proportion of their total income. Government quarters allowances are fully tax deductible without regard to their relationship to the income of the individual.

The President claimed that deductions for home leave for private citizens are more generous than those for government employees. A tax court ruling of recent date stated that not only is travel to the USA deductible for a government employee but also the direct costs to the government employee while he is in the United States on home leave because this is considered to be part of his employment obligation, hence a work rather than pleasure expense. Private citizens do not enjoy such relief.

The most obvious difference in treatment, however, is the fact that cost of living allowances for government employees are not taxable while there are only limited COL deductions for private citizens. The Congress chose to place a ceiling on COL for the private citizen at the level of a middle-grade government employee Any government employee abroad earning more than this cut-off grade salary has a higher, tax-free, allowance for COL than any private citizen abroad.

There is a further problem comparing COL that is given to the government employee and the deduction of a fixed amount granted to a private citizen. In many overseas countries where inflation, or exchange rate movements cause frequent adjustments to be made in real COL differences from the U.S. based standard, the government has adopted a practice of revising the COL allowance levels as frequently as once every month. The private citizen has a COL deduction that is fixed for an entire year, and only adjusted with great delay based upon economic reality at only one reference point in time. Not only does the government employee benefit from the frequent adjustments to new circumstances, he also is insured of protection when there is a cycle of exchange rate fluctuations within any one year period. This is impossible for private citizens under the once-per-year standards now used by the IRS.

ACA's renewed question —ACA would like to ask the President to address several questions. First, why should government officials above the middle bureaucrat level enjoy tax free allowances that are far greater than the deductions for cost of living given to private citizens?

Secondly, why has the COL been pegged to the GS level now in use? What relevance does this have to the economic reality confronted abroad by American private citizens?

Third, why are government employees given more generous tax advantages in their housing allowances than private citizens?

Finally, what form of taxation of these allowances and benefits, if there must be any at all, would give the greatest equity in terms of treatment of private citizens and government employees? Why has there been any deviation from this standard? What should be done to make these two overseas groups comparable?

Issue No. 33

Short title

Tax treatment of income blocked by exchange controls abroad.

Summary of the problem.—Many foreign countries have currencies that are not freely convertible into dollars, or even if convertible have exchange controls that prohibit exporting currency of any kind. The U.S tax code calls for income earned by an American in a country that has blocked currency provisions to be considered as all earned in the year that such income eventually becomes unblocked. This can lead to several years' income being taxable by the United States as if it had occurred in a one-year period. Given the high marginal U S tax rates, this means that the tax liability of such an individual could be much higher than it should be if U.S. law reflected economic reality.

ACA's question —Asked the President to address the question of what definition of equity necessitated such tax practice by the United States?

The President's reply.—"The rules which American residents abroad must observe with respect to blocked foreign income are the same rules which apply to Americans living in the U.S. Blocked income can be taken into income when earned. If taxpayers elect to treat it as income in the year it becomes unblocked, it becomes analogous to receiving a lump-sum payment for services performed in a prior year. The income averaging provisions of U.S. tax law may be used to reduce the tax."

ACA's renewed question.—Why does the United States have a practice that causes such added complications for Americans living overseas? The question is not an idle one, particularly since the 1978 tax law changes brought many more overseas Americans into the tax liability picture through abolition of income exclusion provisions.

Also, why is there not a recognition that living in a blocked currency country is quite different from living in the United States with some income coming from such a country? Why cannot the taxation from such sources be deferred until the income becomes unblocked and then simply have the individual file back returns to pick up the missing years?

Many low income Americans abroad, teachers, and workers at charitable institutions in blocked currency countries face much more complicated tax problems from U.S. taxes than ever before. The U.S. should address this added complexity and find a better solution.

Issue No. 34

Short title

Discriminatory taxation of Americans with an alien spouse.

Summary of the problem.—If an American is unmarried and lives abroad, he files U.S. income tax as a single person and has the maximum tax protection benefit. If he marries an alien, his U.S. tax status changes. Unless he accepts to file a joint return with his alien spouse, who may never have been to the United States and have no intention to ever go there, and accepts to have his spouse also pay U.S. income taxes on all of her worldwide earned and unearned income, he must file as a married-filing-separately individual and he also forfeits his maximum tax protection.

ACA's question.—Why does the United States want to tax non-resident aliens abroad, and why are Americans living abroad with a non-resident alien spouse faced with either paying tax on the spouse's income or losing significant U.S. tax benefits?

The President's reply.—"The rules concerning joint filing status, where one spouse is a non-resident alien are the same for Americans living in the U.S. as they are for Americans abroad. Both spouses must be subject to U.S tax in order to qualify for the benefits of the maximum tax on earned income Married taxpayers who choose not to file a joint return must file as "married filing separately" rather than as single persons. This is the so-called "marriage-penalty" for which there seems to be no solution satisfactory to all. If these rules, including the prohibition against an annual option on filing a joint or separate return, were changed only for U.S. citizens abroad married to non-resident aliens, such citizens could escape tax on their share of the spouse's community income. This is not possible for U.S. citizens living in the U.S. who are married to non-resident aliens."

Once again we don't know how to take the reply given by the President. First of all, it seems to us to say that Americans abroad with an alien spouse must be taxed the same as Americans living at home is one thing, but to say that Americans abroad with a non-resident alien spouse must be taxed the same as an American at home with a non-resident alien spouse is quite another. We wonder just what kind of household it is that has a non-resident alien spouse in the United States. Surely this must be a rare exception rather than the general rule. Abroad, on the contrary this is the rule in almost every case.

Second, why does the United States feel that it has any right to tax a non-resident alien at all? The overseas American has precious little to show for his tax dollar. Surely the non-resident alien abroad has nothing at all. Indeed it is just such non-resident aliens who suffer from our discriminatory citizenship laws and other unfortunate practices. We would ask the President what principle of American or even international law makes such taxation justifiable?

Third, we would ask the President to tell us why an American marrying a non-resident alien abroad must either pay the U.S. Government a full tax on his or her worldwide income or else lose some very important U.S. tax benefits himself? The President has mentioned this as a "marriage penalty" situation. Indeed it is, but not at all the same type as occurring in the United States where both individuals would have a tax liability in any case. The non-resident alien spouse abroad before the marriage did not have such a liability.

ACA's renewed question.—We would ask the President to please address the basic question of why the United States wants to tax overseas non-resident aliens? What is the basis for this tax? Surely it must be the most ambitious reach of any national tax authority in the world.

ISSUE NO. 35

Short title

Denial of right to Americans with an alien spouse to make an annual choice of filing status

Summary of the problem.—Americans who are married with an American citizen spouse, or a resident alien spouse, can decide each year whether or not they choose to file a joint return or separate return for U.S. income tax purposes. Americans with a non-resident alien spouse are denied the same annual option. The overseas American can only choose to file a joint return once. Having made this choice he must continue ever after with the same joint return practice He can discontinue this practice only once. Subsequently he can never file a joint return again.

ACA's question.—Why are American citizens married to non-resident alien spouses not allowed to make an annual option for filing status? What definition of equity justifies such discriminatory treatment?

The President's reply.—"If these rules, including the prohibition against an annual option on filing a joint or separate return, were changed only for U.S. citizens abroad married to non-resident aliens, such citizens could escape tax on their share of the spouse's community income. This is not possible for U.S. citizens living in the U.S. who are married to non-resident aliens."

We wonder, again, just who these U.S. residents are who are married to non-resident aliens. Obviously they are in split households, or perhaps there are the special cases in which the home straddles the border with Canada or Mexico and the spouse lives in the other half of the dwelling.

We wonder, once again, why there is a felt need to tax the income of the overseas non-resident alien at all? What standard of national or international law justifies reaching abroad to tax a citizen of another country in another country abroad for income earned entirely outside of the United States? Not even the Courts could claim that this tax was in payment for any significant benefits because there are no benefits of significance for aliens abroad who have never lived or worked in the United States.

We ask the President why some Americans are given the chance to make an annual option on their income tax filing status and some are not? We seek redress on this glaring inequity issue.

Issue No. 36

Short title

Married filing separately status of Americans with an alien spouse.

Summary of the problem —Americans living overseas with a non-resident alien spouse must file U.S. tax returns as married filing separately unless they file a joint return with their spouse Issue 34 above addressed the inequity of losing the maximum tax protection if a joint return is not filed abroad Issue 35 addressed the inequity of not being able to have an annual option for filing when married to a non-resident spouse abroad. This issue specifically concerns the necessity to file in this least favorable category if the non-resident alien spouse does not also file a U.S. tax return.

ACA's question.—Why cannot an American living abroad with a non-resident alien spouse file either as a unmarried head of household status (if qualifying). or as a single person without loss of one-half of certain deductions when the non-resident alien spouse does not choose to pay U.S. income tax?

The President's reply —"Married taxpayers who choose not to file a joint return must file as "married filing separately" rather than as single persons. This is the so-called "marriage penalty" for which there seems to be no solution satisfactory to all."

We wonder if the basic question of why non-resident aliens should have to pay any U.S. tax at all is finally answered properly by the recognition that they shouldn't have to, if it wouldn't then be most appropriate to allow Americans married to non-resident aliens abroad to file as single persons. or as unmarried heads of households with maximum tax protection if qualifying?

ACA's renewed question.—Once again the first basic question has to be asked of why we want to tax non-resident aliens at all? The subsidiary question of the most appropriate method of taxing the overseas resident American spouse follows. We would hope that ultimately this question would become moot by the United States choosing to conform to the tax practices of all of the other major countries of the world and not tax overseas Americans at all.

Issue No. 37

Short title

Foreign convention deduction problems abroad.

Summary of the problem.—U.S. tax laws allow an individual to deduct for expenses of attending a maximum of two foreign conventions each year. While this limit may meet a legitimate objective of the Congress when it applies to Americans living in the United States, it seems inappropriate and highly discriminatory when it is applied equally to Americans living abroad. Indeed it can mean that Americans are not given tax protection for attending more than two conventions even in the city where they reside abroad.

ACA's question.—Why do U.S. tax rules not recognize the economic realities of the overseas American in this situation?

The President's reply.—"The present rules limiting deductions for expenses incurred in attending foreign conventions to two such conventions a year were introduced in 1976. The Administration considers those rules inadequate to prevent abuse and burdensome on the taxpayer in terms of reporting requirements. In January 1978, the Administration proposed new legislation in which the deduction would have depended on whether it was reasonable to hold a convention at a foreign location. One test of reasonableness was to have been whether a substantial portion of the members resided in that country. That would have alleviated the problem faced by overseas taxpayers who attend conventions in their country of residence. The Congress did not accept the Administration's proposal; no further initiative on this matter is planned by the Administration at this time in view of the recent congressional consideration."

ACA's renewed question —ACA would like to ask the President anew if he feels that the present practice is an equitable treatment of overseas citizens? This needs to be established before any attempt can be made to define suitable redress. While the President chose not to address this question directly, his reply suggests that he does consider there to be grounds for justifying a change

We regret that the President has chosen to take no further action on this issue. We would like to believe that if he feels that there is a problem of equitable treatment of the overseas taxpayer involved he will feel justified in proposing a suitable form of redress.

ISSUE No. 38

Short title

Disallowance of contributions to foreign charities and churches.

Summary of the problem—One of the basic acts of good citizenship and contribution to the life of the local community is the willingness of an individual to make voluntary contributions to local churches and charities.

The U S. tax code permits Americans living in the United States to deduct such contributions from their taxable income. This same deduction is not allowed for Americans living overseas.

ACA's question—What principle of equity justifies this discrimination?

The President's reply.—"The rules pertaining to the deductibility of charitable contributions made by a U.S. taxpayer are the same, regardless of where the taxpayer lives. To be deductible, contributions must be to an organization organized and operated exclusively for charitable purposes and the funds must be used for the same charitable purpose. The Internal Revenue Service requires charitable organizations to be accountable; there would be virtually no way it could make a foreign organization accountable and ensure that the funds are used for charitable purposes. Contributions to U.S. charities which are used abroad may be deducted; thus, while a contribution cannot be deducted if made directly to a foreign charity, deductions can be taken for amounts spent on charitable purposes in a foreign country by a U.S. charity whose books and records are available to the Internal Revenue Service."

ACA's renewed question.—It is hard to understand why such rules and interpretations have so consistently been made other than to harass and abuse Americans abroad. We fail to understand why contributing to local churches and charities is recognized as a tax-deductible expenditure in one location and not in another.

The President's explanation of what constitutes a credible charity or church for IRS deduction purposes is not convincing. Using the same logic, the United States could maintain that no taxes paid abroad can be credited against U.S. taxes at home because the IRS cannot audit the books of the foreign country '

Mr. President, we ask that this issue be examined once again. It is self-evidently unfair to make these contributions abroad ineligible for the same deduction they would have at home. And, our practice is a most unfortunate notice to the rest of the world that we have no concern whether or not our overseas citizens act as good local participants in their communities abroad If they act as generously abroad as they do at home, it will cost them much more in U.S. tax.

We seek redress. Why not simply have the overseas American sign a statement to the effect that he believes the charity to which he is contributing, and for which he is claiming a U.S. tax deduction is a true charity. The United States has to rely on the overseas American's integrity in declaring his income, why not use the same standard in accepting his charitable contributions?

ISSUE No. 39

Short title

Nonrecognition of foreign postmarks for U.S tax submissions.

Summary of the problem.—Many overseas local postmarks have been refused as proof of submissions of U S. tax returns by the relevant deadlines. Postmarks of the United States do not have this same infirmity.

ACA's question.—Why are overseas taxpayers being harassed because of the local postmarks?

The President's reply.—"Foreign postmarks are accepted, provided that it is reasonable to believe that the return was filed on time. The IRS may disallow a foreign postmark if it is of doubtful validity , but in general it is the policy of the IRS to accept foreign postmarks."

We do not know if this is a new policy which has been decided in response to our raising of the issue, but we are happy to learn that our postmarks are now generally acceptable.

ACA's renewed question —We would very much like to know whether the IRS maintains a list of countries whose postmarks are systematically considered of doubtful validity. Overseas Americans have to confront so many unique problems trying to satisfy two competing tax sovereignties that we need all of the clarification we can have on details such as this We hope the IRS will give us further guidance as to how to avoid being challenged on our postmarks in the future.

ISSUE No. 40

Short title

Lack of sufficient time to pay tax from abroad.

Summary of the problem.—While overseas Americans are granted an automatic extension to June 15th to file their tax returns, they are expected to pay their U.S. tax on April 15th. If they pay the tax at the same time they have calculated it, they have to pay interest from April 15th.

Overseas Americans, trying to live with competing tax sovereignties often do not have sufficient information on hand on the 15th of April to complete their tax forms. It seems invidious to give a filing delay and then automatically collect interest on the tax payment that will consequently be late, by definition.

ACA's question.—Why does the United States not give an automatic extension of time to pay U S. tax in parallel with the extension of time to submit the returns?

The President's reply.—"Taxes of U.S. taxpayers payable with the return are due generally no later than April 15 of each year. An extension of time to file the return and to pay taxes due with the return (to June 15) is granted automatically to U.S. citizens and residents living or traveling outside the United States. Taxpayers who are not abroad may receive an extension of time to file their return by submitting the appropriate forms. Taxpayers who utilize an extension of time to file their return are responsible for payment of interest on the tax due from April 15."

The President told us what we already knew. We asked him why this practice was not altered to coincide with the delay for filing. He chose not to address this question.

ACA's renewed question.—Why does the United States not grant an extension of time to pay U.S. tax without interest in parallel with the extension of time for filing the return from which this tax is calculated? The present policy is nothing other than an interest trap which means that overseas Americans will generally have to pay higher taxes than those living at home.

ISSUE No. 41

Short title

Lack of sufficient time to file estimated tax returns abroad.

Summary of the problem.—Overseas Americans are granted an automatic two-month extension of time to file their annual tax returns. But, they are not given a similar extension of time to file their estimated tax declarations which depend upon the same information. Indeed, Congress has suggested the desirability of computing the previous year's tax before estimating future tax.

ACA's question.—Why does the IRS not grant the extension of estimated tax filing deadline to coincide with the June 15 extension for tax returns?

The President's reply.—"Estimated tax returns relating to the current taxable year are due generally on April 15. An extension of time to file the estimated tax return (to June 15) is granted automatically to U.S. citizens and residents living or traveling abroad under proposed regulations which, once final, will be effective for returns due in 1979 and thereafter. Taxpayers who utilize an extension of time to file estimated tax returns are not responsible for payment of interest accruing during the extension period."

ACA's renewed question.—ACA would first like to commend the IRS for making this necessary change. We wonder, however, if it is justified to allow the extension of estimated tax to pass without accumulating interest, why the extension of the deadline for the tax return itself cannot also be congruent with the non-accumulation of interest as per Issue 40 above?

ISSUE No. 42

Short title

Effective loss of January 31 filing benefit when abroad.

Summary of the problem.—Certain penalties for underpayment of estimated tax are eliminated for taxpayers who file their tax return and pay all tax due on or before January 31 of the year following the tax return year. It is frequently difficult for overseas Americans to accumulate the needed information to submit return by January 31. It is also rare that tax forms arrive abroad before the end of January. It is nearly impossible, therefore, for overseas Americans to benefit from this provision of the IRS regulations. It is most unfortunate, also, because overseas Americans have a much greater difficulty accurately estimating their tax liabilities to the United States when dealing in fluctuating exchange rates.

ACA's question.—Why does the IRS not make an allowance for the greater difficulties being faced abroad and grant a more lenient indulgence to overseas Americans with respect to the January 31 filing benefits?

The President's reply.—The President chose not to address this problem.

ACA's renewed question.—ACA would like to ask that this question be addressed by the President in his forthcoming report.

ISSUE NO. 43

Short title

Lack of relevant information guides for taxes abroad.

Summary of the problem.—IRS pamphlets are almost entirely designed to help the domestic American taxpayer prepare his tax returns. Overseas Americans have to confront very confusing tax situations which result from competing tax sovereignties between the United States and more than 150 different foreign nations. The information made available to Americans abroad is not sufficient to meet the tax needs of those abroad.

ACA's question.—Why does the IRS not spend more time preparing relevant tax guides that recognize the problems being faced by Americans abroad in the 150 different nations of the world?

The President's reply.—The President said that the IRS is trying to help Americans abroad. The IRS has prepared five special publications of relevance to overseas Americans and one comprehensive guide exclusively for their use. There are a few IRS employees stationed in key cities abroad who can respond to questions, and there will be longer visits to other Embassies to help local Americans with their returns. Finally, the President stated that: "In 1976, there were only 164,000 tax returns filed from abroad (other than from military post offices) compared to a total of 84 5 million individual tax returns. From that perspective, the publications and personal assistance provided to overseas Americans are substantial when compared to the assistance given to Americans at home."

The last quoted phrase sums up the attitude of the IRS on most questions of why overseas Americans are not receiving better treatment. This is simply that the overseas taxpayer is already getting more than his share of the IRS's time and should be happy with what he has.

ACA's renewed question.—Why does the IRS maintain that overseas Americans must be taxed no matter where they live and then not make a better effort to assist these overseas Americans to comply with their U.S. tax obligations by preparing tax guides that address the tax problems of overseas Americans in each of the overseas countries where they reside?

Overseas Americans need much more help with their U.S. tax returns. We ask the President to consider greatly increasing the budget of the IRS to provide for much more services to Americans abroad.

ISSUE NO. 44

Short title

Difficulty in obtaining tax forms abroad.

Summary of the problem.—Overseas Americans face so many different tax situations that are covered by obscure regulations of the IRS that they often need to use tax forms that are not very much in use in the United States. Most Americans abroad have a very difficult time ever obtaining such forms. The package of tax materials that are sent to overseas Americans often lack even the most commonly used forms. It is rare that overseas Embassies or Consulates have such forms.

ACA's question.—Why is not more care taken to ensure that overseas Americans are provided with all of the tax forms they might need?

The President's reply.—The President replied that the IRS is trying as hard as it can to help overseas Americans. "Widely used specialized forms are mailed to all U.S. taxpayers overseas. If a form is little used, it is too costly to mail to all

Americans living abroad; however, this year the foreign bank account form and the new foreign moving expense form have been added to the mailed package "

The foreign bank account form is one of the items that have caused great inconvenience to overseas Americans for many years. Every overseas American usually has to file such forms but up until 1979 the IRS has refused to place these forms in the standard package When these and other forms are not available the overseas American is still accountable for making the returns on time and subject to all of the penalties for failure to file, or for late filing.

ACA's renewed question.—ACA would like to ask that the President once again take a close look at what the IRS is doing to help overseas Americans comply with U S tax regulations It seems highly inequitable to force overseas Americans to comply with laws and then place great institutional obstacles in their paths for compliance and finally to then go after the overseas Americans who have not been able to so comply.

At the present time, overseas Americans do not have the same ease of access to tax information and tax forms as a citizen at home. We ask the President to consider greatly increasing the budget of the IRS to provide for much more services to Americans abroad.

ISSUE NO. 45

Short title

IRS deficiencies in adapting to overseas tax environment.

Summary of the problem.—Among the typical practices of the IRS that harass, innocently or otherwise, the overseas American are the sending of tax assessment notices by seamail with payment dates that have usually expired before the assessment note has been received.

ACA's question —If the U.S insists on taxing Americans abroad, why is not more care taken to insure that overseas Americans are not being unduly harassed in their taxation?

The President's reply —"Airmail is used to transmit printed material and correspondence overseas, although, admittedly, there have been occasional instances in which the mailing of IRS material has been unduly delayed. Some Americans abroad have also criticized the short ten-day period allowed to pay income tax assessments. IRS is now reviewing this matter to see whether a longer period is warranted for some or all foreign addresses."

What the President didn't add, however, was that in those instances where the IRS material has been "unduly delayed" it is the overseas American who has to expend considerable extra energy to try to protect himself. There is no automatic extension for payment periods when the IRS makes a mistake.

ACA's renewed question.—Why is not more care taken to ensure that overseas Americans are guaranteed an appropriate amount of time to comply with IRS requests for information and tax assessments? Why is there no automatic procedure giving the overseas American an extra amount of time depending upon the date of receipt of the IRS material abroad rather than the date of transmission from the U.S.? For example, letters that have been sent by seamail should give the overseas American an automatic benefit.

Short of changing the U.S. taxation of Americans abroad to conform with the practice of all of the other countries of the world, we would ask that the President consider greatly increasing the budget of the IRS so that more adequate services can be given to overseas Americans.

ISSUE NO. 46

Short title

Lack of adequate IRS assistance abroad.

Summary of the problem —There is a very extensive service organization run by the IRS in the United States to help American citizens and resident aliens prepare their U S. tax returns. There are only a few such offices abroad, located in the capital cities of selected foreign countries.

A very large number of all of the overseas American community does not have any ready access to IRS assistance. While the IRS does also have a travelling assistance program, this usually results in visits abroad to only a selected number of major cities for a very limited period of time. Even when the travelling IRS teams are available, the agents rarely have any knowledge of the special tax problems that Americans resident in these countries have to face which are generated by incompatibilities in the U.S. and foreign tax practices.

ACA's question.—Why does the United States not take more care to ensure that IRS assistance is available to Americans abroad?

The President's reply.—"In addition to premanently stationing IRS personnel in key embassies overseas, IRS tax specialists visit a number of principal cities to respond to questions and to provide other assistance. In 1979, there will be more and longer visits due to the change in law in 1978. Complaints of a lack of adequate assistance have probably been due to the uncertain status of the law in the last couple of years: now that new legislation is in place, the tax forms should remain relatively unchanged from year to year."

The problem with inadequate assistance from the IRS for tax problems abroad is far more extensive than the suggestion the President offered as having been "probably due" to the uncertain status of the U.S. tax law in recent years. This is but a small portion of the problem. Every year there are changes to tax practices at home. New tax court rulings are constantly being made that can impact on the tax status of Americans abroad. Even more distressing is the fact that the overseas countries of residence are also constantly changing their tax codes and practices and an overseas American's U.S. tax status may well change due to changes in the foreign country's laws.

ACA's renewed question.—Despite the claims that IRS is giving us adequate service abroad, and perhaps even giving us more than our fair share of their total resources, it is evident to all Americans overseas that IRS assistance abroad is woefully inadequate.

We would like to ask the President to please take another look at the mandate of the IRS for serving Americans abroad. If the U.S. persists in taxing overseas Americans it should assume a parallel obligation of ensuring that the overseas American has the same "quality" of service from the IRS abroad that he would have at home. He also deserves not only the same quantity of service but also its convenient proximate availability.

We ask the President to consider greatly increasing the budget of the IRS to expand the taxpayer services that are offered abroad.

ISSUE NO. 47

Short title

Problems in taxation of partnership income when abroad.

Summary of the problem.—U.S. tax practice concerning partnership income can lead to inequitable situations. A taxpayer living in a foreign country who does not enter the U.S. during an entire tax year, but who is a partner in a U.S. Partnership, has his earnings treated as if they were U S. source income to the extent that the partnership's total earnings were from U.S. sources. Since this portion of his income is considered as being of U.S. source, even though he worked the entire time abroad, it will be taxed by both the United States and the foreign country and there will be double taxation in many cases.

ACA's question.—Short of doing away with the unfortunate practice of taxing overseas Americans, why does the United States not change its source of incomes rules to allow treatment by a partner in a partnership to have the source of his income determined with regard to his physical location when performing his partnership duties?

The President's reply.—The President admitted that cases can occur where there is double taxation of such income. Foreign countries tax income earned in their domains. The United States will not give a foreign tax credit for taxes paid on what the United States defines as U.S. source income even if this income so defined is entirely earned abroad! The President offered the consolation of the following redress: "Where such problems of double taxation occur, they can be resolved in a tax treaty. When a problem arises under an existing treaty, relief can be provided in a special protocol."

ACA's renewed question.—Is there really a need to resort to the negotiation of international treaties or protocols to existing treaties to resolve an arbitrary definitional problem in IRS regulations?

We would urge the President to take another look at this entire question of the taxation of partnershhip income. In its present form it can lead to substantial tax problems for many overseas Americans, and can lead to international competitive problems for American partnerships competing with those of other nationalities where such unfortunate tax practices have not been introduced.

We urge the President to propose a more appropriate form of redress.

94

Short title

Double taxation of income for days worked in the United States.

Summary of the problem.—When the United States negotiates a bilateral tax treaty with a foreign country there is generally a provision that enables residents of each country to visit the other for a specified period of time each year, or within a specified income limit for services performed in the other country each year, without these residents being held liable for income tax by the treaty partners. Then, the United States adds a clause that says that these provisions do not give any protection to American citizens living in the foreign country.

The United States has unilaterally defined all work performed in the United States by a U.S. citizen as giving rise to U.S. source income even if the overseas American is being paid for this work by a foreign employer in the foreign country.

This can lead to double taxation of the overseas American's income unless the overseas country is willing to forfeit its priority right to also tax this same income.

When problems of such double taxation occur, it is up to the individual American abroad to try to negotiate tax relief with the foreign tax authorities. Greatly complicating such negotiations are incompatible dates for the submission of tax returns to the U.S. and the foreign countries, and different definitions of total income, deductions, credits, etc., which make identification of the precise amount of the double taxation very difficult.

ACA's question.—If the United States insists on taxing the overseas American, why does it not accept to define overseas residence in conformity with the tax treaties it has negotiated and permit overseas Americans the same opportunities to work in the United States with tax protection against double taxation as enjoyed by all other residents of the overseas country?

The President's reply.—"Where such problems of double taxation occur, they can be resolved in a tax treaty. Tax treaty negotiations include consideration of this issue along with other aspects of double taxation. When a problem arises under an existing treaty, relief can be provided in a special protocol."

There are a number of special problems that can arise abroad even in cases not so clear cut as those addressed by the President in his generic response. For example, Switzerland will recognize U.S. source income that is taxable by the United States as non-taxable in Switzerland. But, the Swiss tax practice is to include this income in the total for the determination of the tax rate that is to be applied to the rest of the taxable income. This inflation of the rate on taxable income is a manifestation of the double tax problem that has not been resolved by treaty or protocol but which nevertheless harms the overseas American and subjects him to additional tax.

ACA's renewed question.—Why does the United States not take better care of overseas Americans in the tax treaties that are negotiated with foreign countries? Citizens of these foreign countries are more equitably treated by the United States, than are Americans living in the treaty-partner's foreign domain.

ISSUE No. 49

Short title

Problems of overseas estate taxation.

Summary of the problem.—Americans living overseas can have severe difficulties from conflicting claims on the estates of relatives who die in either the United States or abroad. In some cases wills in one country are held to be invalid in others.

ACA's question.—Why does the United States not take more care to recognize that problems such as these could impede the willingness of many Americans to go abroad?

The President's reply.—The President chose not to address the problem of foreign estate taxation of overseas Americans.

ACA's renewed question.—Does the United States have a concern for protecting overseas Americans from problems of double taxation of estates?

ISSUE No. 50

Short title

Denial of a deduction for "rates" tax paid by Americans in the United Kingdom.

Summary of the problem.—U.S. citizens living in the United Kingdom are required to pay a tax that is peculiar to the English tax code. This tax, called "rates" is essentially a property tax, but it is levied on the occupant rather than the owner of the lodging. The IRS will neither give a credit nor a deduction for "rates" taxes paid abroad.

ACA's question.—Why is the IRS harassing the U.S. taxpayer by refusing to recognize a tax that has been paid abroad?

The President's reply.—"Residents of the United Kingdom, whether living in their own home, or rented quarters, pay a residency tax called "rates". Since the resident, not the owner, bears this tax, the IRS has ruled that "rates" are not real estate taxes. The Internal Revenue Code permits deducting property taxes, but not occupancy taxes."

The President shows us another instance of how it is the overseas American who suffers because of the lack of congruence between the U.S. tax code and the foreign tax practice. If the United Kingdom were to change its tax practices and call this tax a property tax, presumably then a deduction would be given by the IRS for the same amount of foreign tax paid.

ACA's renewed question.—Having insisted on the need to tax overseas Americans, why does the United States feel it is equitable to ignore econnomic reality abroad and simply pretend that the foreign payment was not a recognizable U.S. type tax hence not eligible for tax relief in the United States.

We ask the President to take another look at this unfortunate practice. This license that has been given to the IRS to define what are taxes paid abroad and what are not for credits or deductions from U.S. tax on the same income base had led to a whole series of abuses in the past.

Not only are Americans abroad being hurt in their ability to compete against individuals of other nationalities because of the double taxation they face, they are being nickeled and dimed to death by such IRS interpretative games. We urge redress. If the IRS has trouble defining such a tax as "rates" as a property tax, perhaps it is time to define a new category of overseas tax payments of a miscellaneous nature for which due credit or an equitable deduction should be allowed.

ISSUE No. 51

Short title

Inadequacy of the 4-year rule for sheltering capital gains from the sale of a residence abroad.

Summary of the problem.—Congress has decided to allow Americans to shelter some of the capital gain realized from the sale of an owner-occupied dwelling if the proceeds of the sale are reinvested in a new owner-occupied dwelling within a specified period of time. The length of time during which a new home can be purchased for an American living abroad has been extended to 4 years.

While more generous than the earlier time limit, the new 4-year rule still causes considerable problems for a number of Americans living overseas and cause a loss of international competitive ability because of the restrictions on how long any assignment can be accepted in certain countries, and what new assignments can be accepted subsequently.

Suppose an overseas American is assigned to a country where it is not possible to purchase a dwelling. This American can only reside in this new country for less than four years. Otherwise if he has a capital gain from the sale of a residence to shelter he will have to pay considerable U.S. tax on this gain after 4 years. Many corporations now find that they would prefer to have their overseas executives stay in a given location for longer periods of time than was the former practice. An American may have a great financial disincentive in accepting any assignment longer than 4 years.

A related case occurs when an American living in a country with a housing purchase restriction nears the end of his 4 year tour. He is not fully mobil for subsequent assignment because his next tour of duty must be in a country where the purchase of a residence is possible. Failing such a new assignment he will have to pay U.S. capital gains on a shelter dwelling sale.

ACA's question.—Why does the United States accept such tax provisions that manifestly make Americans have a great disincentive to be as mobile for employment abroad as individuals of all of the other Free World nationalities? As the United States is the only country that taxes overseas capital gains at all it would seem imperative that a method for such taxation be found that does not harm the competitive ability of American executives abroad.

We ask the President to consider a policy for sheltering capital gains from the sale of a residence abroad in such a manner that no overseas American loses international job mobility which will bring potential harm to himself as an individual, to his employer and ultimately to the entire Unted States.

ISSUE No. 52

Short title

Inadequacy of rules for capital gains tax shelter on sale of a home retained in the U.S.A. by Americans assigned abroad.

Summary of the problem.—Some American citizens, when they are assigned abroad, retain possession of their residence in the United States with the intention to return to reside in them after the overseas assignment is terminated. It often occurs that upon completion of the overseas assignment, during which no residence was purchased abroad, the American is assigned to a new location in the United States remote from the residence that was maintained while abroad

U.S. tax practice insists upon the fact that a residence that is sold can only be protected for capital gains if the owner resided for a requisite period of time in the dwelling before the sale. The returning American cannot qualify for this residency period and hence has no sheltering of any capital gain from the sale of the retained residence for the purpose of purchasing a new residence where he will be henceforth employed.

ACA's question.—If sheltering capital gains from the sale of a residence is the intent, why does the present U.S tax practice penalize overseas Americans who cannot meet the stipulated residency tests, but who in all other respects meet the intent of the statute? Does not this unfair treatment of overseas Americans constitute just the sort of disincentive to being willing to move abroad that we should be preventing?

We ask the President to consider modifying the capital gains shelter rules to help overseas Americans be more willing to accept new assignments at home and abroad without fear of being abused by inflexible tax treatment. Specifically, we suggest that consideration be given to allowing overseas Americans to maintain a principal abode in the United States while they are abroad, and to be credited with constructive residence in this abode while they are abroad for purposes of meeting the prior residence or occupancy test when the dwelling is sold upon their return from abroad.

We suggest that this rule apply not only to those who go abroad maintaining a dwelling at home, but also suggest that the rule be so structured as to permit Americans living overseas who need to shelter such capital gains from sale of a residence at home or abroad but who are precluded from doing this by the purchase of a residence abroad be also enabled to purchase a suitable residence in the United States which is intended for subsequent use upon return to the United States from abroad.

ISSUE No. 53

Short title

Discriminatory customs treatment for purchases of gifts abroad by Americans resident abroad returning for a holiday in the U.S.A.

Summary of the problem.—Whenever it is to the advantage of the United States overseas Americans have to fulfill obligations on the basis of citizenship. When it comes to rights, or benefits, however, there is frequently a discrimination on the basis of where an American resides.

This discrimination exists in the Customs Rules that apply to how much dollar value purchases of gifts abroad can be brought duty-free into the United States. Returning U.S. residents are allowed up to $300 under the new Customs Rules. Americans who are residents abroad are treated the same way as foreigners who are resident abroad and are limited to only $100 of such duty-free gifts.

ACA's question.—Why is there this discrimination in the Customs Rules against Americans abroad? What definition of equity necessitates this discrimination?

ISSUE No. 54

Short title

Problems of obtaining rulings of overseas residence status for customs purposes when returning from residence abroad.

Summary of the problem —Each year thousands of overseas Americans move back to the United States after having lived for various periods of time abroad

These returning Americans must decide in advance whether to bring back possessions that have been purchased abroad, or whether to sell these goods abroad. One of the principal factors that will often determine this choice is whether or not duty must be paid on the goods when they arrive in the U.S.A.

It is very difficult to obtain a ruling from the Customs Service in advance concerning the overseas residence status that will be considered to apply to any U S. citizen returning from abroad. While there are some Customs Service representatives assigned to Embassies abroad, they are most reluctant to give any such rulings, and usually insist that the returning American wait until he arrives at the Port of Entry to the U.S. for a definitive ruling from the Customs Inspector who is met upon entry.

This situation is a major, and unnecessary, inconvenience for overseas Americans. It can cause needless confusion, anxiety and economic loss.

ACA's question.—Why cannot the Customs Service define overseas residence requirements in such a way that such determinations can be easily made abroad?

ISSUE No. 55

Short title

Discriminatory treatment of some overseas Americans in the definition of overseas residence for customs purposes.

Summary of the problem.—In addition to the problem of obtaining an advance ruling on overseas residency status for an American planning to return to the U.S. after residing abroad for Customs purposes (see Issue 54 above), there is a discriminatory distinction made between those returning from foreign employment when the government is the employer and those returning from civilian employment.

Returning Government employees are generally considered to have qualified for duty-free entry of goods acquired abroad if the period of residence abroad was 140 days. Returning Americans who do not work for the government usually have to prove that they have been abroad at least three years.

ACA's question.—What principle of equity justifies making such a discriminatory distinction? And, why has this distinction been made?

ISSUE No. 56

Short title

Use of voting from abroad as a criteria for determining the overseas residence status of Americans returning from abroad.

Summary of the problem.—In addition to the problems of returning overseas residents for U.S. Customs purposes (see Issues 54 & 55 above) already mentioned, there is a further practice of the Customs Service that is a threat to the overseas franchise.

One of the most difficult rights that overseas American have fought to obtain is the right to be able to vote in Federal Elections in the United States. This right was finally established in 1975, but many overseas Americans refused to exercise the franchise in 1976 because of ambiguities in State tax laws. It came as a most unpleasant surprise to learn that the Customs Service also has adopted a practice of using the right to vote from abroad as a criteria for determining whether or not an American living overseas was a resident for Customs purposes.

One of the questions that a returning American can be asked at the Port of Entry is whether or not he registered and voted in U.S. elections while he was abroad. A positive reply can be used to disallow a claim that this American was really a resident in a foreign country for Customs duty purposes.

ACA's question.—Why are the myriad bureaucracies of the U.S. Government allowed such unencumbered license to ask such questions about the use of the overseas voting right? This question should be forbidden to the Customs Service and to any other bureaucrat for any definitional purposes.

ISSUE No. 57

Short title

Nonavailability of toll-free telephone access to IRS help when abroad.

Summary of the problem.—In addition to the ubiquity of IRS offices in the United States, the IRS also has established a toll-free telephone inquiry service whereby any American living in the United States can call, without charge, and receive an explanation of his tax situation

Overseas Americans, who typically have much more complicated tax problems due to the incompatible nature of two conflicting tax sovereignties, are not offered such toll-free telephone assistance benefits.

There are few IRS offices abroad. Typical telephone charges are much more expensive abroad than in the United States. It therefore costs much more for an American abroad to obtain tax advice from the IRS than it does in the USA Indeed, it is free at home and very expensive abroad

ACA's question.—What definition of equity justifies offering toll-free tax assistance at home and denying this same assistance abroad ?

ACA contacted the Director of International Operations of the IRS with this question. His reply was: "We regret that the costs of such service, ie. equipment costs, line and mileage charges, and additional personnel, are beyond our budgetary means at the present time."

ACA wonders why budget considerations suffice as a justification for the discrimination faced by Americans abroad? We hope that the President will either recommend that taxation of Americans abroad be terminated, or will request a sufficient augmentation of the IRS budget be made to insure that the same quantity and quality tax assistance service be available to Americans abroad as is provided to American citizens at home. If taxation on the basis of citizenship is our policy, so should all of the related benefits be based upon citizenship without regard to "budget constaints" etc.

ISSUE No. 58

Short title

Discriminatory treatment of Americans abroad who do not contribute to medicare while abroad despite denial of medicare benefits abroad.

Summary of the problem —At age 65, Americans who are eligible for medicare must enroll and pay a fee for some of the benefits. Enrollment can only take place during the first three months of any given year Overseas Americans are denied medicare benefits while they are abroad But if they do not enroll and pay the fee anyway, they will have great difficulties becoming eligible for medicare if they return to the United States.

The first surprise that the medicare program has for the overseas American coming home is that he has to pay 10 percent more fee for every year that he did not contribute while abroad Secondly, if he comes home at the wrong time, in addition to the extra fee penalty, he will also have to wait up to 15 months in some cases before medicare benefits can be obtained.

ACA's question.—Why has the medicare program been conceived with so many different penal clauses for the overseas American? Why is there a penalty for those who do not enroll and contribute while they are abroad when there are no benefits while one is abroad? Why is the enrollment period restricted to only three months of each year?

ACA wonders what principles of equity necessitate this unfortunate practice?

ISSUE No. 59

Short title

International competitive problems for Americans due to lack of special tax rules for construction companies.

Summary of the problem —Since the oil crisis of 1974, there has been a much more intense scramble underway to win contracts in the construction markets of the Middle East.

While the United States was going about increasing the tax that would have to be paid by its workers abroad, our major foreign competitors were busy trying to find ways to make their own construction companies more competitive in these markets.

Workers who have an overseas tax domicile do not have to pay any income tax to their home countries if they come from France, West Germany or Italy. Usually workers who go abroad for only a short period of time while retaining a tax domicile in their home country do continue to have an income tax liability for their overseas earned income. It was here that all three of these countries sought to give their construction industries a competitive edge. All three of these countries have now modified their tax laws to allow special overseas income exclusions for workers who are temporarily abroad working on construction projects.

This means that not only are their workers who are abroad for a full tax year not liable to any home country tax on their overseas incomes, but even those workers who go abroad for shorter periods of time and who retain a tax domicile at home are also allowed a tax free income abroad if they are working on construction projects

American construction companies have a double competitive disadvantage today in these same markets. Their workers who are abroad for a full tax year still have tax obligations to the United States. While some deductions have been introduced to shelter extraordinary costs associated with overseas work, for most individuals their base income remains fully taxable. There is an option to use a flat income exclusion of $20,000 if the workers are living in a camp, but almost no worker abroad can use this exclusion because the IRS chose to define camps abroad in such a way that there were almost no qualifying camps!

The tax faced by those domiciled abroad, even in the slightly attenuated form after allowance for the Sections 913 or 911 provisions is bad enough. But, American employees who are abroad for less than a full tax year have no special deductions or exclusions at all! Their counterparts of French, West German or Italian nationality have a full exclusion of their overseas incomes even when only temporarily abroad. The temporary American employee in the construction industry is a very heavy cost liability for American construction companies.

ACA's question.—Why is the United States unwilling to give the same tax treatment to construction workers abroad as is afforded by our competitors? Is there no concern for the implications on the U.S. economy of having made our companies so evidently non-competitive abroad?

Issue No. 60

Short title

International competitive problems for American teachers abroad because of U.S. tax laws.

Summary of the problem.—Many foreign countries unilaterally give special tax treatment to teachers of foreign nationalities working in their countries as a special incentive to improve the quality of their schools and encourage better understanding among nations.

Teachers of every nationality except Americans can benefit from these special incentives. The overseas American remains fully liable to the U.S. Government for taxation of his worldwide income, and if a tax advantage would be offered by an overseas country it will be nullified by the tax liability to the U.S.

Under the pre-1976 tax laws of the United States, overseas Americans had either $20,000 or $25,000 income exclusions. Since salaries for teachers abroad are usually modest, most Americans were sheltered from U.S. tax, and could benefit from the overseas tax incentives. When Congress passed the 1978 Tax Amendments, U.S. teachers were among those who were hurt the most by the elimination of any tax excludable income earned abroad.

ACA's question.—Is the United States willing to have its teachers abroad be uniquely non-competitive for teaching assignments? Would it not be in the best interest of the United States to take better care of our overseas teachers and permit them to be as cost competitive as those of other nationalities?

Issue No. 61

Short title

Discriminatory preference to some American citizens in conferring citizenship on adopted children abroad.

Summary of the problem.—Section 323 of the Immigration and Nationality Act, which establishes the conditions under which a child adopted by an American citizen abroad can acquire American citizenship, makes a distinction between two classes of American citizens living abroad.

One class, including those in the Armed Forces, employed by the U.S. Government, research institutions, U.S. companies, international organizations, or serving as ministers or priests, is given the opportunity of having children adopted abroad acquire American citizenship without any prior residence in the United States by the child. The other class, containing all others including doctors, lawyers, engineers, consultants, architects and poets, etc. is not given the same rights. Children adopted by the underprivileged class cannot obtain American citizenship while the parent is abroad and before the child has lived for two years in the United States.

This discrimination can lead to very difficult problems for the American citizen parent and for the child abroad. It is not clear how the United States benefits from this discrimination.

ACA's question —Why are some American citizens, and their adopted children, given more benefits abroad than others? Why are not all U.S. citizens abroad equal before the law in terms of being able to give U.S. citizenship to their adopted children? What definition of equity makes such discrimination necessary, or justified?

Issue No. 62

Short title

Internatonal competitive handicaps caused by American citizenship laws.

Summary of the problem.—There are a number of professions that are closed to American citizens living in foreign countries. In some countries, one must have local citizenship to practice law. In others, one must be a local citizen to practice medicine, or accept a post as a professor in the Universities.

Under present American law, if an American citizen acquires another nationality, for whatever reason, he is subject to loss of his American nationality.

A number of countries against whom the United States competes in the major markets of the world do not have such stringent laws. England, for example, allows its citizens to acquire another nationality and still remains English. Switzerland has a similar practice. France will tolerate a number of instances of voluntary acquisition of a second nationality without loss of French citizenship.

ACA's question —Is it really in the best interest of the United States to have such a strict policy concerning the acquisition of another nationality? If an American citizen is living abroad and wants to practice a profession whose foreign qualifications require the acquisition of another nationality, why must it be assumed that the individual does not retain loyalty to the United States if he acquires a second nationality? America loses some of its best, and most talented citizens this way. Is it really necessary? And if so, why?

Issue No. 63

Short title

Additional tax problems for overseas Americans.

Summary of the problems.—In addition to the various taxation issues already mentioned which afflict overseas Americans, there are two other problems that also need to be addressed because of their impact on American competitiveness abroad.

The first problem comes from the U.S. policy of taxing overseas unearned income. The United States is the only major country of the Free World that taxes the overseas unearned income of its overseas citizens. Many in the United States feel that this is perfectly proper. Yet, those who suffer severe hardship from this tax practice are those usually who have worked to accumulate a nestegg for retirement. Overseas retirees, living mainly on the fruit of such capital accumulation are treated much worse under present U.S. law than those earning an income abroad. Sections 911 or 913 give some relief from U S. taxes for those abroad by recognizing extraordinary overseas cost of living, housing, etc. There are no similar provisions giving any tax relief for unearned income

The impact of this unfortunate tax practice of the United States is so severe in some cases that overseas Americans who are about to retire must seriously consider abandoning their U.S. citizenship and acquiring another nationality merely to be able to survive economically during their last years of life.

The second problem is of a different nature The United States defines overseas taxpayer status either on the basis of an individual having been abroad for an entire tax year, or having been abroad for seventeen out of eighteen consecutive months under the physical presence test. It should be readily apparent that this second definition of eligibility for relief from U.S taxes for work abroad can cause very serious complications for Americans working abroad.

Take the case of an individual in a high technology company who, in order to shelter some of his income from double taxation, must remain physically outside of the United States for seventeen out of eighteen months. His mobility in terms of direct contact with his colleagues at home is seriously impeded Or take an architect, or engineer, or anyone else whose work abroad might require frequent contact with his company at home.

There are always good reasons for adopting rules such as those concerning the overseas taxation of Americans. The difficulty is that there are also dangerous side-effects that can destroy the economic health of individual Americans, their employers, and the entire United States.

ACA's question.—In its quest to ensure that there can be no possible abuse of the U.S. tax system, and to ensure the maximum possible collection of revenue from Americans abroad, a number of unfortunate tax practices have been adopted. We wonder if this has not become an intense process of straining our gnats and swallowing camels?

Citizens of other countries working abroad can help their home countries and still build up a capital and income base for their retirement years. The U.S. has chosen tax practices that will severely hurt any overseas American who would like to do the same thing. We doubt the wisdom of such practices. And, we wonder if the President and the Congress are really convinced that such practices are necessary?

On the physical presence test practices of requiring an American to stay out of the United States for seventeen out of every eighteen months, we recognize that this was a brilliant way to stop provocative abuse of the earlier laws by a few movie stars, but we also recognize that it places some absurd burdens on the vast majority of overseas Americans who are trying to do a job abroad in competition with those of other nationalities. Consider also that it means that any company, American or foreign, will have much less difficulty sending employees of every nationality other than Americans to work with colleagues at their home company offices in the United States. We wonder at the wisdom of such policies.

Finally, on this physical presence test, we wonder if the President or the Congress have taken account of the fact that here again we have set up some landmark criteria which are not used by any of the foreign countries against whom we compete around the world. Indeed, to take the case of the United Kingdom, this country will give tax relief to any British resident if he is out of the United Kingdom for only one month during any tax year. The United Kingdom recognized the need to stimulate exports and was ready to give relief even to those domiciled at home for this stimulative purpose. We, on the contrary, will not give any relief to those abroad less than one year, and stretch the period out to seventeen months for minimum qualification for relief for those who cannot claim a bonafied residence abroad.

We are, and shall continue to be, paying dearly for such unenlightened policies. We hope the President will address these additional two issues in the full new analysis of how we treat Americans living abroad.

ANNEX 1

[From the Congressional Record—Senate, Jan. 23, 1979]

ISSUES CONCERNING AMERICAN CITIZENS LIVING ABROAD

Mr. McGOVERN. Mr. President, last year I proposed, and Congress enacted, an amendment to the Foreign Relations Authorization Act calling upon the administration to analyze and report to Congress on the subject of Americans living abroad. The purpose of the amendment was to cause the executive branch to focus on the myriad of issues which arise in fairly determining the rights and obligations of our citizens who, for one reason or another, live in foreign countries. By January 20, as stipulated in the amendment, the President will submit the required report for congressional consideration. As supplemental material on this complex subject, I submit for the RECORD an analytic compendium of issues prepared by a group called American Citizens Abroad. It would, of course, be improper for me to endorse this report without further study, but I believe it provides useful information on a broad range of questions which will require careful study and deliberation during the 96th Congress.

The compendium follows:

AMERICAN LAWS AND REGULATIONS THAT DISCRIMINATE AGAINST AMERICAN CITIZENS LIVING ABROAD: A COMPENDIUM OF ISSUES PREPARED BY AMERICAN CITIZENS ABROAD

AMERICAN CITIZENS ABROAD,
Geneva, Switzerland, December 18, 1978.

Mr. JIMMY CARTER,
President of the United States,
The White House, Washington, D.C.

DEAR MR. PRESIDENT: The 1979 Foreign Relations Authorization Act, which you signed on October 7, 1978, contains a special section (611) which asks you to submit a report to the Congress by January 20, 1979, concerning American laws and regulations that discriminate against Americans who live abroad.

American Citizens Abroad (ACA) is a group of American citizens living around the world who feel that improving the way those living abroad are treated is in the best interest of all Americans, especially those living in the United States.

We have been working for the past several months to collect information to assist you and the members of your staff and Administration in the preparation of this report that you must submit to the Congress. We have been aided in our work by a multitude of ideas and suggestions that we have received from Americans around the world including those living on all of the major continents and those living behind the Iron Curtain.

We are proud to present these ideas and suggestions to you in the form of the book that is being sent under separate cover. We would very much like to be able to help you in any other way that you might find appropriate. Should members of your staff find it useful, we would be prepared to arrange for meetings with groups of Americans abroad in different countries to provide a fuller development of the issues that we have presented.

Your concern for the human rights of mankind is greatly appreciated by those of us who live abroad, and it certainly makes us proud to be able to claim that this is what America is really all about. We would only hope that this concern would be also translated into new policies which would extend the same guarantees of human rights to American citizens who happen to live abroad. Sadly enough such guarantees are not at present in existence.

Our kindest regards to you and your family and our hopes that you will have a joyful holiday season.

Most sincerely,

FRANCIS PRIBULA,
ANDREW P. SUNDBERG,
STEVEN M. KRAFT,
DON V. W. PERSON,
JOHN IGLEHART,
EUGENE EPSTEIN,
ROBERT W. SHEETS,
Directors.

中

INTRODUCTION

America is a land of immigrants. Most of her citizens left their home countries to seek a new life in what was believed to be a promised land, specially endowed and especially favored in the eyes of deity.

America was built by immigrants, and by the gifts of individuals who were willing to come, some for only a limited time, to create this new entity out of a nearly virgin wilderness.

One cannot understand the history of America without stumbling over countless instances of special people who came from abroad to participate in the fight for independence and in the creation of a new form of government. Count Pulaski came from Poland, Baron von Steuben came from Hesse, Lafayette came from France, Albert Galatin from Switzerland, and so on.

But, many of those who came also returned to their home countries, or to other lands. Lafayette went back to participate in the French Revolution, John Paul Jones who is called the "Father of the American Navy" went to Russia and became an Admiral in Katherine the Great's Navy Yet these were undeniably vital people in the building of America.

Other individuals who we cannot conceive of as other than "Americans" spent many years abroad in the service of the United States. Benjamin Franklin and Thomas Jefferson created ties of affection between the fledgling new Union and France. John Adams was in Holland, others built ties to the other powers in Europe.

And, finally, throughout our short history many Americans have continually gone abroad to build the links of commerce and social affection which have brought the United States into a full sense of harmony and participation with the other nations of the world.

Yet, throughout all of this period America has been principally busy building inside, rather than looking outside. It has been growing and absorbing new waves of immigrants arriving to meet the continuing need for more labor. And, each new wave of immigrants has felt a keen need to prove quickly that they are as much the incarnation of patriotism and dedication to the ideals of the United States as those who preceded them.

America remains a land of immigrants. Most of its commercial activity is internal rather than external. And the basic traits of the American character still remain dominated by a patriotic machismo which attributes praise to those who come to play our game.

It is not surprising, therefore, that even today the role of expatriates, those who have gone abroad from America is still little understood, and even less accepted with equinamity. For if immigrants are to be praised, what are we to think of emigrants, even those who are abroad for only a short period of time?

Thus it is that unlike almost every other country of the world, America has not affection for its expatriates, but rather hostility and mistrust. For isn't there something fundamentally wrong with those who might choose to live in any other country?

Today there are over 1.5 million American citizens living outside of the United States as private citizens. If those working for the U.S. Government, the Armed Forces and their dependents are added the total would approach nearly three million.

The population of civilian expatriates, without any contractual ties to the Government exceeds the population of 14 different States in the United States, and in fact is larger than the combined population of the three smallest political units added together.

Yet, for all intents and purposes the American expatriate community and its problems are almost totally unknown to the average American citizen, and the indifference if not subliminal hostility that would be manifested if the question of expatriates were to be raised is rather well represented in the attitudes and opinions of many of the individuals who are chosen to conduct the legislative business of the United States.

Americans living abroad have generally been a forgotten constituency. And, for many who are abroad this was a situation that did not have too many inconveniences, although certain severe problems inevitably occurred for individuals who came into confrontation with specific laws applying to expatriates.

However, in 1976 the roof fell in on those living abroad. The Congress, impelled by a tax reforming zeal, decided that it was time to start applying much more severe pressure on the taxation of those living abroad. A plan was proposed for essentially doing away with any exclusion of income earned abroad for U S tax purposes, and coincidental with this Congressional action the U.S. Tax Courts ruled that any allowances or services paid to Americans working abroad had to be declared as income at the full value of the facilities or services provided, not at whatever nominal cost an employer might charge.

The result was an enormous extra tax burden. The Treasury Department did a great misservice to those abroad by grossly underestimating what impact the 1976 law would have. Treasury's initial estimate was extra revenue of about $50 million, which implied extra tax of a few hundred dollars per expatriate taxpayer. But the uproar from the expatriate community following enactment of this bill was stunning. Under pressure from Congress which began to receive voluminous complaints from those abroad and from their employers, the Treasury made a new estimate of the revenue to be earned from changes in taxation of those abroad and this time, based upon different data, the estimate came close to $400 million. The Congress had required the typical overseas taxpayer abroad to pay an extra several thousand dollars, not the much smaller sum they had originally believed.

The stage was obviously set for a new form of relief from this mistake. But much hyperbolic rhetoric had been expended at the expense of those living abroad, and this could not be retracted. There was no way to go back toward the old practice of excluding part of the income earned abroad from U.S. tax, so a new form of special deductions was chosen. Alas, for those in many countries this is not an improvement at all.

The Congress had also been considering whether those living abroad, and being taxed, should not be granted a better opportunity to exercise the right to vote in the United States. A new law was enacted to guarantee all expatriates the right to vote in Federal Elections and this took effect in 1976. However, there was no rush to the polls from abroad, because expatriates were becoming very wary of gifts from Washington. One obvious trap was the fact that registering in a State in the USA could lead to the State using this as a justification for wanting income tax to be paid at the State level. Those abroad, already badly bruised with Federal tax had little interest in an even greater tax burden. It was finally recognized in 1978 that the law, to be meaningful, had to be amended to forbid States to use the voting registration as any claim by the State to be able to tax the overseas voter. But, of course, many of those who live abroad are not willing to take any chances any more with income, or estate tax liability from voting, and many will probably never use this new franchise.

The situation today concerning expatriates is still very confused. The United States has a peculiar philosophy of insisting that obligations of citizenship are ubiquitous but that many rights and benefits of citizenship must stop at the water's edge.

The expatriate community, on the other hand, has finally been awakened from its political torpor by the recent rape of the pocketbook. And now awake, the community is taking a much closer look at other problems which face those living abroad.

AMERICAN CITIZENS ABROAD (ACA)

During the last few years, a group of American citizens living in Geneva, Switzerland, has been concerned with a number of problems that afflict expatriates.

During the summer of 1977, members of the group decided to seek help for those living abroad by appealing directly to the White House for assistance. A special request was sent to the President asking him to establish some sort of Commission to look at problems facing those living outside of the United States. Members of the group met with some of the members of the President's staff and found some initial encouragement from the personal views of these staff members. But, eventually, when asked for a final verdict on what could be expected, the reply was given that the President does not like Commissions and there would be no special help from the White House for expatriates.

Indeed, in early 1978, the Administration's new position on how the tax laws should be amended concerning those living abroad proved to be so unfair that all hope of help from the Administration was quickly dissipated.

Fortunately, there are a number of Members of Congress in both Houses who have been more sympathetic with the plight of those living away from home. Americans in Geneva had the opportunity to meet with Senator George McGovern in 1977, and he and his staff were particularly concerned that there seemed to be no overall policy in the United States toward expatriates and this was continually giving rise to all sorts of new problems which not only had an impact on individuals abroad, but which also could be much more profoundly important to the future of the United States.

Senator McGovern forwarded the request that had been sent to the President for a Commission on Expatriates to the State Department for its comments. The reply was that while such a Commission or study of expatriate problems could be useful, it should not be confined to State since the problems that would be raised would reach many other departments of the Government

Having found that the White House was not going to do anything voluntarily for expatriates, and that State did not feel fully competent to deal with the need for analysis of expatriate policy, Senator McGovern decided to help Americans abroad by convincing other Members of the Congress to accept an amendment to the 1979 Foreign Relations Authorization Act which required the President to report to the Congress on expatriate problems.

The text of Senator McGovern's amendment is as follows:

EQUITABLE TREATMENT OF UNITED STATES CITIZENS LIVING ABROAD

Section 611(a) The Congress finds that—

(1) United States citizens living abroad should be provided fair and equitable treatment by the United States Government with regard to taxation, citizenship of progeny, veterans' benefits, voting rights, Social Security benefits, and other obligations, rights, and benefits; and

(2) such fair and equitable treatment would be facilitated by a periodic review of the statutes and regulations affecting Americans living abroad.

(b) Not later than January 20, 1979, the President shall transmit to the Speaker of the House of Representatives and the chairman of the Committee on Foreign Relations of the Senate a report which—

(1) identifies all United States statutes and regulations which discriminate against United States citizens living abroad;

(2) evaluates each such discriminatory practice; and

(3) recommends legislation and any other remedial action the President finds appropriate to eliminate unfair or inequitable treatment of Americans living abroad.

This amendment was accepted by Members of the House of Representatives and Members of the Senate and it became law with the full bill on October 7th, 1978 when signed by the President.

To insure that there would be proper attention paid to this study, and to the identification of all of the issues that were felt to be particularly unfair by those living abroad, it was decided to create a new organization which would work to bring as many Americans living overseas as possible into the arena for this project.

In July 1978, after the amendment had been accepted by the Senate, American Citizens Abroad, was founded in Geneva, Switzerland, by a number of private American citizens. The organization is a non-profit association of Americans who are striving to create a better understanding in the United States of the value of the expatriate community, and of the need for the United States to take a more concerted effort to insure that expatriates were being fairly and equitably treated while they were living abroad.

ACA publicised the fact that the Study on Expatriate Discrimination was to take place, and invited Americans from all over the world to send in information and suggestions of issues to be covered. Replies to this request were received from hundreds of individuals including residents in all of the continents of the world, from those behind the Iron Curtain, and from those in North America especially in Canada and Mexico. But, of equal interest was the volume of replies from those abroad working for the U.S. Government who also felt that there were laws and regulations that discriminated against Government employees abroad.

ACA has volunteered to help the White House in the preparation of its study, and remains at the disposal of the President for whatever additional contributions might be found to be appropriate.

THE PRESENT REPORT

The present report is a compilation of issues that have been identified by American citizens living abroad which are felt to be discriminatory against expatriates.

Each issue has been individually addressed in a form which will hopefully assist those responsible for the preparation of the President's study. Each issue has a short title, a background discussion, a presentation of the problem of discrimination, and some suggestions as to how a solution could be reached for each problem.

This report is by no means complete in its identification, and should not be taken to suggest that any issues not herein contained need not be addressed. It is rather the first effort at a preliminary catalog of vital issues as seen from those living abroad.

A NOTE ON DISCRIMINATION

There are really two different aspects to discrimination that are important to consider when analyzing laws and policies that affect expatriates. The first is in terms of equity between citizens living in the United States and those living abroad. The second concerns the extent to which laws enacted for expatriates create a situation abroad in which American citizens face problems which are not the same as those facing other nationalities abroad. In this second case it could well be that discriminatory American laws and regulations are not only hurting individual Americans, but they also may be hurting those who hire Americans, and ultimately they may be doing major harm to all of the citizens of the United States, particularly those living at home.

ACKNOWLEDGEMENTS

ACA would like to thank the many generous members of the overseas American community who have contributed their time and thoughts to help make this present submission as full and complete as possible.

We would also like to particularly thank the many individuals in Washington who have given sympathetic support to our cause and who have given invaluable suggestions as to how to better promote the interests of Americans abroad and thereby of all Americans.

And, of course, a special thanks is due to the most kind generosity of Senator McGovern and the members of his staff without whom this report would not have been necessary, or possible

ISSUE No. 1

SHORT TITLE

Constitutional Right Denied to Children Born Outside of the United States.

BACKGROUND

In 1971, the Supreme Court by a five-to-four majority decided that there are two classes of citizens of the United States, those with full Constitutional rights, and those who are to be denied some of these rights. The distinction is made strictly on the basis of where the individual is born.

At issue is this case, *Rogers* v. *Bellei*, was whether a law was Constitutional which required American children born abroad (if only one parent was an American citizen and the other was an alien) to return to the United States and live for a certain period of time or face involuntary loss of American citizenship.

In an earlier decision of the Court in Afroyim vs. Rusk, it was stated that the Congress has no "power, expressed or implied, to take away an American citizen's citizenship without his assent." This ruling was based upon an individual's Constitutional rights as expressed in the first sentence of the 14th Amendment

The Court, in *Rogers* v. *Bellei*, had a different composition than when the earlier case had been decided. The new Court, was at pains to uphold the right of Congress to set special burdens upon those born abroad, but did not want to overrule the import of the earlier case. Resort was therefore made to a most extraordinary interpretation of the 14th Amendment's first sentence:

"All persons born or naturalized in the United States and subject to the jurisdiction thereof, are citizens of the United States and of the State wherein they reside."

According to the Court, this definition excludes those born abroad. Said the Court, "The central fact, in our weighing of the plaintiff's claim to continuing and therefore current United States citizenship is that he was born abroad. He was not born in the United States. He was not naturalized in the United States. And he has not been subject to the jurisdiction of the United States. All this being so, it seems indisputable that the first sentence of the Fourteenth Amendment has no application to plaintiff Bellei. He simply is not a Fourteenth-Amendment-first-sentence citizen." By this judgment, not only Mr. Bellei, but every other American child born abroad will spend the rest of his life deprived of some of his constitutional rights.

It is interesting to recall the dissenting opinion of Justices Black, Douglas and Marshall in this case. Said Justice Black on behalf of himself and the others, "I cannot accept the Court's conclusion that the Fourteenth Amendment protects the citizenship of some Americans and not others. Indeed, the concept of a hierarchy of citizenship, suggested by the majority opinion, was flatly rejected in *Schneider* v. *Rusk*, 377 U.S. 163 (1964) : "We start from the premise that the rights of citizenship of the native born and of the naturalized person are of the same dignity and are coextensive."

Justice Black further commented, "Under the view adopted by the majority today, all children born to Americans while abroad would be excluded from the protections of the Citizenship Clause and would instead be relegated to the permanent status of second-class citizenship, subject to revocation at the will of Congress. The Court rejected such narrow, restrictive, and super-technical interpretations of the Citizenship Clause when it held in Afroyim that that Clause "was designed to, and does, protect every citizen of this nation."

THE PROBLEM

The problem with the present status of children born abroad is obviously one of having to spend the rest of one's life with less Constitutional protection against involuntary loss of citizenship than all other citizens of the United States. The practical import of this second-class status was that up until October 10th, 1978, some children born abroad had to fulfill subsequent residence requirements in the United States or face involuntary and automatic loss of American citizenship. This provision has now been stricken from the law. But there is no protection for children born abroad from some future decision on the part of Congress to impose a similar burden, or one of another form. The Congress would not be able to impose any such burden on any other citizen, born in or naturalized in the United States, however, because these individuals have greater Constitutional rights than those born abroad.

The inequity of this situation is apparent when it is recalled that many children born abroad are in alien latitudes and longitudes at birth precisely because their parents have been sent there by the U.S. Government or by their American employers. And, at the same time these children are born into second-class citizenship status, children born in the United States to casual tourists acquire full U.S. citizenship rights which those born abroad will never enjoy.

This is an example of a discrimination based solely on the latitude and longitude of an individual's place of birth.

THE SOLUTION

There is no simple solution which is evident for this discrimination short of an amendment to the Constitution which would guarantee that there shall be no second-class category of American citizens, and that all citizens shall be equal regardless of race, religion, color, creed or place of birth.

ISSUE No. 2

SHORT TITLE

Eligibility of an American child born abroad with American citizenship at birth to run for the office of President of the United States.

Article II, Section 1 clause 5 of the United States Constitution states:
"No Person except a *natural-born* Citizen, or a Citizen of the United States, at the time of the Adoption of this Constitution, shall be eligible to the Office of President; neither shall any Person be eligible to that Office who shall not have attained the age of thirty-five years, and been fourteen years a resident within the United States."

THE PROBLEM

The problem facing children who are born abroad with American citizenship acquired automatically at birth is that there is no legal Constitutional definition of "natural-born Citizen."

In recent years there have been several potential Presidential candidates who were not born in the United States and whose candidature would have been in doubt due to this definitional lacuna. Among these potential candidates were: George Romney (born in Mexico), Governor Christian Herter of Massachusetts (born in France) and Franklin D. Roosevelt, Jr. (born in Canada).

There has been much legal debate on whether those born abroad were intended by the Founding Fathers to be eligible for this office. There is no recorded discussion of the Fathers' opinions However, during the First U.S. Congress, just after the Constitution was adopted, the first citizenship bill concerning those born abroad was passed. This bill stated that:
"And the children of citizens of the United States, that may be born beyond the sea, or out of the limits of the United States, shall be considered as natural-born citizens: PROVIDED, That the right of citizenship shall not descend to persons whose fathers have never been a resident in the United States." [1]

Equally significant in this bill and its use of the term "natural born citizen" is the fact that twenty members of the First Congress had been delegates to the Constitutional Convention, and that among these twenty were eight members of the Committee of Eleven at the Constitutional Convention which drafted the presidential qualification clause.

THE SOLUTION

Congress should act to remove the ambiguity that presently persists concerning the eligibility of children born abroad with American citizenship acquired at birth to hold the office of President of the United States.

One form of redress would be for Congress to enact legislation which repeats the use of the term "natural-born citizen" in the Immigration and Nationality Act. One appropriate place for this term to be used would be in the first sentence of Section 301 of the present Immigration and Nationality Act. In its amended form this first sentence would read:
"SEC. 301. (a) The following shall be nationals and *natural born citizens* of the United States at birth :—" (new wording italic).

Discussion of the intent of this change in the Congressional Record would establish that it was for the purpose of clarifying the issue of Presidential eligibility.

The weakness of this solution is that as an Act of Congress it could just as easily be changed by a future Congress.

A better solution would be in a clarification of the definition of citizenship in the Fourteenth Amendment to the Constitution. Rewording of this section could be as follows:
"Section 1. All persons born or naturalized in the United States, and subject to the jurisdiction thereof, are citizens of the United States and of the State wherein they reside. *All United States citizens who acquire their United States citizenship at birth are natural-born citizens.*—" (new wording italic).

American citizens born abroad should not have to spend their whole lives in doubt about this basic right of citizenship in the United States.

---

[1] Act of March 26, 1790. ch 3, 1 Stat 103, 104

ISSUE No. 3

SHORT TITLE

Congressional Representation for Americans Living Abroad.

BACKGROUND

There are over 1.5 million American citizens living outside of the United States. This number exceeds the population of 14 different States of the United States, and actually exceeds the combined population of the three smallest political units.

Americans living abroad have many common problems that are directly due to their being away from the United States, but at present these expatriates have no unique representation in the Congress.

Recent changes in American voting laws have enfranchised all of those living abroad for all Federal elections. And, this, of course, means that there is access to Members of the House of Representatives and to Senators, but most will concede that those living abroad form only tiny marginal percentages of their total constituencies, and those living at home must come first.

It is not to be suggested that the Congress has ignored the American expatriate community. Quite the contrary is the case, but it is very apparent that despite the good will and concern of many members of both Houses of the Congress there are still significant problems that have not been addressed and there are still many myths about the expatriate community which have not been successfully destroyed. Indeed, it is quite significant that there is no Committee, or even sub-Committee in either House of the Congress which addresses itself to questions of policy or practice toward those living abroad. Thus, at present, there is no established mechanism whereby expatriates have any possible continuing attention in the Federal legislature.

THE PROBLEM

The problem with the present situation is that despite the goodwill and intentions of many Members of the Congress, the problems of Americans living abroad are not being fully appreciated. Individual members who might be sympathetic to one particular problem or another often have to consecrate valuable staff time and resources to issues that are only of marginal interest to their basic constituencies. And, often such resources are being diverted in parallel with those of other Members of the Congress when a greater amount of coordination could be more efficient and productive.

THE SOLUTION

One useful solution would be for the Congress to consider granting Americans living abroad at least one non-voting delegate in the House of Representatives. This individual would act like those of the same title who now represent Americans living in Guam, the Virgin Islands and Washington, D.C.

The utility of this delegate for those living abroad would be the fact that there would be henceforth one central reference point for contact with the legislature for transmitting comments to Washington, and for feedback to those living abroad.

But the utility would also be great for the other Members of Congress who today do not have such a resource for acquiring broad information about expatriate problems, nor for obtaining proposed solutions to such problems that would be fair and effective for all Americans living abroad. Thus, this would be an asset of major importance to those abroad and to the Members of Congress.

The right to have such a delegate would not need to impair the right to participate in regular Federal elections either, for those living abroad would not really be doubly represented. The delegate has no *vote*, hence those who vote for Congressmen and Senators in their home districts vote once only in terms of real representation in the Congress, but have a delegate to help focus on problems affecting 1 5 million citizens in unusual circumstances who can initiate legislation and serve on Congressional Committees to the benefit of everyone.

ISSUE No. 4

SHORT TITLE

Discrimination Against Certain American Citizens in the Ability to Transmit Citizenship to Children Born Abroad.

Children born abroad to an American citizen parent are not automatically American citizens at birth in all circumstances. The right to transmit citizenship to a child born abroad depends upon an individual's marital status, and upon the nationality of the spouse. In this respect, American law differs from that of almost every other major country of the world.

The law has not always been this way. From 1790 until 1940, an American father could always transmit American citizenship to a child born abroad provided only that the father had ever resided in the United States. In 1934, this same right was given also to American women under the same conditions.

In 1940, however, the law was abruptly changed. Henceforth, if only one parent was American, the child born abroad could not have American citizenship unless the American parent had lived for ten years in the United States, five of which must have been after the age of sixteen. In 1951, when the most recent overhaul of the citizenship laws took place, the ten year qualification period was retained but five needed to have been only after the age of fourteen (vs. sixteen).

The present law also sets different qualifications for transmission of citizenship to children if a mother is not married, if the birth takes place in an outlying possession of the USA, if one parent is a citizen and the other is an American national but not a citizen, etc. The different standards of qualification are shown below in a summary table.

QUALIFICATIONS FOR TRANSMITTING AMERICAN CITIZENSHIP TO CHILDREN ABROAD

Abroad: Both American; One must have had a residence in theU.S.A. prior to the birth of the child.

Abroad: One American citizen and one American national who is not a citizen; The American citizen must have had a residence in the United States or an outlying possession for *one continuous year* before the child's birth.

Abroad: One American citizen and one alien; American citizen parent must have been physically present in the United States or an American possession for *ten years,* five of which after the age of fourteen years before the child's birth.[2]

Abroad: An unmarried American mother; The mother must have been physically present in the United States or in an American possession for *one continuous year* prior to the birth of the child.

In an outlying possession of the United States: One American citizen and one alien; The American citizen must have been physically present for *one continuous year* in the United States or an outlying possession prior to the birth of the child.

The Problem: The problem with this law is that it sets up a number of different categories of eligibility for one of the most basic of all human rights, that of transmitting citizenship to one's child. By failing to meet the necessary qualifications many American citizens face the dilemma of having children who are born stateless.

The inequity of this law become even more starkly apparent when it is recalled that any child born in the United States, no matter what the nationality of the parents might be, is automatically an American citizen at birth with all of the same rights and privileges of this citizenship. Thus while an American may be living abroad, working for the United States Government, or serving in the Armed Forces, he could still have a stateless child.

The law also makes it impossible for any American citizen who is under nineteen years of age to transmit citizenship to a child born abroad if the spouse is an alien. However, if the American is a woman, and not married, she might well be able to transmit citizenship to her illegitimate child even if she is under age nineteen, but she would not have the same facility if she were married and the child was legitimate. As an unmarried mother she need only have previously lived in the United States for one year, not ten which is required of a married woman.

Statelessness is widely recognized to be a major human rights tragedy. The United Nations over thirty years ago adopted a "Universal Declaration of Human Rights" in which Article 15 states, "Everyone has the right to a nationality".

---

[2] Certain Americans living abroad are allowed to count their years abroad toward this qualification period. See further details of this and the discrimination involved in this practice in Issue No 5.

Going further in declaring the importance of the family and what States should do on their behalf, Article 16(3) of the same Declaration states, "The family is the natural and fundamental group unit of society and is entitled to protection by society and the State." The United States has not yet ratified this Universal Declaration and is still one of the major offenders in the area of permitting statelessness to occur for children of its citizens.

There was a further effort made by the United Nations specifically addressed to the question of statelessness and what member countries should do to insure that no one is ever cast into such a situation. The United States has not ratified this Convention either nor has it amended American laws to remove the remaining areas that still generate involuntary statelessness.

THE SOLUTION

The United States should give the same human rights to its citizens abroad that it gives to any casual visitor or tourist at home. Every American citizen living abroad should be allowed to transmit American citizenship to his/her children born abroad. Discrimination based upon latitude and longitude should be ended.

ISSUE No. 5

SHORT TITLE

Discriminatory Preference Shown Toward Certain Individuals Living Abroad in Qualifying to Transmit Citizenship to Children Born Abroad.

BACKGROUND

The basic question of when an American living abroad should be able to transmit citizenship to his child born abroad has already been raised in Issue No. 4. This present discussion concerns a subordinate issue of discrimination that is present in the law as it now stands. Should the solution proposed in Issue No. 4 be adopted, this present issue would also be met. Should the solution of Issue No. 4 not be adopted, this issue remains for redress.

Section 301(g) of the Immigration and Nationality Act of 1952 sets the conditions under which an American citizen married to an alien can transmit American citizenship to a child born abroad. The requirement is that the American citizen must have previously lived in the United States for a period of ten years, five of which after the age of fourteen years.

However, certain individuals living abroad can meet this residence requirement even while actually being outside of the United States. Such individuals are:

Those serving honorably in the Armed Forces of the United States,
Those working abroad for the United States government,
Those working abroad for an international organization, or
Those living abroad as dependent unmarried sons or daughters of the above.

THE PROBLEM

The discrimination manifested in this provision is obvious. Some individuals working abroad have more basic human rights than others, namely a greater chance to insure that their children will not be born stateless.

THE SOLUTION

The preferable form of solution to this problem would be to accept the proposal suggested as the solution of Issue No. 4. This would do away with the prior residence requirement for American citizens married to aliens to qualify to transmit American citizenship to children born abroad.

Failing this preferred solution, the law should be modified so that anyone working or living abroad can be given credit for the years required for transmission of citizenship to children no matter what his profession abroad, and no matter who his employer might be.

ISSUE No. 6

SHORT TITLE

Retroactivity of the Elimination of Subsequent Residence Requirements of Certain American Children Born Abroad.

BACKGROUND

In 1978, through the enactment of Public Law 95-432, a major discrimination against American children born abroad was eliminated from American law. This concerned children born abroad to only one American citizen parent. Such children, prior to the 1978 law, were required to return to the United States for a period of continuous residence between the ages of fourteen and twenty-eight years, or else their American citizenship would be automatically and involuntarily stripped away.

Such a requirement for subsequent residence in the United States to protect citizenship which was acquired at birth abroad was not a part of American law for most of the history of the Republic. It was an innovation of the law which was passed in 1934, which at the same time granted the right to American mothers to transmit citizenship to children born abroad when the father was an alien. The 1934 law set a requirement for children born to only one American parent abroad to spend the five year period from age thirteen to eighteen in the United States, or else citizenship would be lost. This requirement never really took effect, however, because the law was changed in 1940 to allow for five years of residence in the aggregate between ages thirteen and twenty-one. The effect of this law reached back to those born after 1934. Thus, it was not until 1950 that children started losing their American citizenship for failure to comply with such residence requirements.

Shortly thereafter, however, the law was once again changed. In June 1952, a new requirement was instituted, again reaching back to those born after 1934, this time calling for five years of continuous physical presence in the United States between the ages of fourteen and twenty-eight years. The effect of this new requirements did not begin to be felt until 1957 (those born in 1934 did not reach age 23 until 1957). Then the harshness of a five year continuous residence without any allowable break became apparent. The Congress relaxed this requirement in 1957 by allowing up to twelve months of absence from the United States during the five year period without loss of continuity. However, as the length of time period, and the qualifying ages during which residency had to occur did not change, 1957 started the period from which involuntary loss of American citizenship for children began.

According to the State Department, approximately two thousand children have been stripped of their American citizenship for failing to come to live in the United States for the prescribed period of time. The fact that they might have been ill, or had any other reasonable cause for such failure did not bring any relief.

When the Congress decided to eliminate this subsequent residency in 1978, there was discussion of the possible problems from making the effect of this change retroactive to pick up those who had previously lost citizenship due to this requirement. Several Members of Congress felt that great complications would possibly result from such retroactivity of the eliminated requirement, and convinced the other Members of Congress to deny this retroactivity.

It is most significant, however, that in the denial of retroactivity, the Congress was acting contrary to the practice that had been followed when the 1952 residency requirements proved to be more generous than those of the 1940 Act. In an important case finally decided by the Supreme Court, the more generous provisions of the 1952 Act were made retroactive to those who had not complied with the provisions of the 1940 Act, hence closing the hole which had occurred from 1950 to 1952. Subsequent to this decision, those who had lost their citizenship in 1950–1952 could still retain their American citizenship by complying with the 1952 requirements. The case in question was *Fee* v. *Dulles*, 236 F. 2nd 855 (C A. 7. 1956). In lower Federal Courts, the decision went against those who had lost their citizenship because the court upheld the original administrative position that a person who had not complied with the conditions prescribed by previous statutes had lost his citizenship and derived no benefit from the more generous retention provisions of the 1952 Act.

However, upon consideration of this issue when it reached the Supreme Court the Solicitor General confessed error, taking the position that a person who could comply with the terms of section 301(b) and (c) would retain his American citizenship, even though he had not fulfilled similar provisions of the earlier statutes The Supreme Court reversed the lower court, and thus adopted the view projected in the Solicitor General's confession of error. (Refer to 355 U.S. 61)

THE PROBLEM

The problem caused by these circumstances is the fact that those born abroad before October 10th, 1952 (date of the effective remission of the subsequent residency requirement from the law signed Oct. 10th, 1978) do not have the same rights as those born after this date. Further, while the benefits of an easier compliance situation were conferred administratively for the 1952 changes (although it took court cases to establish this right) is a retro-active fashion allowing those who had lost their citizenship under the 1940 law to get it back to comply with the 1952 Act, this same retroactive possibility was not granted in 1978.

The problem is not a large one in that the total number of persons who would be affected directly or derivatively would probably not exceed three thousand. The State Department does not feel that the granting of this return to American citizenship of those deprived for failure to comply with earlier requirements of residency would create a major difficulty. Indeed, the State Department recommended that this be made retroactive as did the Justice Department.

THE SOLUTION

The effect of the 1978 changes in the citizenship laws which eliminated loss of citizenship for those who failed to live in the United States after birth abroad to one American parent and to one alien parent should be made retroactive to 1934, the date at which the first such requirements were set.

This solution would give back citizenship to those who have lost it since 1957, covering a total which would probably not exceed two thousand individuals. (Perhaps three thousand if their children were also considered).

ISSUE NO. 7

SHORT TITLE

Loss of Citizenship by Children Because of Actions of Their Parents Abroad.

BACKGROUND

Section 349(a)(1) of the Immigration and Nationality Act of 1952, states that anyone who is an American national by birth or naturalization shall lose his nationality by obtaining naturalization in a foreign state upon his own application, upon an application filed in his behalf by a parent, guardian or duly authorized agent, or through the naturalization of a parent having legal custody of such person.

There is some control on this loss by a child, however, in that the law further states that he can remain American if he returns to the United States before age twenty-five to establish a permanent residence.

THE PROBLEM

There are several problems associated with this section of the law. The first has to do with the notion of involuntary expatriation. The second has to do with the suitability of the protection that is offered.

There is some question as to whether the involuntary expatriation called for in Section 349(a)(1) is really Constitutional. Some recent Supreme Court cases have established that an individual cannot lose his citizenship unless he voluntarily desires to renounce it. This is obviously not the case for someone who is less than age eighteen (the actual age of majority for voting now in the USA) who has no control over whether his parent or guardian takes out another citizenship for him, and it is doubtful if an individual under the age of twenty-one has much effective control either. Thus, it may well be that this automatic loss of citizenship is not Constitutional.

It is also valid to question whether the requirement to make such individuals who have acquired a second nationality return to commence permanent residence in the United States before age twenty-five is really an appropriate form of relief. In many overseas countries one could well be still completing one's education at age twenty-five, thus the requirement would mean rupturing this education. It could also be the case that the individual is just beginning his work career and has not yet acquired a skill that could be easily transferred to the United States. Finally, it would not necessarily be easy for such an individual to come to the United States and find suitable employment before age twenty-five.

What seems to be the obvious intent of the present law is the requirement of a child who has acquired a second nationality to prove a valid nexus to the United States.

Such a nexus could be easily proved by a requirement for such an individual to take an oath of allegiance to the United States when he first applies for an American passport after attaining the age of twenty-one years.

ISSUE No. 8

SHORT TITLE

Loss of nationality for a naturalized citizen who goes abroad within five years of naturalization.

BACKGROUND

Section 340(d) of the Immigration and Nationality Act of 1952 provides that any person who is a naturalized citizen and who takes up a permanent residence abroad in any foreign country within five years of naturalization in the United States shall be considered to have demonstrated prima facie evidence of a lack of intention to reside permanently in the United States at the time of filing his application for naturalization. In the absence of countervailing evidence, it shall be sufficient in the proper proceeding to authorize the revocation and setting aside of the order admitting such person to citizenship and the cancellation of the certificate of naturalization as having been obtained by concealment of a material fact or by willful misrepresentation.

THE PROBLEM

Naturalized citizens do not have the same right to live abroad as other citizens until they have lived an additional five years in the United States. The effective period of residence to obtain such citizenship with full rights is therefore not five years, but ten years.

THE SOLUTION

Naturalized citizens should be treated with the same standards and conditions as any other citizen. This automatic assumption of fraud or misrepresentation on the part of a naturalized citizen who moves abroad within five years of nturalization should be stricken from the law.

ISSUE No. 9

SHORT TITLE

Immediate naturalization of an alien spouse permitted only to certain American citizens living abroad.

BACKGROUND

Section 319(b) of the Immigration and Nationality Act of 1952 allows an alien spouse of an American citizen to be naturalized as an American citizen without any of the usual prior residence requirement in the United States if the American citizen is working abroad:

In the employment of the Government of the United States,

In the employment of an American institution of research recognized as such by the Attorney General,

In the employment of an American firm or corporation engaged in whole or in part in the development of foreign trade and commerce of the United States, or a subsidiary thereof,

In the employment of a public international organization in which the United States participates by treaty or statute,

As one authorized to perform the ministerial or priestly functions of a religious denomination having a bona fide organization within the United States,

As a missionary of a religious denomination, or of an interdenominational mission organization having a bona fide organization within the United States.

All such individuals can bring their spouses to the United States and have them immediately naturalized as United States citizens. All others must have their spouses reside in the United States for three years to qualify for this same naturalization.

THE PROBLEM

The problem is self-evident. Wives or husbands of some American citizens have rights that are denied to those of other citizens solely on the basis of the employment status of the American citizen. Bureaucrats and employees of corporations have rights that individuals in a liberal profession such as doctors, lawyers, consultants and poets are denied.

THE SOLUTION

The discrimination against those working abroad in certain professions or for certain employers that this provision of the law incorporates is arbitrary and unfair.

All American citizens living abroad should have the same rights to have their spouses immediately naturalized in the United States.

ISSUE No. 10

SHORT TITLE

No Provision for Education of American Children Residing Abroad.

BACKGROUND

While a certain amount of Federal Revenue is expended to assist in the provision of adequate elementary and secondary education to children living in the United States, no such expenditure is made on behalf of children living abroad. The United States does not provide any funds to provide schooling for American children abroad unless these children are dependents of government employees.

American practice in this regard is much at variance with many other foreign countries.

For example, France has a publicly stated policy of wanting to provide at least as much annual expenditure per child abroad for education as for the child living in France. Indeed, the Government of France recently agreed to spend even more per capita for children abroad because of extra costs concerned with education abroad.

The Government of West Germany annually spends more than $100 million for elementary and secondary education for the children of expatriates.

The Government of Japan spends considerable amounts of money also for this purpose.

THE PROBLEM

The problem caused by this differential policy of various governments, is that Americans living abroad have much higher costs for educating their children in home country type schools than do expatriates of other nationalities.

This makes it more difficult for Americans to compete economically with those from these other countries.

Indeed, it was only in 1978 that the Congress finally agreed to stop *taxing* Americans living abroad on the education allowances being paid by employers. In all previous years, while other nationality expatriates were being given subsidized educational benefits for their children, and not being taxed, the United States was giving nothing at all to expatriate children, and taxing the allocations that employers were giving to help with this education!

THE SOLUTION

The United States should consider whether there should not be some sort of contribution made to help with the education of children of expatriates. This would not only be of benefit to the children, but could help equilibrate the competitive balance between American expatriates and those of a number of other countries who all compete in the international employment markets.

ISSUE NO. 11

SHORT TITLE

Revocation of APO Privileges for Certain American Schools Abroad.

BACKGROUND

During recent years, the United States has been willing to allow certain American schools which have been set up abroad by American citizens for use by children of Americans who are working abroad to use the APO (an official overseas postal system whereby letters and packages which are destined for abroad are sent to special post boxes in New York, or San Francisco and the subsequent postal costs for further transmission abroad are borne by the U.S. Government).

THE PROBLEM

Recently, the United States has started taking these privileges away from these schools and refusing them to new schools being set up abroad. This has not only added materially to the cost of operating these overseas schools, but in some cases insures that the supply of materials will be very difficult in the future due to the unreliability of the local mail services.

THE SOLUTION

This policy should be reviewed to determine whether revocation and refusal to grant APO privileges is really in the best interest of the United States.

ISSUE NO. 12

SHORT TITLE

Eligibility of American Embassy and Consulate personnel stationed in select cities throughout the world to send their children to the school of their choice and still be entitled to an allowance to cover tuition and charges.

BACKGROUND

American Embassy and Consulate personnel in various cities in the world are being forced by the United States Government to send their children to Department of Defense schools. In many of these cities alternative schooling is available in non U.S. Government schools. The Government enforces this by refusing to pay heavy tuition and other charges if the parent decides to send their child to a non Government school. In effect, the parents are being denied the right to select an appropriate school for their child relative to educational philosophy, proximity, school facilities and academic program. The position of the Department of State is that they are enforcing a "Congressional law".

THE PROBLEM

American Embassy and Consulate personnel are not entitled to both an appropriate educational allowance and the freedom of choice of where to send their children to school.

THE SOLUTION

Congress should review the law referred to above to determine in what way it denies parents who are American Embassy and Consulate personnel the freedom of choice of the most desired schooling for their children. If it is found that the law directly or indirectly infringes on the parents' right of choice of the most desirable schooling for their children, the law should be repealed or amended to ensure rather than inhibit the eligibility referred to above.

ISSUE NO. 13

SHORT TITLE

Eligibility of American students attending foreign higher education institutions for Federal student aid programs.

BACKGROUND

American students attending colleges and universities in the United States are Eligible for a Variety of Federal student aid programs including Basic Educational Opportunity Grants (BEOG), Supplemental Educational Opportunity Grants (SEOG), College Work-Study (CWS), State Student Incentive Grants (SSIG), National Direct Student Loan (NDSL) and the Guaranteed Student Loan Program (GSLP). These programs were originally established under Title IV of the Higher Education Act of 1965.

THE PROBLEM

American students attending foreign higher education institutions are ineligible for all but the Guaranteed Student Loan Program (GSLP). The General Provisions (Title VIII) of the Higher Education Act of 1965 states that to be eligible, an institution of higher education must be located "in any State", with the term "State" referring to, in addition to the several States of the Union, the Commonwealth of Puerto Rico, the District of Columbia, Guam, American Samoa, and the Virgin Islands.

Thus far the eligibility status of foreign institutions with American Students has been discussed with the Accreditation and Institutional Eligibility Staff of the U.S.O.E., the House Subcommittee on Postsecondary Education, and the Senate Subcommittee on Education, Arts and Humanities. These efforts have been to no avail.

At the present time, the eligibility of American students for Federal student aid programs is based entirely on the location of the institution they are attending. This automatically denies the eligibility for Federal student aid programs to American students living outside the U.S. The problem was stated most succinctly by Senator Claiborne Pell: "It does not make sense to me that students in foreign institutions which are accredited by American accrediting associations should be denied student aid benefits which they would otherwise be eligible to receive if they attended college in the United States."

Sadly enough, each year there are thousands of American students around the world who are discriminated against by the existing Federal higher education legislation. This dilemma takes on increasingly greater proportions when one considers the recent College Board Report stating that 70% of the American students enrolled in institutions of higher education in the United States received some form of financial aid during the 1977-78 school year.

THE SOLUTION

Amend the wording of that part of the Higher Education Act of 1965 which defines the eligibility of institutions who can administer Federal student aid programs. Besides, or instead of, a geographical definition, general criteria would be listed under which an institution's eligibility would be established. The primary criterion should be that the institution is accredited by an American accrediting association.

The above solution would not solve the problem but it would be a first step to rectification. It would expand the eligibility of American students for Federal student aid programs but it would not be granting the eligibility to all. There would still be American students attending non-accredited foreign higher education institutions who would not be eligible. This is a more difficult problem because eligibility for Federal student aid programs, as now defined, depends on both the nature of the student receiving the aid and the nature of the institution administering the aid program. Ultimately, the legal foundation for Federal student aid programs should apply to all American students wherever they are living and going to school. Only by eligibility being based on nationality alone will all discriminatory acts be eliminated.

ISSUE No. 14

SHORT TITLE

Expiration of CHAMPUS for Military Retirees Living Abroad at Age 65 Leaves Them Without any Health Benefits.

BACKGROUND

One of the major benefits given to those who retire from military service is a range of medical and hospitalization options for which the government pays all or part of the cost. Military retirees can obtain medical care almost without cost at military installations, and they can also obtain care from civilian doctors and hospitals with the government paying much of the cost.

The civilian part of this medical benefit is covered under a program called: Civilian Health and Medical Program of the Uniformed Services (CHAMPUS).

CHAMPUS benefits are available to retirees who live in the United States, and also to those who live abroad. However, these benefits stop when the retiree reaches age 65, because the individual would then be eligible for Medicare benefits which are similar.

THE PROBLEM

The problem for military retirees living abroad is that there is no Medicare for anyone outside of the United States. Hence military retirees lose CHAMPUS at age 65 and have nothing to replace it abroad. At an age when they are more likely to have need for medical and health services, they lose much of their coverage and could only regain this by moving back to the United States.

THE SOLUTION

The United States should not abandon military retirees living abroad who grow older and more in need of care. As there is no Medicare to replace CHAMPUS abroad, the CHAMPUS program should be extended to cover all retirees living abroad no matter what their age.

Issue No. 15

SHORT TITLE

Denial of VHA Benefits to Veterans Living Abroad.

BACKGROUND

One of the important veteran's benefits is the VHA program whereby the Government guarantees part of a home purchase loan which enable a veteran to buy a home with a lower downpayment and at a lower rate of interest.

THE PROGRAM

The problem is that VHA does not apply to veterans living abroad.

THE SOLUTION

While there are a number of problems which could occur with extending VHA to overseas locations, a satisfactory method for extending this benefit to veterans abroad could possibly be found.

One such possibility would be to consider using overseas branches of American banks as loan vehicles for the VHA with master agreements with the banks' headquarters in the USA as to how the overseas loans could be worked out.

Issue No. 16

SHORT TITLE

Denial of Vocational Rehabilitation Benefits to Veterans Living Abroad.

BACKGROUND

American veterans who retire with a disability are eligible for vocational rehabilitation benefits which are designed to prepare these veterans to assume a new career in civilian life. Among the possible forms of such benefits are subsidized education at the graduate level for advanced university degrees.

THE PROBLEM

The problem is that Vocational Rehabilitation Benefits are not available to veterans who live abroad. While education for a future career might be equivalent to that available in the USA, or might be uniquely available abroad these benefits cannot be used abroad.

THE SOLUTION

It should be possible to conceive of at least some vocational rehabilitation benefits which could be offered to veterans living abroad. For example, education at the university and post-graduate level at American type institutions abroad could be eligible for VA support.

ISSUE NO. 17

SHORT TITLE

Discriminatory Hiring Practices Against American Citizens in U.S. Military Status of Forces Agreements With Foreign Countries.

BACKGROUND

The United States has negotiated a number of special agreements with foreign governments concerning the stationing of American Armed Forces in these foreign countries. Most of these agreements were made many years ago when the United States was a rich country and the overseas locations were relatively much poorer.

These agreements often called for preferential hiring of local nationals for many jobs to be performed for the American Forces. In cases where local nationals were not found to be qualified, nationals from other countries of Europe were to be given the next preference.

THE PROBLEM

The problem is that today there are many American citizens living in overseas countries where American Forces are located who cannot be hired by the American Forces because the local nationals and nationals of all other foreign countries in the area have preference.

What may have been prudent political policy in the former era of dollar supremacy is today an unfortunate tragedy for many Americans who live on dollar retirement salaries.

THE SOLUTION

The United States should reconsider the wisdom of continuing to discriminate against American citizens in hiring for many jobs associated with overseas forces of the United States.

It would seem basic justice to get the United States back into the role of an "Equal Opportunity Employer" abroad, and to stop the unfortunate policy of discriminating against Americans for employment abroad.

ISSUE NO. 18

SHORT TITLE

DOD Regulations That Deprive Americans Living Abroad of Some Work Opportunities.

BACKGROUND

The Department of Defense has issued a number of regulations that control the amount and type of work that individuals can engage in abroad.

Two such rules have been called unjust by Americans living abroad. These concern restrictions on outside jobs for individuals working for quasi-governmental organizations, and restrictions on individuals selling life insurance.

The first problem involves regulations that prohibit individuals who work for the Armed Forces for activities that are paid for from Non-Appropriated Funds (NAF), from also working for civilian firms dealing with U.S. military personnel.

The second problem is a DOD rule that individuals cannot sell life insurance to U.S. Military Personnel unless the seller has worked in the United States in this profession for at least one year.

The problem with these two regulations is that they impede the opportunities that Americans have to earn additional income while living abroad. In the first case those working for NAF organizations often make a bare living wage since salary levels are in dollars, not in the local cost of living currency levels. The diminished moonlighting opportunities means that such individuals are precluded from the jobs where they could most easily earn additional income.

The problem in the second case concerns those who retire, are married to local nationals, and who would like to (or have to for economic survival reasons) take on a second job as a life insurance salesman. The DOD regulations would force them to spend a year in the USA to qualify to sell life insurance abroad, and this is often economically impossible to accomplish.

The Department of Defense should reconsider whether the prohibitions on outside employment that are involved in these and possibly other regulations are really necessary and absolutely necessary in their present form today.

In the case of the first problem there is a probable issue of potential conflict of interest. Could not some other form of resolving such potential problems be found short of an absolute ban?

In the case of the second problem, could not some form of approved training program be found which would permit individuals who retire abroad to become qualified for the selling of life insurance to members of the Armed Forces without the individual having to work for a year in the USA?

Eligibility of United States citizens abroad to participate in U.S. social security programs if working for an American corporation's foreign subsidiary or for a foreign corporation.

The United States Code of Federal Regulations under title 20, Chapter III, Part 401 et seq. specifically provides that work by a U.S. citizen outside the U.S. for a foreign subsidiary of a domestic corporation is covered by social security, if:

(a) The domestic corporation arranges for coverage by entering into an agreement with the I.R.S.; and,

(b) The agreement applies to all U.S. citizens employed outside the U.S. by the foreign subsidiary and all citizens subsequently employed by the subsidiary if their work would be covered if performed in the U.S.

If a domestic corporation does not arrange for coverage for its subsidiary, the U.S. citizens working for that subsidiary are denied the opportunity to participate in the U.S. social security program if they should so wish. This delegates the decision as to the right to participate in the program to the domestic corporation rather than to the U.S. Government or to the individual U S. citizen resident abroad.

If the American citizen works for a foreign corporation abroad, he is not permitted in any circumstances to voluntarily participate in U.S. social security programs.

If the U.S. citizen_resident abroad is not permitted to participate in the social security program and he has not yet accumulated the 40 quarters of coverage required under the program to be "fully insured for life", he would not be eligible for social security benefits.

This situation could create discriminatory and tragic problems for these American citizens, for example:

(a) If disabled while working abroad neither he or his family would be eligible to receive social security benefits in the United States even if he had accumulated up to 39 quarters before leaving the U.S. He and his family might, however, be eligible to receive benefits from the country where he was working and likely paying social security taxes. He and his family might be obliged, therefore, to remain outside of the U.S. in order to avoid destitution. In those cases in which no such benefits from another country were available, the family may be simply left destitute.

(b) If he should die while overseas, his family would not receive social security benefits from the United States. If not eligible for benefits from another country his family would be in a difficult and tragic situation.

THE SOLUTION

Any American citizen resident abroad should be permitted to *voluntarily* participate in the U.S. social security system, at least until he has accumulated the 40 quarters necessary for "fully insured for life" status.

ISSUE No. 20

SHORT TITLE

Eligibility of American citizens working outside of the United States for a foreign government or international organization to participate in United States social security programs.

BACKGROUND

The United States Code of Federal Regulations under title 20, Chapter III, Part 401 et seq. specifically excludes from coverage by social security work carried on outside of the U.S. as an employee of a foreign government or of an international organization. If work for these entities was carried out within the United States, however, the income would be included as earnings from self-employment.[3]

THE PROBLEM

If the U.S. citizen resident abroad is not permitted to participate in the social security program and he has not yet accumulated the 40 quarters of coverage required under the program to be "fully insured for life", he would not be eligible for social security benefits.

THE SOLUTION

Any American citizen resident abroad should be permitted to *voluntarily* participate in the U.S. social security system, at least until he has accumulated the 40 quarters necessary for "fully insured for life" status.

ISSUE No. 21

SHORT TITLE

Problems of compulsory social security coverage of self-employed American citizens resident abroad.

BACKGROUND

The Social Security Handbook states in paragraph 1246 that the "income of a U S. citizen from a trade or business carried on in a foreign country or in a possession of the U.S. is includable in his net earnings from self-employment except to the extent that such income is excludable from gross income under sections 911 or 931 of the Internal Revenue Code of 1954 for Federal income tax purposes". Section 911 previously permitted the exclusion of up to $20,000 of earned income for the taxable year ($25,000 after 3 years).

THE PROBLEM

The revision of section 911 in 1978, however, has eliminated this foreign earned income exclusion (except in very special cases). The exclusion in the

---

[3] Reference paragraphs 948 + 9 of *Social Security Handbook,* 1973.

past had permitted many self-employed Americans abroad, especially those with modest incomes, to avoid or at least decrease the amount of double social security taxation; i.e., the payment of social security taxes to the U S. *and* to the country of residence. Now *all* self-employed Americans resident abroad will be compelled to pay social security taxes in the United States without any exclusion of foreign earned income. This will result in many more cases of double social security taxation and could damage the competitive position of many of these Americans overseas. As many of these Americans have a direct and substantial influence on the development of export opportunities for American goods and services, consideration should be given to eliminating this and other examples of double taxation of self-employed Americans resident abroad.

THE SOLUTION

Self-employed Americans resident abroad should *not* be compelled to pay U.S. social security taxes on foreign earned income. They should be permitted, however, to voluntarily participate in the U.S. social security program.

ISSUE No. 22

SHORT TITLE

Discriminatory regulations concerning the "7-Day Foreign Worktest".

BACKGROUND

The United States Code of Federal Regulations under title 20, chapter III, Part 401 et seq. specifies that inside the United States a beneficiary may not have earnings in excess of a yearly exempt amount which is adjusted annually on the basis of the cost of living. If a beneficiary is outside the United States, however, and his work is not covered by the social security program, he must pass the socalled "7-day foreign work test".

The Social Security Handbook describes this test in paragraph 1828 as follows:

"Under this test, a monthly benefit payment is withheld for each calendar month in which a beneficiary, under age 72, works:

A. On any part of 7 or more days;
B. In "noncovered remunerative activity";
C. Outside the U.S.

This test is based solely on the number of days on which the beneficiary was employed or self-employed, and not on the amount of his earnings. . . .

If benefits are not payable under this test because of a retirement insurance beneficiary's work, no benefits are payable to such individual's spouse or children, if they are entitled on his social security earnings record".

THE PROBLEM

Such disparate "tests" for excess earnings of U.S. resident and non-resident beneficiaries is clearly discriminatory. For example, should a beneficiary resident abroad wish to work part-time for 2 hours a day, 7 days a month, he and his family would lose their total social security benefits for that month. If resident in the United States, however, he would:

(a) be permitted a specified level of dollar earnings (adjusted annually for the cost of living), and

(b) be permitted to average that income over an entire year rather than observe a monthly limit.

A specific example of the effect of such discriminatory provisions was reported by Miss B. J. Swayze, the Director of the American School of Languages and Art in Istanbul, Turkey. This school was originally started by the YWCA and has remained in Turkey under the present name since 1924 when the nation was secularized. The school provides secretarial training to Turkish women and girls. To provide a high level of training they required a qualified secretarial teacher from the United States. Mrs. D. Gehring of North Carolina offered to go to Turkey to teach in order to help the school in return for their paying her enough Turkish liras to cover her room and board. She had retired early and had reached the age of 62 in July 1978 and began receiving social security payments. In addition, she received social security support for a 30-year-old handicapped son. It was a great shock for Mrs. Gehring to be informed by her social security adviser that if she worked more than 7 days a month she would not only lose *her* social security benefits, but also the amount designated for her son.

Mrs. Gehring has decided to borrow money in the U.S. to support her son and other obligations in order to remain at the school for eight months. The Director of the School would have liked Mrs. Gehring to stay for the two years she originally had offered. In the circumstances, however, that will not be financially possible. If Mrs. Gehring was in the United States she would be permitted to work and earn up to $3,240 per year, but in Turkey she is penalized by losing her social security benefits and her son's because she is earning her room and board (well below $3,240).

Letters from retired Americans living abroad cite example after example of the difficulties they face with the devaluation of the dollar, the lack of Medicare benefits overseas, and unfair restrictions on foreign work.

THE SOLUTION

Americans living abroad should be allowed to choose whether they want to have their Social Security pension linked to fixed dollar earning ceilings, or whether they desire the 7-day work test to apply.

ISSUE No. 23

SHORT TITLE

Payment of Medicare benefits for services provided outside of the United States.

BACKGROUND

The United States Code of Federal Regulations under title 20, chapter III, Part 405, Regulations No 5, Federal Insurance for the Aged and Disabled, provides for two primary types of health services; hospital insurance benefits and medical insurance benefits. The *Social Security Handbook* indicates in paragraph 2201 that:

"Hospital insurance benefits may ordinarily be paid only for services furnished in the United States".

Paragraph 2401 states that:

"Medical insurance benefits are not paid for services outside the United States under any other conditions than . . .".

The text goes on to cite an exemption similar to one provided for hospital insurance benefits which permits payment for services in a Canadian hospital if traveling between Alaska and the United States or if a Canadian or Mexican hospital is "closer or substantially more accessible to his residence" than the nearest participating U.S. hospital.

THE PROBLEM

Any American outside of the United States, even if for a brief trip, sacrifices his Medicare coverage. An American resident abroad is not permitted to enroll in the Medicare program and therefore does not pay for those services. An American resident in the United States who travels outside of the United States, even if enrolled and paying his dues, however, still has *no* Medicare coverage.

The harmful effects of these regulations upon overseas Americans are frequently encountered in today's world of rapid and inexpensive travel.

An emergency illness abroad without any medical insurance whatsoever can quickly destroy the financial independence of a pensioner. The purchase of comparable private medical insurance coverage before traveling abroad is often ignored because citizens are insufficiently aware of the residency requirements.

For American citizens resident abroad the resulting extra medical insurance expenses, added on to the problems arising from exchange rate fluctuations and the 7-day work restrictions, explains the difficult plight of many United States retired citizens living abroad.

THE SOLUTION

First of all, action should be taken to ensure that Medicare participants are fully aware of the implications for their Medicare coverage if they travel outside of the United States. In the future, however, provision should be made either through national, bilateral or multilateral agreements to at least protect American residents who are participants in the Medicare program while traveling temporarily abroad. This protection could take the form of permitting such residents to submit claims to be repaid on the basis of a "basic minimum rate" which they would have received if these services had been provided within the United States.

United States citizens resident abroad who would be eligible for Medicare if resident in the United States might be permitted, on a reciprocal basis, to enroll in the comparable medical program of the country in which they are resident (if available) without fulfilling the necessary rules for eligibility. This would, of course, require a series of bilateral or multilateral agreements.

A temporary measure to assist United States citizens resident abroad may be to allow them to submit claims for a "basic minimum rate" repayment as suggested for U.S. residents temporary abroad. If this were not possible, consideration could perhaps be given to allowing an additional monetary exemption to the permissible earned excess income to compensate for the additional medical insurance costs required for United States pensioners resident abroad.

ISSUE NO. 24

SHORT TITLE

Eligibility of United States citizens resident abroad for unemployment insurance.

BACKGROUND

The unemployment insurance program provides partial income replacement for a limited period to persons who become unemployed. It is a State-administered program with Federal participation Each State is required to specify in its laws ·

A. Who may receive unemployment benefits;

B. How each worker can qualify for benefits;

C. The amount of the weekly unemployment benefit;

D. The maximum number of weeks for which unemployment benefits may be paid.[4]

A key criterion in all State programs is either past work history in that State or other States. In fact procedures are available for the local office to forward a claim to another State for payment. Federal workers and ex-servicemen may also be covered by local States with the cost of the benefit paid from a Federal appropriation from general revenue.

United States citizens resident abroad, however, have no access to unemployment insurance within the United States.

THE PROBLEM

In the present economic environment, some Americans resident abroad are being forced to return to the United States as a result of the new tax regulations. exchange rate fluctuations or other economic conditions. In some cases it is very difficult to find new employment within the United States while still resident abroad. When a citizen returns to the United States, however, he does not receive unemployment benefits to assist him and his family as he searches for new employment.

THE SOLUTION

United States citizens resident abroad should have the option to participate in a Federal unemployment insurance scheme. Such a scheme could permit him to make the required payments into the Federal general revenue fund and have States disburse unemployment benefits in a manner similar to the procedure used for Federal workers and ex-servicemen.

ISSUE NO. 25

SHORT TITLE

Loss of Social Security Benefits Due to Dollar Limits on Outside Income, Problems From Floating Exchange Rates.

---

[4] Cited in *Social Security Handbook;* 1973

BACKGROUND

Retired individuals who are eligible to receive pensions from U.S. Social Security face limits on the amount of outside income they can earn without loss of these benefits.

The limits for these outside sources of income are expressed in dollars, and refer to levels of aggregate earnings (pension plus other earned income) which are relevant to the cost of living in the United States. For every dollar of outside earned income above these limits, one half-dollar of benefits are lost.

American Social Security Retirees living abroad are in some cases subjected to these same dollar ceilings on outside income (in some other cases the 7-day work test applies, See Issue No. 22).

However, in many overseas countries there are some severe problems that have to be faced due to higher cost of living than in the United States, and due also to the fluctuations of exchange rates.

THE PROBLEM

The first problem (the higher cost of living abroad) is treated separately in Issue No. 26.

The problems that arise from floating exchange rates are different. Suppose an individual needs to earn outside income because the size of the pension is too small. Suppose also that a job is found that will provide sufficient extra income, but will also fall within the dollar ceiling. Everything will be in order until the foreign currency starts to fluctuate. If as occurs in many overseas countries the dollar starts to weaken, the foreign currency earnings begin to grow larger and larger when translated into dollars. Thus, while the amount of foreign currency that can be purchased by the Social Security pension declines due to the devaluation of the dollar, the constant value of the foreign earnings start to grow larger when translated into dollars. The pensioner is being hit twice, losing from a diminished pension and losing part of this smaller pension (in foreign currency terms) because the outside earnings appear larger.

THE SOLUTION

Some method should be found to protect American pensioners abroad from loss of their Social Security pensions due to phantom increases in the value of their outside earnings due to exchange rate fluctuations. Perhaps these outside earnings should be allowed to float with reference to some acceptable neutral standard rather than being fixed in dollar terms that can vary the apparent value from day to day.

ISSUE No. 26

SHORT TITLE

Irrelevance of Dollar Limits on Outside Income for Social Security Pensioners Abroad in High Cost of Living Countries.

BACKGROUND

Retired individuals who are eligible to receive pensions from U.S. Social Security face limits on the amount of outside income they can earn without loss of these benefits.

The limits for these outside sources of income are expressed in dollars, and refer to levels of aggregate earnings (pension plus other earned income) which are relevant to the cost of living in the United States. For every dollar of outside earned income above these limits, one-half dollar of benefits are lost.

American Social Security Retirees living abroad are often subjected to these same dollar ceilings on outside income (in some cases the 7-day work test applies, See Issue No. 22).

THE PROBLEM

The problem facing those living abroad is that in many countries, the local cost of living is much higher than in the United States. The dollar limits on outside earned income that permit a minimum standard of living in the USA are too low to permit the same minimum standard of living for those abroad.

As more extra income must be earned abroad in such high cost countries to attain a comparable level in the USA, the limits are surpassed and the retiree loses benefits, which, of course, means that he must earn even more to catch up and this leads to even more loss!

THE SOLUTION

The U.S. Government recognizes that there are cost of living differences facing its employees abroad. It has prepared cost of living compensation tables and pays extra allowances to those abroad to protect them from the impact of these cost differences.

How much more important it would seem to be to protect those who are retired with much lower benefit incomes from the same cost-of-living differences.

The dollar limits on outside earned income for those abroad should be indexed to the State Department's cost-of-living tables so that those who are retired abroad will be able to live at the same standard as those who retire in the USA.

ISSUE No. 27

SHORT TITLE

World-Wide Nature of U.S. Tax System Which Taxes on Basis of Citizenship Rather Than Residency.

BACKGROUND AND PROBLEM

The United States is the only major industrialized nation which taxes its citizens on a world-wide basis and not just on the basis of residency. This was not always the case, however. Between 1926 and 1962, the United States did not tax at all the foreign earned income of its citizens living and working overseas. It was not until 1963 that the amount of foreign earned income excluded from taxable income became limited in amount. First, a $35,000 exclusion limit was set for two years which was then reduced to $20,000 or $25,000, depending upon length of residence abroad. Recent tax legislation has generally eliminated the foreign earned income exclusion substituting limited deductions for certain excess living costs. The anticipated effect of this new law is a substantially higher tax bill for American taxpayers abroad and, where they are reimbursed for the excessive tax cost, their employers.

Our competitors are not faced with this additional cost of reimbursing their employees for the home country excess taxes incurred relating to an overseas assignment. As a result of this competitive disadvantage, companies must consider replacing their American employees overseas with foreign nationals who would understandably not be as sympathetic to purchasing and promoting U.S. goods and services. Some 50% of total U.S. exports are sold to or through U.S. companies abroad. In addition, many U.S. firms are losing contracts in foreign countries where American expertise is imperative and a foreign national would be inadequate.

It is also estimated that 40,000 jobs in the U.S. depends on every billion dollars in U.S. exports. Also, Americans, if forced to return to the U.S. from abroad, are competing for U.S. jobs.

It would seem, therefore, that there could be a significant adverse impact on the U.S. economy as a result of continual taxation of U S. citizens on a world-wide basis. This form of discrimination against Americans overseas actually discriminates against the United States and citizens living within its borders as well, as a result of the above. In addition, the costs of administering a world-wide and increasingly complex taxation system for American taxpayers residing abroad seem certainly excessive and should be considered in the light of the revenue generated.

SUGGESTED SOLUTION

Taxation of Americans on the basis of residency only rather than on a world-wide basis by virtue of citizenship.

ISSUE No. 28

SHORT TITLE

Inadequate Credit Given For Taxes Paid By American Citizens Living Abroad

BACKGROUND

While the United States insists on making American citizens continue to pay United States income taxes while they live and work abroad, there is no willingness on the part of the United States to recognize that these same citizens are paying many different forms of taxes to overseas countries on this same income, and in effect are being taxed twice.

The present tax philosophy of the United States is to allow credit only for income tax that is paid abroad, but not for any other form of tax paid abroad.

THE PROBLEM

The problem with this practice is that no other country of the world has exactly the same form of revenue generation as the United States. Each country chooses a mix of direct and indirect taxation which is the result of history, tradition, and different belief of how the common economic burdens should be shared. But, since the United States will only recognize one form of tax paid abroad as equivalent to tax owed to the United States, the American living abroad is protected against double taxation only to the extent that the overseas country relies on income tax and not on tax of any other form.

The following table shows how the revenue generation mix of eight countries varies in terms of what proportion of total national tax revenue comes from personal income tax, personal social security contributions, general sales taxes (or value added taxes) and specific goods taxes, and taxes paid by individuals on property.

COMPARATIVE TAXATION OF INDIVIDUALS IN 8 MAJOR WESTERN COUNTRIES

Country	Per capita tax in 1975	Personal income tax	Social security payment	VAT/ sales taxes	Specific goods taxes	Individual property taxes	Regressivity indexes (percent) 4 / 2+3	5 / 2+3	4+5 / 2+3
	(1)	(2)	(3)	(4)	(5)	(6)			
U.S. dollars:									
United States_____	$2,044	1 $644	$202	1 $137	1 $192	$154	16	23	39
United Kingdom_____	1,495	565	113	117	218	73	19	32	51
France_____	2,348	1 291	201	548	215	23	111	44	155
West Germany_____	2,420	728	363	356	253	16	33	23	56
Italy_____	997	1 150	90	136	134	_____	57	56	113
Switzerland_____	2,494	1 870	347	194	1 266	14	16	22	38
Sweden_____	3,890	1 1,783	_____	464	442	_____	26	25	51
Japan_____	919	1 230	85	_____	1 145	_____	46	46	
Percentages									
United States_____	100	31.5	9.9	6.7	9.4	7.5	_____		
United Kingdom_____	100	37.8	7 6	8.7	14 6	4 9	_____		
France_____	100	12.4	8.6	23.4	9 2	1 0	_____		
West Germany_____	100	30.1	15.0	14.7	10.5	.7	_____		
Italy_____	100	15 1	9.0	13.7	13.5	_____			
Switzerland_____	100	34.9	13.9	7.8	10 7	.6	_____		
Sweden_____	100	45.9	_____	11.9	11 4	_____			
Japan_____	100	25.0	9.2	_____	15.8	_____			

1 Including State and local taxes.

The per capita tax is the total tax revenue of the country divided by the population. The other items are their respective contributions to total tax revenue on a per capita basis. The regressivity indexes show the extent to which total per capita tax revenue comes from indirect taxes felt by individuals (VAT or sales taxes and other indirect taxes of specific goods and services, excise taxes, etc.).

Source· OECD Revenue Statistics of OECD Member Countries 1965–75, OECD 1977.

Despite the fact that the United States allows resident citizens to deduct State sales tax s from their gross taxable income, it denies this same possibility to those American citizens living abroad. Thus, those living abroad in highly regressive tax countries are faced with tax credit (or deduction) losses that can exceed what they pay in direct income tax. (See France above.)

The table is based upon data from 1975, and was compiled by the OECD on a per capita basis.

The upper part of the table shows the amount of taxes collected from individuals (as opposed to corporations) through the various different types of taxation. The amounts that were collected per capita from corporations are not shown on this table, but are included in the first column of total revenue collected per capita during 1975.

It is quite apparent that the eight countries place very different emphasis on raising revenue from income tax and other forms of taxation than the United States. This difference of emphasis is more clearly shown in the lower part of the table where each tax's contribution to total revenue is shown in percentage terms.

To show an overall comparison of revenue from income tax and social security contributions as opposed to indirect forms of taxation of individuals, a simple regressivity index has been prepared (shown at the right of the table). The first column of the index shows the ratio of general sales tax (or value added tax) to tax revenue from income tax and social security contributions. While such general sales taxes (including tax at the State level in the USA) contributes only 16% of the amount from income tax and social security contributions in the USA, it contributes an equal amount (in Switzerland) or greater amount (in every other country except Japan) elsewhere. And in the case of countries such as France more per capita tax is raised each year from this single form of general sales tax than from income tax and social security tax combined. Curiously, those American citizens living in the United States are allowed a deduction from taxable income from sales taxes (which only amount to 16% of tax on income and social security) but for those Americans living in France, there is neither a credit nor even a deduction for taxes which exceed on a per capita basis the amount paid to France on income and for social security.

If one looks at the second column of the index, the ratio here is revenue from specific goods taxes (on gasoline, liquor, cigarettes, etc.) to revenue from income tax and social security. Here again this form of tax is low in the United States (and Switzerland) but twice as big in countries such as Japan and Italy. Again the American citizen living in countries where much more tax is collected from these sources than in the United States is again deprived of any recognition that tax has been paid abroad.

Finally, column three of the index shows the combined revenue from general sales taxes and specific goods taxes as a ratio of revenue per capita generated from income tax and social security contributions. Again the United States and Switzerland are comparable, but countries such as France and Italy appear all the more strikingly different in their tax policy. France collected one and a half times as much revenue per capita from general and specific sales taxes as from income tax and social security contributions. Yet, as far as the United States is concerned, American citizens who have paid this amount of tax have not thereby earned any right to a credit for this tax or even a deduction.

The problem is thus rather evident, United States citizens paying taxes abroad are not recognized as having paid taxes, unless the tax they pay abroad is an income tax. Yet, most overseas countries rely less heavily on income taxes for total revenue than does the United States Americans living abroad face effective double taxation to the direct extent that their overseas country of residence does not have a tax mix that is exactly congruent with that of the United States.

To take an extreme example, let us suppose that one of these countries, say France, were to decide to get rid of income tax entirely, and to generate all government revenue from several different forms of indirect tax on individuals and from taxes on corporations. And, for sake of further example let us assume that the tax on individuals would be such that its effective rate would be 30 percent of total income. The American taxpayer in this country would be told by the United States that he had not paid any tax overseas that is either creditable, or even deductible for U.S. tax purposes. The overseas income would thus be fully taxable by the United States as well.

THE SOLUTION

The ideal solution, of course, would be to recognize that each overseas country is sovereign in its tax policy, and to also recognize that American citizens living in each overseas country are effectively being taxed by all of the individual forms of tax each such country chooses to impose. Thus, if the United States still wants to insist on the American expatriate paying U.S income tax the full value of overseas tax paid should be recognized.

One obvious objection to this practice would be that it would be nearly impossible to ever calculate how much tax had really been paid abroad, for which credit or some form of deduction should be given. The present response to this problem is to simply ignore that any tax other than income tax has been paid.

Another alternative, which is followed by every other civilized country of the world, is to recognize the inherent inequity in requiring overseas citizens to pay tax twice on portions of the same income and to simply stop taxing Americans living abroad.

Lest this radical solution seem ridiculous, it should be recalled that this is precisely what the United States did from 1926 until 1962.

ISSUE No. 29

SHORT TITLE

American Tax Laws Impede the Purchase of American Goods by Americans Living Abroad.

BACKGROUND

There are over 1.5 million American citizens living outside of the United States. This total aggregate population exceeds the population of fourteen different States in the United States, and constitutes a very large potential market for American goods.

Present American tax laws require Americans living abroad to pay American income tax on all foreign income, earned and unearned. At the same time the United States will not give either a tax credit, or even a deduction for much of the tax that is paid to overseas countries.

Included in the category of tax for which no credit is given are tariffs, sales taxes and other goods related taxes that must be paid by an American living abroad if he wants to purchase American made products.

THE PROBLEM

The problem created by this American tax policy is that in many instances there is a heavy tax penalty to be paid if the American expatriate wants to purchase an American made product rather than a product of local origin.

Let us take the example of the purchase of an automobile. And, let us assume that there is some marginal ability on the part of the American in question to work a little harder to earn whatever extra money would be required to buy either a local car, or a car made in the United States. For simplicity, let us also assume that the individual is earning enough money to be paying U.S. tax at the marginal rate of 50%, assume that the overseas country has no income tax, has an import duty of 100% of the cost of the car, and a local sales tax of 30%. The CIF cost of the American car is equal to the ex-factory cost of the local car.

To buy the American car, the American must be willing to pay the cost of the car, plus 100% (for import duty) plus 30% of this duty paid amount for sales tax, or a total of 260% of the CIF car value. To buy the local car the cost is only 130%, or just half of the American car price.

But, since the American is going to have to work an additional amount of time to earn this extra money he will also have to pay to the United States Treasury extra income tax.

Here is where the U.S. tax policy penalizes him for buying American. If he earns enough to buy the foreign car, he will have to pay the United States half of this amount in extra tax (50% of the cost of the car plus the overseas sales tax) or 65% of the CIF cost of the American car.

If the American wants to buy an American car, however, he will have a much greater amount of tax to pay to the U.S. Treasury. For the cost of the American car is double that of foreign car after duty and sales tax, and the U.S. will make him pay twice as much U.S. tax if he buys the American car, than he would have to pay to buy the foreign car.

THE SOLUTION

There is an enormous potential in the overseas American community for selling much greater amounts of American made goods. Not only is the expatriate market a large one, but it is also an invaluable demonstration market for showing American products to others.

The Congress should seriously consider whether it would not be in the best interest of the United States to stop penal taxation of those who earn more to buy American products.

One possible solution would be to grant tax credits for overseas tariffs and sales taxes paid to purchase American origin goods.

If one considers that the result of the present system is to make the American pay the U.S. Treasury more than the value of the American car (in the example above), this is effectively a U.S. excise tax which the expatriate has to pay, which he would not have to pay on this same car if he was living in the USA. And, for this reason the present situation is quite wrong.

ISSUE No. 30

SHORT TITLE

Taxation of "Phantom" Income Resulting from Fluctuating Exchange Rates.

BACKGROUND AND PROBLEMS

An individual living in a foreign country should not be penalized solely due to the fluctuation in value of local currency in terms of U.S. dollars. However, Americans residing in, say Switzerland have seen their income for U.S. tax purposes inflated by approximately 160% since 1971 for a given unchanged nominal income expressed in Swiss francs, the country in which their normal living expenses are incurred. An earned income of SFr. 100,000 was equal to $22,300 in 1971 but at today's exchange rate (December 1978) is worth about $60,000. While the individual's purchasing power in Swiss francs has actually decreased since 1971 due to inflation, his income for U.S. tax return purposes has artificially increased by $37,000 which amount is included in his taxable income. In addition, his other income has been pushed up into a higher tax bracket due to the graduated tax rate system.

SUGGESTED SOLUTION

This is a problem for which there seems to be no practicable solution short of changing the system to taxing on the basis of residency only.

ISSUE No. 31

SHORT TITLE

Taxation of "Phantom" Capital Gains Resulting from Fluctuating Exchange Rates.

BACKGROUND AND PROBLEM

When an American residing overseas sells a capital asset, such as his home, translation must be made into U.S. dollars at the exchange rate in effect at date of purchase and sale to determine purchase price and sales price in dollars for purposes of calculating gain or loss on sale. Assuming the taxpayer resides in Switzerland and he received the same amount of Swiss Francs on sale in December 1978 as he paid upon purchase in December 1970, or SFr 500,000, he would, nonetheless, have a capital gain to report on his U.S. tax return of $178,000 (the difference between translation of SFr. 500,000 at SFr. 1.70=$1 exchange rate at date of sale and SFr. 500,000 at SFr. 4.32=$1 exchange rate at date of purchase $294,000—$116,000=$178,000). Assuming no deferral of the gain through the appropriate repurchase of a new principal residence, the full $178,000 would have to be currently included as capital gain with the appropriate tax paid regardless of the fact that the Swiss Francs, the currency of the taxpayer's country of residence. there was not appreciation in value. In addition, assuming the property had been mortgaged, two other inequities might exist. First, as is possible in Switzerland, there may have been no repayments on tne principal of the mortgage. In that situation, little or no money may have been exchanged on the sale with the mortgage being assumed by the purchaser. Even though little or no cash might be received by the seller, he would still have to report the $178,000 of capital gain. Second, assuming the seller had made mortgage repayments over the years at increasing amounts in terms of dollars, translating at the exchange rate in effect at time of repayment would result in dollar repayments being greater than the original dollar liability, or a currency loss on mortgage repayments. The resulting currency loss would not be deductible from the $178,000 capital gain on sale since the house sold was a personal (rather than business or investment) asset.

SUGGESTED SOLUTION

Short of changing the system to taxing on the basis of residency, Americans residing overseas should not be taxed on capital gains resulting from exchange fluctuations relating to the sale of personal assets.

ISSUE No. 32

SHORT TITLE

Taxation.—Preferential Treatment Given to Government Employees.

BACKGROUND AND PROBLEM

While non-government employees are taxed on all income and allowances regardless of source, U.S. Government employees are not taxed on all allowances and benefits received for additional costs incurred while residing overseas. This situation is highly inequitable. The average non-government employee residing overseas is considered himself to be an unofficial ambassador. He comes into contact with foreign nationals on a daily basis and is looked to as being representative of Americans in the United States. In this day and age of importance of international communications we cannot afford to take an isolationist attitude by substantially reducing the size of our American communities abroad through inequitable treatment of government and nongovernment employees overseas.

SUGGESTED SOLUTION

Short of changing the system to taxing on the basis of residency, government and nongovernment employees overseas should be treated equaly.

ISSUE No. 33

SHORT TITLE

Taxation.—Exchange Controls.

BACKGROUND AND PROBLEM

Currency restrictions imposed by foreign governments may "block" the conversion of foreign currency earned abroad into U.S dollars. The Treasury gives taxpayers a special election to defer reporting blocked foreign income until the foreign currency can be readily converted into U S. dollars. A taxpayer makes the election by filing a separate income tax return covering the deferred income and related deductions. Whenever the income can be changed into dollars, or into a foreign currency or property that can be converted into U S. dollars. A taxpayer makes the election by filing a separate income tax return covering the deferred income and related deductions. Whenever the income can be changed into dollars, or into a foreign currency or property that can be converted into dollars, the taxpayer becomes liable for income tax on all the income on which no tax had previously been paid. The problem, however, is that the tax liability is computed as though the taxpayer had earned that income in the year in which his income became convertible or unblocked Several years income can therefore become taxable all in one year, resulting in considerably higher marginal tax rates than had the income been taxed in the year actually earned.

SUGGESTED SOLUTION

Short of changing the system to taxing on the basis of residency, when earned income becomes unblocked, the tax on that income should be determined in accordance with the other income, deductions and tax rates applicable to the earlier year in which actually earned.

ISSUE No. 34

SHORT TITLE

Taxation —Maximum Tax Treatment With Non-Resident Alien Spouse.

BACKGROUND AND PROBLEM

A married individual is not entitled to benefit from the maximum tax on earned income rates unless he files a joint tax return. A U.S. citizen taxpayer married to a non-resident alien prior to the Tax Reform Act of 1976 was not entitled to file a joint return and therefore not eligible for that tax benefit. While the Tax Reform Act of 1976 enabled taxpayers to file jointly with their non-resident alien spouse and therefore enabling benefit from maximum tax rates, it also causes, by electing such treatment, the non-resident alien spouse to be treated as a resident alien for tax purposes and therefore to be taxed on a world-wide basis Thus forcing income which would be otherwise not taxable by the U.S to be taxable, just for the purpose of the U.S. citizen spouse benefitting from maximum tax rates on earned income.

SUGGESTED SOLUTION

Short of changing the system to taxing on the basis of residency, U.S. citizens married to non-resident aliens should be allowed to benefit from the maximum tax rates on earned income without having to make an election to have their spouse taxed as a resident alien.

ISSUE No. 35

SHORT TITLE

Taxation.—Joint Filing Status With Non-Resident Alien Spouse.

BACKGROUND AND PROBLEM

A U.S. citizen residing overseas does not have the right to make an annual election to file a joint return as a domestic taxpayer has, if he is married to a non-resident alien. Under the Tax Reform Act of 1976, he has the right to make an election to treat his non-resident alien spouse as a resident alien for tax purposes, making the spouse taxable on a world-wide basis. However, once the election is made, if it is broken it can no longer be made again in the future, whereas the taxpayer in the U.S. can annually choose whether or not to file a joint return with his spouse.

SUGGESTED SOLUTION

Short of changing the system to taxing on the basis of residency, a U.S. citizen married to a non-resident should be allowed to make an annual election to file a joint U.S. tax return.

ISSUE No. 36

SHORT TITLE

Taxation—Married to Non-Resident Alien Spouse—Treatment as Married Filing Separately.

BACKGROUND AND PROBLEM

A U.S. citizen overseas married to a non-resident alien spouse who does not choose to elect to treat her as a resident alien and causing her otherwise non-U.S. source income to become taxable in the U.S., must use the filing status married filing separately (unless he qualifies as an unmarried head of household, i.e. dependent child living in household). Having to file as married filing separately is a distinct disadvantage due to higher tax rates and certain deductions which are limited to only one half the normal amount (i.e. deduction for capital loss against ordinary income limited to $1,500 instead of $3,000).

SUGGESTED SOLUTION

Short of changing the system to taxing on the basis of residency, a U.S. citizen married to a non-resident alien who does not elect to have the spouse treated as a resident alien should be allowed to file (if not qualifying for unmarried head of household status) as a single person and not lose one half of certain deductions as if filing as married filing separately.

SHORT TITLE

Taxation—Foreign Conventions.

BACKGROUND AND PROBLEM

An individual is allowed a deduction for expenses limited to attendance at two foreign conventions per year. A taxpayer residing overseas might attend several such conventions in the foreign country in which he resides and yet he would still be limited to a deduction for two conventions per year since what to him is his home country of residence is for purposes of the related tax deduction considered to be a foreign country.

SUGGESTED SOLUTION

Short of changing the system to taxing on the basis of residency, taxpayers residing overseas should have no deduction limitation for the reasonable cost of "foreign" conventions attended.

ISSUE No. 38

SHORT TITLE

Taxation—Nondeductibility of Foreign Charitable Contributions.

BACKGROUND AND PROBLEM

No deduction is allowed for contributions made to charities in foreign countries even though the ultimate beneficiaries and objectives may be the same as those charities for which tax deductions are allowed in the U.S. (such as churches, the Red Cross, etc.).

SUGGESTED SOLUTION

Short of changing the system to taxing on the basis of residency, it is suggested that a deduction be allowed for contributions to foreign charities which would be considered to qualify for tax-exempt status in the U.S.

ISSUE No. 39

SHORT TITLE

Taxation—Non-Recognition of Foreign Postmark.

BACKGROUND AND PROBLEM

Unlike domestic taxpayers, the local postmark is not accepted as date of filing for tax returns submitted by Americans overseas. Only a U.S. postmark is evidence of timely filing. As a result, overseas taxpayers never know with certainty exactly when their tax returns are considered filed since there can be significant delays incurred in some foreign country postal systems. Such delays can cause significant penalties as well as interest charges to be imposed for late filing, even though the taxpayer may have mailed the return well before the due date.

SUGGESTED SOLUTION

Short of changing the system to taxing on the basis of residency, foreign postmarks should be accepted as evidence of timely filing.

ISSUE No. 40

SHORT TITLE

Taxation—Lack of Sufficient Time To Pay Tax.

BACKGROUND AND PROBLEM

While taxpayers overseas are entitled to an automatic extension to June 15 in which to file their returns, they must pay interest on the balance of tax due from April 15. Since the later filing date is necessitated by the additional time needed to accumulate tax information and supporting documents while overseas and also by the IRS due to the delay in overseas taxpayers receiving tax forms, it is inequitable not to extend the date for payment of the tax as well. The overseas taxpayer may indeed be prevented from filing due to unavailability of tax forms, or as we experienced for 1977 tax returns, an uncertainty as to what would be the applicable law.

SUGGESTED SOLUTION

Short of changing the system to taxing on the basis of residency, an automatic extension of time for payment of the tax due should be granted to coincide with the automatic extension of time for filing the returns.

ISSUE No. 41

SHORT TITLE

Taxation—Lack of Sufficient Time for Filing Estimated Tax Return.

BACKGROUND AND PROBLEM

Although overseas Americans are granted an automatic two-month extension of time to file their tax return for the previous year, there is no similar extension of time beyond April 15 for filing an estimated tax declaration and for paying the estimated tax for the current year. Congress has suggested the desirability of computing the tax liability for the previous year before estimating income tax for the current year by adopting Section 1012 of the 1976 Tax Reform Act in order to make the filing date for the declaration of estimated tax by a non-resident alien coincide with the June 15 filing date for the non-resident alien tax return. Non-resident citizens can reasonably expect to be treated equitably with non-resident aliens.

SUGGESTED SOLUTION

Short of changing the system to taxing on the basis of residency, the due date for declaring and making the first payment of estimated tax should be June 15 instead of April 15.

ISSUE No. 42

SHORT TITLE

Taxation—Effective Loss of January 31 Filing Benefit.

BACKGROUND AND PROBLEM

Certain penalties for underpayment of estimated tax are eliminated for taxpayers who file their tax return and pay all tax due on or before January 31 of year following the tax return year. Since tax returns typically are not delivered either to overseas taxpayers or U.S. embassies at best until the very end of January or beginning of February, the potential tax benefit is, for practical purposes, unavailable to overseas Americans, even for those who are aware of it.

SUGGESTED SOLUTION

Short of changing the system to taxing on the basis of residency, the date for qualifying for this benefit for Americans overseas should be extended to March 15 from January 31.

ISSUE No. 43

SHORT TITLE

Taxation—Lack of Relevant Information Guides.

BACKGROUND AND PROBLEM

While the IRS publishes a large number of pamphlets to guide domestic taxpayers, most of these are of little use to Americans overseas because they do not address themselves to the problems encountered by taxpayers in foreign countries. There are a few pamphlets designed specifically for overseas taxpayers but it is fair to say that the information is neither the equivalent of that provided for domestic taxpayers nor nearly adequate to explain to the average overseas taxpayer how his return should be properly prepared, given the additional complexities of foreign tax credits and treatment of foreign-earned income.

SUGGESTED SOLUTION

Short of changing the system to taxing on the basis of residency, the IRS should review and revise its existing information guides with the objective of providing as informative pamphlets for overseas taxpayers as for domestic taxpayers. To be more meaningful, pamphlets should be prepared on a country-by-country basis.

ISSUE No. 44

SHORT TITLE

Taxation—Difficulty in Obtaining Tax Forms.

BACKGROUND AND PROBLEM

While the IRS sends a supplementary package of tax forms to taxpayers who have filed from overseas the previous year, they are usually inadequate. For instance, the form for reporting foreign bank accounts is not included even though nearly every taxpayer residing overseas has a foreign bank account and is therefore required to file such form. In addition, the package of forms does not include Form 2210, required to be completed in cases of underpayment of estimated tax, or the form for computing maximum tax on earned income (to be used when earned taxable income exceeds 50% tax bracket) which income level is frequently exceeded if for no other reason due to fluctuating exchange rates resulting in a devalued dollar.

Taxpayers overseas must request such form from the local consulate or embassy. When not locally available, they must be requested from the Office of International Operations. This involves considerable delays, particularly where forms are sent by seamail and where it causes filing beyond April 15 interest must be paid.

SUGGESTED SOLUTION

Short of changing the system to taxing on the basis of residency, the tax form package for overseas filers should be revised and made more complete.

ISSUE No. 45

SHORT TITLE

Taxation—IRS Deficiency in Adapting to Overseas Taxpayer Situation.

BACKGROUND AND PROBLEM

The IRS often sends tax assessment notices and other communications by seamail, requiring four or more weeks for receipt by the taxpayer overseas. The notice itself normally requires payment within ten days of the date of the notice or a date well prior to receipt by the taxpayer. Not complying with the IRS request results in penalties and interest occurring.

SUGGESTED SOLUTION

Short of changing the system to taxing on the basis of residency, it is suggested that the IRS be required to send notices to overseas taxpayers by airmail. allowing a reasonable period of time from date of receipt in which to reply.

ISSUE No. 46

SHORT TITLE

Taxation—Lock of, and Cost of Obtaining Assistance in Preparation of Tax Returns.

BACKGROUND AND PROBLEM

While an extensive advisory service is provided for domestic taxpayers, including the use of toll-free telephone answers for federal tax questions, overseas a limited amount of IRS tax advice is available. It is generally limited to a few embassies on a continent. It is certainly not available in every country except for a few days around tax filing time and then not adequate to be of much specific help for a taxpayer's particular situation.

As a result, the overseas taxpayer who is obviously faced with a much more complex tax preparation situation than he had in the U.S. must seek outside professional assistance. This is certainly not available on every street corner as it is in the U.S. As a matter of fact, for the most part, this professional assistance is only available from international accounting firms. The individual who would never think of using, or require, the services of such a firm when living inside the U S. is left little alternative, if his return is to be done properly, but to go to such firms, with the resultant cost of preparation being ten times or more than what he might have to pay in the U.S.

SUGGESTED SOLUTION

Short of changing the system to taxing on the basis of residency, it should be incumbent upon the IRS to ensure that adequate assistance in preparing tax returns is available. If the IRS itself cannot provide adequate assistance for overseas taxpayers, there should then be allowed a credit rather than a deduction for the excess cost of such assistance. Toll-free telephone answers should be available as is the case for domestic taxpayers.

ISSUE No. 47

SHORT TITLE

Taxation—Source of Income—Partnership.

BACKGROUND AND PROBLEM

Due to U.S. rules determining source of income and the related effect on the foreign tax credit limitation inequitable situations can arise. For example, a taxpayer living in a foreign country who does not enter the U S at all in a particular year, and who is a partner in a U.S. Partnership has his earnings treated as U.S. source income to the extent of the partnership U.S. source earnings even though he was physically present in the foreign country while performing his services. This "U.S. source" income even though it is taxed by the foreign country may not benefit from relief from double taxation by virtue of the foreign tax credit.

SUGGESTED SOLUTION

Short of changing the system to taxing on the basis of residency, source of income rules should be changed to allow treatment by a partner in a partnership to have the source of his income determined with regard to his physical location when performing his partnership duties.

ISSUE No. 48

SHORT TITLE

Double Taxation on Income Earned Relating to Days Worked in U.S.

BACKGROUND AND PROBLEM

Under U.S. tax law, the source of earned income is determined by where the individual is physically located when the services are performed. An American living and working overseas who spends some time on business in the U.S. must treat his earned income relating to those business days as U.S. and not foreign source income. This is the case even though no payments were made to him specifically with regard to his time in the U.S Due to the foreign tax limitation, the U.S. tax on income generated from U.S. working days cannot be reduced by the foreign tax credit. This is the case even though the foreign country in which the taxpayer resides may tax that earned income, which the U.S. considers to be U.S. source income, by virtue of his residency there. As a result of the foreign country taxing that income for which the U.S. does not allow a foreign tax credit, double taxation of income occurs.

SUGGESTED SOLUTION

Short of changing the system to taxing on the basis of residency, a foreign tax credit should be allowed for all income taxed by a foreign country for which no relief is provided from double taxation by treaty.

ISSUE No. 49

SHORT TITLE

Estate Taxation.

BACKGROUND AND PROBLEM

Depending on individual foreign countries and related if any treaties with the U.S. taxpayers residing overseas risk double estate taxation or even annulment of seemingly valid wills.

SUGGESTED SOLUTION

Further study must be made of this complex situation to determine areas where inequity exists and recommendations made for appropriate relief.

ISSUE No. 50

SHORT TITLE

Failure of the U.S. Tax Laws to Recognize Special Residents' Taxes Paid by Some Americans Living Abroad.

BACKGROUND AND PROBLEM

American citizens living in England whether they live in rented quarters or in their own home, are required to pay a tax on the residence they occupy. This tax is called "Rates".

In the United States, real estate taxes are deductible from taxable income for Federal Income tax purposes. However, the IRS has ruled that "Rates" cannot be considered a real estate tax because U.K. tax practice is that the resident rather than the owner bears this tax burden.

THE SOLUTION

Short of changing American tax laws to taxation on the basis of residence rather than citizenship, a deduction should be allowed for those living in countries such as England that have residents' taxes such as "Rates". The nit-picking of the IRS on many small issues such as this is what eventually aggregates into grossly unfair overall tax treatment of those living abroad.

APPENDIX C

U.S. SENATE,
Washington, D.C., September 13, 1979.

THE PRESIDENT,
The White House.

DEAR MR. PRESIDENT: Section 407 of the recently-enacted Public Law 96–60 mandates that you prepare a report with respect to how U.S. law and regulations affect the ability of American citizens to compete in the major international markets of the world. Having initiated this legislation, as well as previous legislation (Section 611 of P.L. 95–426) requiring a report analyzing the status of American citizens abroad as compared with those living in the United States, I believe it may be of help to explain what I hope the new report will contain.

A perception widely shared by the nearly two million American citizens residing abroad is that the United States has no overall policy objectives regarding our overseas citizens—neither with respect to the rights, duties and benefits they should retain while away from home, nor with respect to what competitive status they should have vis-a-vis citizens of other nationalities living abroad. Unfortunately, this perception was not ameliorated by the Administration's recent report (in response to Section 611 of P.L. 95–426) entitled "Equitable Treatment of United States Citizens Abroad," which identified a number of present laws and regulations but which did not attempt to frame an overall and coherent policy. I therefore believe that the forthcoming report should begin with, and be based upon, a clear statement of the overall policy orientation and objectives of the United States Government with regard to how our overseas citizens should be treated while they live abroad: the rights, duties and benefits they should retain or be denied, and a justification for any differences from treatment they would have received at home.

In the course of its analysis, the report should compare the U.S. Government's approach to American citizens overseas with the approach taken by the major foreign countries with whom we compete in international markets, in order to determine what competitive advantages or disadvantages our policies now cause our citizens abroad. Then, any competitive disadvantages which exist, and which you feel ought to be maintained, should be explained and justified.

Finally, of course, the report should contain those legislative and other changes you propose to bring your recommended policy into effect.

Should you require Congressional assistance in this endeavor—as perhaps through the creation of a Presidential Commission—I will be pleased to meet with you or your representatives to discuss the alternatives.

I trust you will agree that what we need is not simply another report restating present tax policy, or the history or individual pieces of legislation in other areas such as social security, voting rights, and citizenship. What we need is a fresh, comprehensive look at the problems and opportunities facing our overseas citizens, and a careful analysis of how the United States should deal with these citizens—who collectively constitute a vital national asset—in the context of our nation's current objectives abroad.

With all good wishes, I am

    Sincerely yours,

GEORGE MCGOVERN.

APPENDIX D

[From the New York Times, Feb. 19, 1980]

COSTLY FALL IN EXPATRIATE JOBS : TAXES AND A WEAK DOLLAR LEAD TO COSTLY DECLINE IN U.S. JOBS ABROAD

(By Robert D. Hershey, Jr.)

LONDON, February 18.—Tax penalties, a weak dollar and soaring inflation have made it so expensive to employ Americans overseas that large numbers of them are being replaced by other nationalities at what appear to be major economic and political costs to the United States.

American executives say the problem, which has been building for many years, now jeopardizes billions of dollars of exports and hundreds of thousands of jobs at home and abroad.

A recent report issued by the President's Export Council, an advisory group headed by Reginald H. Jones, chairman of the General Electric Company, echoed that view. The council declared that the trend of Americans being taxed out of competing in foreign markets had produced a "sharp" loss of business, contributing to the balance-of-payments deficit, a loss of American jobs and a decline in "presence and prestige" abroad.

Not only are United States and foreign companies increasingly reluctant to subsidize American workers overseas, but the workers themselves are rejecting job offers because of the financial burdens posed by such a move.

The expatriates say that many laws and practices tend to make second-class citizens of the two million of them who live overseas, but income taxes are regarded as the most damaging factor. The United States is the only major country that taxes income earned abroad, a fact that increasingly places Americans and their companies at a competitive disadvantage. Americans overseas often pay foreign income taxes as well, but they receive a credit for such levies when they file their American tax returns.

"What we're seeing is a form of discrimination against Americans by our own Government," said John G. McCarthy Jr., vice president of Russell Reynolds Associates, an executive recruiting company. "It means Americans seeking to work abroad are burdened with cost factors which other nationals do not have."

Mr. McCarthy, who runs the firm's Middle East operation from London, said the company had conducted searches for about 35 Middle East clients last year, all of whom would have preferred an American. In all but three cases, however, the jobs were filled by Britons for reasons of cost. Other American jobs overseas, he said, are being taken by Canadians, who pay no income tax at home so long as the employee is accompanied abroad by his family.

American companies are confronted by the same problem William Ferguson, a senior manpower manager for General Electric here, said it could cost G.E. $90,000 or more in pay and allowances to maintain an American overseas who is paid only $30,000 at home .

"It's really disturbing," said Mr. Ferguson "We can hire two fully qualified British nationals and afford to train them in our products for less than we can put one American on the payroll."

He added that five years ago the United States was the leading exporter to Saudi Arabia, but that it had slipped to third or fourth position because of the high cost of doing business there. "We would love to double our sales and marketing operation in the Middle East, but we just can't afford it," he added.

While a British employee can quadruple his after-tax earnings by going overseas, his American counterpart usually fares no better than he would have at home. At times, the American is actually penalized by taxes levied on allowances for what in many cases are astronomic costs for housing and education. In some cases, an American's tax liability may exceed his basic salary before adjustments.

One group of activists, the Geneva-based American Citizens Abroad, has listed 63 ways in which they say the Government discriminates against them. They range from taxes on "phantom" income arising from currency fluctuations and loss of Social Security benefits to the sometimes bizarre rules governing the citizenship of children born abroad.

The latest frustration for overseas Americans is the Carter Administration's response late last month to a Congressional demand that it identify and evaluate all the statutes and regulations that treat expatriates differently and that it recommend action to eliminate discrepancies.

Critics say, however, that the Treasury report fell far short of its mandate. The report found that while taxation of Americans abroad could have adversely affected United States exports, "it is not clear how prevalent this type of situation is or what its impact is." It added that the studies done so far did not permit decisions about what changes, if any, should be made.

The Treasury's report was characterized by Andy Sundberg of American Citizens Abroad as a "red herring that the White House has just dragged across the path that was supposed to lead toward an unambiguous statement of where overseas Americans are supposed to fit into the political, social, economic and ideological life of the United States."

He said that what he called inconclusive findings on the relationship between income taxes and exports were "a silly answer to the wrong question."

A task force of the President's Export Council, headed by Robert Dickey 3d of the Dravo Corporation, recommended that the United States align its tax policy with that of its competitors, none of which now taxes its citizens who meet overseas residency tests.

This would restore to Americans abroad the status enjoyed by most of them until 1962, when income of less than $20,000 was tax-exempt. By the mid-1970's, inflation, the decline of the dollar and rising salaries and benefits put heavy financial pressure on Americans overseas.

Instead of liberalizing the exemptions, Congress decided in 1976 to eliminate them altogether. At the same time, the Internal Revenue Service decided that any goods or services workers received, even housing in the Saudi Arabian desert, had to be declared and taxed at full market value.

"It's not just a matter of dollars and cents," said Mr. McCarthy, the recruiter. "If you don't have American people of some stature on the ground, you're just not going to get across the American point of view. You can project power with aircraft carriers, but you can also spread American influence with businessmen."

O

Capital Preservation Through Global Investing

Investing globally is one of the most successful ways to accomplish capital preservation and growth. In books such as *The Complete Guide to Tax Havens* and *The Conservative Wealthbuilder: Capital Preservation Through Global Investing*, Adam Starchild reveals how you can create an ultimate global portfolio of investments to hedge against inflation, taxes, confiscations, market, fluctuations, currency devaluations, economic and political turmoil...

Starchild reveals the little-known investment secrets that he has been giving to his clients for the past few decades. His recommendations are not high-flying investment tips, but rather solid, conservative recommendations that over time will help build a healthy nest-egg for you.

You will learn how to build a secret stash of cash that:

- *You can access at any time*

- *Is tax-free and seizure proof*

- *Pays competitive dividends and interest*

- *And has no government reporting requirements (even for Americans)*

In fact, if you had put $ 10,000 each year into this investment or the last twenty years you would have $590,697 today!

You will also discover:

- *How to accumulate income tax-free*

- *Why offshore mutual funds should form a vital part of your global portfolio*

- *How to invest in gold, silver and platinum and the investor potential of these precious metals*

- *Why Switzerland should play an essential part in any global nest-egg strategy*

- *How and where to best form an offshore trust in order to provide tax and creditor protection for your investments*

- *How to invest tax-free in the United States*

Everything you need to get yourself started on a global path to a secure fortune is in *The Conservative Wealthbuilder.* Starchild's techniques have been used by many of the world's wealthiest people for decades, including presidents, kings, Arab sheiks... And now for the first time they are available to you. They have been tested and proven over time. You will not find a safer, surer path to financial security than that mapped out for you in this unique work!

Just published (ISBN 0894990500), *The Conservative Wealthbuilder* is available through major bookstores and online booksellers. Also recently published (ISBN 1893713105) *The Complete Guide to Tax Havens* provides a wealth of information on forming offshore corporations and trusts.

The following sections are excerpts from *The Conservative Wealthbuilder* and other books by Adam Starchild:

Investing for the Offshore Entity

Investing for the offshore entity is just as important as creating the corporation or trust in the first place. Failure to invest the corpus and reinvest the income is one of the surest ways to squander the benefits that come from creation of an offshore corporation or trust. Astute choices in investment can lead to the realization of personal financial goals and, potentially, financial freedom. A problem often arises when one considers where to invest his money because there are so many options. Selecting the wrong ones can, at best, hinder the achievement of financial goals, and, at the worst, result in financial ruin. It is important to bear in mind that the investing is as important as the creation and structuring of the offshore entity.

Asset Allocation — The Key To Successful Investing

One of the newest forms of investments in America is called asset allocation. Basically what it means is that one investment is "allocated" to a number of different types of investments by a professional investment allocator. The reason for this allocation is that no one type of investment is the best in all investment climates, and no one type of investment is usually appropriate for all of one person's investment money.

By using an asset allocation program, a person can invest a large amount of his principal in one place, gaining ease of tracking the investment, while attaining the advantage of having a number of different investments to serve his different investment objectives.

The asset allocator performs the service for the investor of allocating varying amounts of a total investment into different areas of investing, such as income stocks, growth stocks, small capitalization stocks, etc., and a variety of fixed income securities.

For modest to medium-sized investments, one method of attaining even more diversification of investments, and expertise in the actual details of the investments, is to allocate the investment among various top-rated mutual funds. As is well known, mutual funds can perform a number of important tasks for the investor. Diversification among a large number of stocks is possible for even a relatively small sum of money. Expertise is available on any type of investment at a relatively low price. Last, there is great liquidity with ease of purchasing and selling.

The actual allocation into different mutual funds will depend upon three principal criteria:

(1) What is the risk to reward profile of the individual investor,

(2) What is the need of the investor for predictable current income as opposed to the desire for capital gains, and

(3) What is the state of the economic and investment cycles at the particular moment in time.

The first and most important criteria are clearly the needs of the investor. These outweigh any thoughts of where any market may be going or where an allocator believes that the most money can be made. The first need which needs to be addressed is the risk which the investor is prepared to accept. All investment involves some degree of risk, but that risk can rage from the minor risk of how inflation can impact an investment in the next 90 days, to the risk of a high flying initial public offering in a company which may have no earnings and no prospect for earnings in the foreseeable future.

The amount of risk which is appropriate for an individual investor depends upon both the investors actual economic situation and his psychological attitudes towards risk of loss. Human temperament plays a very large role in determining risk tolerance. For example, if a person remembers a period of his or her past where they did not have enough money to make ends meet, they may be very adverse to taking any risk at all. Their attitude may be, "We worked hard for that money, and we don't want to lose it."

Others may have almost the opposite approach. They may never have known deprivation, and may have earned a good income all their life. Their attitude may be that they can live very well on their current earnings, and so any savings can be used to speculate. If the speculation turns out to be successful, that will be great and they can raise their standard of living even further. But if the speculation doesn't work out, that's OK too because they will simply continue living as they have.

Thus a good investment allocator will first determine what the needs of his clients are with respect to risk. One method is to determine first how much money is needed to maintain the current standard of living of the investor, and if he or she is not yet retired, how much of the investment will be needed when they do retire. Whatever amount is needed for these purposes is then designated as income producing principal and is invested accordingly into low-risk, high-yielding investments.

The balance can then be invested according to the investor's wishes into areas which can offer the promise of large capital gains in the future. This is the risk portion of the principal, and care must be taken so that the allocator and the investor agree on what amount of risk is to be taken.

The third and equally important task of allocating is to attempt to maximize the return to the investor from the changes in the economic cycle. When business has been in a slump and starts to turn up with both interest rates and inflation low, the largest profits are typically made in the stock market. But as the economy continues to expand, interest rates will rise and so will inflation. These factors make the prognosis for the economy less rosy, and the stock market may start to gyrate, and then fall. Perhaps gently at first and then more rapidly. So the stock market is definitely not the place to be.

At the same time that the stock market is suffering from inflation, the price of hard assets such as gold, oil, and real estate could well be rising rapidly. It is in these areas that fortunes are made during inflationary periods in the economy.

And then as the economy finally begins to cool down due to the effect of high interest rates, interest rates will begin to fall nd the big money may be made by investing in long-term non-callable bonds.

Thus a good allocator must keep in mind the needs of the individual investor and the current status of the economy. And of course he must have an intimate familiarity with specific investments which are available to investors. Whether they be stocks, bonds, or fixed income securities, the allocator must know which are appropriate for the investor and which will likely do well in the present stage of the economy.

As with options in the preceeding chapter, the expertise of Max G. Ansbacher is once again quite useful. His credentials in the stock market are equally impressive. The second book he wrote is titled *How to Profit from the Coming Bull Market* and it was published in the summer of 1981 near the bottom of the long bear market which had actually begun in 1973.

This book explained how and why a strong bull market was about to start on Wall Street. At the time it was published the book was largely ignored by a public which had grown cynical about a stock market which seemed to do nothing but go sideways or down, year after year.

But just one year after Mr. Ansbacher's book was published, the market suddenly took off like a rocket in August 1982, igniting one of its greatest bull markets ever and establishing Mr. Ansbacher's reputation as an insightful student of the stock market.

We recently asked Mr. Ansbacher what his philosophy was concerning asset allocation. He replied, "Asset allocation is probably the most important single aspect of any investment program. And yet what is so strange about it is that it is often not even considered by investors. Some people will have most of their money in the stock market most of the time, unaware of the large risks which the market sometimes contains. Others believe in bonds, and continue to invest most or all of their money there, apparently unaware that in the 1970's and early 1980's the bond market was the biggest money loser of any investment. I would say that asset allocation is not just important, it is the key to successful investing."

Mr. Ansbacher went follows a deliberatly planned, carefully crafted strategy when handling an asset allocation account for a client. "The first thing I do is to talk to the client in whatever depth is necessary to determine the proper risk profile for the client. This depends upon his current financial situation and what he foresees for his future situation as well as his psychological feelings towards money and the potential loss of money. The second thing I do is to make an outline of the client's need for current income. This naturally has a great deal of influence on how we can invest the funds."

"Only after this has been done, do I then discuss with the client where I think the financial markets are heading and where the best returns are likely to be made in the future. The first step in actually making the investments are to decide upon the proportion of money going into each class of investments. The second part is to select the actual investments. For a number of reasons, I select from among the thousands of mutual funds which are available in the U.S. They range all the way from bond to preferred stocks, to common stocks of all types. There is usually a time and a place for almost all of them, but we try to pick the best one for that particular client at that particular time in the client's life, and in the life of the markets."

Mr. Ansbacher explained that his minimum investment is $100,000, and that he works with some of the biggest mutual fund organizations in the U.S., including Fidelity, Dreyfus and other mutual fund management firms. He does not bill his clients for a fee or commission for the work he does, because his compensation is paid to him by the mutual funds.

We have always believed that to be a good asset allocator is one of the most difficult tasks in the investment world, because it requires so many different considerations. To see just what kind of factors Mr. Ansbacher considers we asked him how he would go about planning an asset allocation program we asked him about a potential (though fictitious) client: a 50-year-old German married man who earns the equivalent of $200,000 a year and has a well-funded pension plan with his company. He is in good health and plans to retire at about the age of 65. We asked Mr. Ansbacher to assume that this man comes to him with $300,000 to invest. Here is how Mr. Ansbacher went about making his asset allocation process.

Mr. Ansbacher's recommendation? "The first question I have is about the amount of $300,000. Since he has a pension plan with his company, it is obviously not pension money. It is also a rather large amount for a person earning $200,000 to want to invest in the U.S. Is it inherited money? Does his wife earn money? Is this his life savings? Did he make a successful investment? The reason I ask this question is that it is very important to know if the money is replaceable. If it is inherited, will there be more to follow, or is this all? First I would want to know whether there will be more money coming in or not."

"Second, I would want to know more about his potential future obligations. Do he or his wife having living parents or other relatives who may need financial support in the future? How much support, if any, does he expect that his children will need in the future? Does he have disability insurance or a company plan in case he becomes disabled before he retires? Is there some specific financial goal that he has, such as acquiring a vacation home, yacht or other item which will require a substantial amount of ready cash. All these factors related to the amount of risk which I would want to take."

"The next set of considerations center around his financial situation now. Since he lives in Germany, this means that he pays a high tax on income such as dividends and interest, but pays no capital gains tax. Right away that sways me into investments which are likely to have high capital gains. I would want to know whether the $200,000 he earns covers all of his current expenses, or whether his current standard of living is so high that he needs extra income each year."

"Once we have the answers to these questions, we can begin to solve the problem of how best to allocate this investment. If there are no likely financial needs coming up in the future, and if at the time of the investment I decide that the stock market is not over priced or likely to decline for other reasons, I would place most of the money into various stock funds. I am particularly fond of funds which use value investing, which means that they pick stocks based upon how large an amount of earnings one gets for each dollar invested. This is another way of saying that they seek out stocks with high quality and low price/earnings ratios."

"The reason I like value investing is that many studies have shown that low price/earnings stocks outperform other stocks in normal markets. And in down markets heir inherent value keeps them from falling as far as others. The second group of stocks I would pick would be senior growth stocks. This means stocks which grow year after year because they are gaining market share, or because they are in a solid growth industry. Examples of this are some pharmaceutical companies which are constantly creating new and better drugs, or highly efficient national retail chains which are constantly gaining market share over local competitors."

"One advantage which growth stocks have for this particular client is that they usually don't pay a very large dividend, which fits right in which his local tax structure. Depending upon the wishes of the client, we would consider some gold stocks as a hedge against inflation. And we might add some mutual funds which specialize in large capitalization companies, because these are the tried and proven winners among all the competition in the economy, and often outperform other stocks when the economy softens."

"I would also place a portion of the assets into a short or medium term bond fund for three reasons:

(1) This could be a source of money in case an emergency arose which required a withdrawal from the fund,

(2) It is a reserve in case some outstanding bargains come up for investment, and

(3) It is a hedge against a downturn in the stock market."

Of course the actual percentage allocations would be discussed with the client. The actual funds selected would depend upon their performance records at the time of the investment. And in general, much of the allocation would depend upon the state of the economy at the time of the investment."

Good advice. From a man well-qualified to give it.

Investing in Options

Another vehicle to consider investing your money is in options. Specifically, trading options on stocks or on a stock index (such as the Standard & Poor's 500 Index). This is route is particularly appealing to foreigners, since the gain or loss from trading in options is a capital gain, and any profits made by a foreigner from trading in such options are free from any tax imposed by the United States.

But, as many investors already know, options are notoriously speculative and most people who try trading in them wind up losing money. Therefore, in order to take advantage of this tax benefit, it is first imperative to find a method of trading options which has a good probability of actually making money.

Almost any method of trading options which has the chance of making an above average return also carries a commensurate high degree of risk. But some practitioners of the arcane art of options trading do manage to do better than others over the years. One such person who has done very well for his clients is Max G. Ansbacher, Chairman of Ansbacher Investment Management, Inc., located in the prestigious Rockefeller Center complex in New York City.

Mr. Ansbacher has a long and distinguished involvement with options. In fact, he is the author of the first book published on the modern form of options, titled *The New Options Market, Revised and Enlarged Edition,* first published in 1975. Today, he manages accounts for investors in both the U.S. and overseas.

What sets Mr. Ansbacher apart from many others is that he has an excellent record of bringing in above average profits for his clients. Since most people who buy options seem to lose money, we asked Mr. Ansbacher what the key was to his success. He replied, "Yes, I agree that most people who buy options do seem to lose money. But what many people don't realize is that the money which the options buyers lose, doesn't disappear from the face of the earth. Rather it becomes the profits of the options *sellers.* And therefore, I concentrate in *selling* options."

What Mr. Ansbacher was saying is that options trading is actually a zero sum game when one looks at the total overall economic effect. This means that buying and selling options has no overall impact on the economy. It neither creates any money or lose any (except transaction costs). If the sellers make money, the buyers lose money. And if the buyers make money, then the sellers must lose money.

Since the options *buyers* tend to be the ones who lose money, it therefore must be true that the options *sellers* are the ones who make money over the long run. "The options buyers tend to be less sophisticated than the sellers," Mr. Ansbacher explained. "They don't always carefully assess the chances that their stocks will really go up enough to make money when they buy a call. Similarly, if people think a stock or a stock market is going to go down, they often over estimate how much it is going to go down. They will buy a put which is going to lose money unless the stock makes a really unusually large move within a relatively short period of time. These are the options I sell."

Of course there is not an investment program yet invented which makes money on every single trade, and option selling is no exception.

Mr. Ansbacher said, "Certainly there are times when we have losses, but we believe that the probability lies with the sellers. And so we usually find that every loss is matched by many more winners."

If you do become involved in selling options, the best advise is: proceed with caution! Never forget that the risk factor is high. How does a veteran like Mr. Ansbacher control this risk? He said that the first defense was to control the number of options which he sells. "I usually sell only about one fifth the number of options which margin rules permit me to do. The second line of defense is that I use stop loss orders, which in most instances will automatically get me out of the options before the losses rise to a point which I consider unacceptable."

He continued, "The most interesting line of defense and the most important from the point of view of making money, is that I sell out-of-the-money options. This means that I sell options which have a strike price which is a distance away from the current price of the underlying security." We should point out that a strike price is the level at which an option becomes effective.

What Mr. Ansbacher means is that if a stock is 100, for example, he will not sell the 100 strike price call, because it is tool likely that the stock will go above 100 and he might lose money. Instead, he might sell the call with a strike price of 120. The stock would have to be above 120 at the option's expiration for the seller of the option to sustain a loss. Obviously it is less likely that a stock will go up 20 points than it will merely go up a few points. So, by selling out-of-the-money options, Mr. Ansbacher is able to shift the probabilities in his favor.

Another major decision which an options trader has to make is whether to be trading calls, which go up in price when a stock goes up, or puts which go up in price when the stock goes down. Mr. Ansbacher said that he makes this decision based upon a number of factors, including his long experience in the field. "One of the factors I rely upon, is my own Ansbacher Index. This Index tells me whether the puts or the calls are higher priced. Since I am selling these options, I will generally choose to sell the ones which are higher priced. I believe the Index also gives an indication of which way the stock market is likely to go in the intermediate future." Thus, Mr. Ansbacher can sell options on the stock market which will be profitable for his clients if the market moves as The Ansbacher Index indicates it is likely to do.

The minimum account which Mr. Ansbacher accepts is US$100,000, and he accepts accounts from people residing anywhere in the world. Depending upon the type of account, the investor will receive monthly or quarterly statements giving the exact value of the account.

For more information contact:

Ansbacher Investment Management, Inc.

Attn: New Clients Information

45 Rockefeller Plaza, 20th Floor

New York NY 10111

telephone: (212) 332-3280

fax: (212) 332-3283; Attn: New Clients Information

Swiss Financial Experts

Swiss investment managers are experienced in working with investors from around the world. Most are fluent in English and have substantial experience in managing various types of investments. They are comfortable managing an investor's entire portfolio if he wishes; however, for investors who prefer to make their own financial decisions, Swiss advisers are happy to offer their expertise to the degree it is required. They can help you manage your investments, or manage them for you whichever arrangement makes you feel more comfortable. For the entrepreneur who devotes much of his energy to building his venture, the efficiency and competence of Swiss investment managers can be a major attraction.

A fine example of a Swiss money management company is JML Swiss Investment Counselors. Founded by Jurg M. Lattman, who has been providing expert financial advice to investment professionals, bankers, economists, and private investors around the world since 1973, JML experts monitor global economic indicators and trends and provide their clients with some of the best financial advice available anywhere. They make it a simple matter to invest in Swiss annuities as well as take advantage of other global investment options.

One of the leaders in Swiss financial management is JML Swiss Investment Counsellors, a firm which offers a unique style of financial management. Clients can customize and control their own portfolios and still receive comprehensive management advice from some of the world's best experts on financial matters.

Recognizing that investors have differing goals, time frames, and tolerance for risk, JML's managers work with their individual clients to help them target their unique objectives. This naturally requires continued surveillance and analysis of worldwide economic trends, political events, financial markets, currencies, and other factors which could make some investments particularly attractive and others most unfavorable. Few individuals have the time or

expertise to undertake this kind of evaluation themselves.

In any event, JML clumps the various opportunities that are available to investors into five separate categories for consideration by its Personal Portfolio Management Program clients:

- *Cash Equivalents. Principal and interest are guaranteed for finite terms are provided.*

- *Blue Chips. The investment portfolio consists of high-quality securities purchased for long-term capital appreciation potential.*

- *Trading. The portfolio consists of securities which are bought and sold for short-term capital appreciation.*

- *Trends. Often referred to a cyclical portfolios, securities are selected on the basis of economic forecasts by industry, sector, or country. The investor normally needs to wait about six years to realize significant annual returns.*

- *Visions. The most speculative of the five categories, investments are selected from opportunities in emerging markets and new technologies. It may take ten or more years to realize larger annual yields.*

For more information on JML write:

JML Jurg M. Lattmann AG

Swiss Investment Counsellors

Germaniastrasse 55, Dept. 212

CH-8033 Zurich, Switzerland

telephone: +41 1 368 8233

fax: +41 1 368 8299;

marking the fax "Attn: Dept. 212"

While there are many excellent Swiss investment financial managers, another one of particular note is the management firm of Weber Hartmann Vrijhof & Partners. Offering management services for the portfolios of both individuals and companies, the firm excels at providing personal attention to its clients. Weber Hartmann Vrijhof & Partners was established in 1992 by Hans Weber, Robert Vrijhof, and Adrian Hartmann. The three men have substantial experience in finance and investment. Weber managed Foreign Commerce Bank (FOCOBANK) in Switzerland for nearly 30 years as its president and CEO, Vrijhof was a former vice president and head of FOCOBANK'S portfolio management group, and Hartmann was head of FOCOBANK'S North American subsidiary in Vancouver. Weber Hartmann Vrijhof & Partners offers specialized investment services designed to meet the individual needs of their clients.

The minimum opening portfolio to be managed by this firm is $250,000 or equivalent. The management team here normally recommends that a portion of the portfolio be invested in hard

currencies other than the U.S. dollar including the Swiss franc, French franc, German mark, and Dutch guilder. Respected for their conservative approach to portfolio management, the partners assist clients with opening a custodial account at one of the major private Swiss banks, so that all client securities are held by the bank, not the investment manager.

A large percentage of their clients are based in the United States. One of their main goals has always been to get a certain portion of their clients' wealth out of the U.S. dollar and into European hard currencies such as Swiss francs, Deutschmarks, and Dutch guilders, and then build a portfolio with a mix of bonds and shares.

If you wish to learn more about the services the firm offers, contact them at:

Weber Hartmann Vrijhof & Partners, Ltd.

Attn: New Clients Department

Zurichstrasses 110B

CH-8134 Adilswil

Switzerland

Tel: +41 1 709 11 15

Fax: +41 1 709 11 13, please mark fax "Attn: New Clients Department"

Even though many investors recognize that Switzerland is a center of finance and investment, they do not realize the vast scope of the investment options offered by Swiss financial institutions and companies. Switzerland is a prime spot for investment for numerous reasons, most importantly for the strength of its currency, security of its financial system, and steady returns on investment.

Dunn & Hargitt: Offshore Managed Commodities Accounts

An offshore managed commodities account is typical of the type of investment that is available to an offshore corporation or trust, but is not available to Americans.

The Dunn & Hargitt International Group, founded in 1961, has specialized in doing research for developing Portfolio Management Programs that have the potential of providing investors with a high return on their capital by investing in a diversified portfolio trading in the commodity, currency, precious metals, and financial futures markets in the United States and throughout the world.

The Dunn & Hargitt group offers investors the possibility of participating in several of the different pools that are managed by them by investing through the investment programs that are offered by their affiliate, Winchester Life in Gibraltar, but which are actually managed by The Dunn & Hargitt International Group.

At the time of publication they are offering three possible investment alternatives, including The Winchester Life Umbrella Account (which allows 100% of a client's money to be invested in a diversified futures portfolio), The Winchester Life 100% Guaranteed Investment Account (in which Lloyds Bank acts as custodian trustee and US Government Zero Coupon Treasury Bonds are set aside to guarantee the client's capital), and The Winchester Life 150%

Guaranteed Investment Account (which is a similar program, but guaranteeing that the client will receive at least 150% of the value deposited with a maturity date at least ten years in the

future).

The average net return for the 150% Guaranteed Investment Account over the last six years would have been 22% a year. The average net return on the 100% Guaranteed Investment Account over the last six years would have been 27% a year. The average annual net return for The Winchester Life Umbrella Account over the last twelve years would have been 35% a year.

The minimum accounts accepted are $20,000 for The Winchester Life Umbrella Account, $20,000 for The Winchester Life 100% Guaranteed Account, and $50,000 for The Winchester Life 150% Guaranteed Account.

Although commodities are a speculative form of investment, investors everywhere are diversifying part of their portfolios to take part in the considerable potential profit opportunities that are available in the commodity, currency, precious metals and financial futures markets. The programs devised by the Dunn & Hargitt International Group will make profits if significant trends develop in either direction; i.e. up or down. This does not mean that short term results are always profitable, however the Dunn & Hargitt proven trading systems can provide above average returns over the longer term. Their objective is to make a profit for their clients of between 20% and 40% per annum and their computer trading systems are geared to this level of performance.

For more information, contact:

The Dunn & Hargitt International Group

Department S 697

P.O. Box 3186

Road Town, Tortola

British Virgin Islands

The structure of the Dunn & Hargitt Group has been established so that no taxes are withheld from the client's investment on the international commodity, currency, precious metals and financial futures markets. Because of this they can only manage money for investors who are neither citizens nor residents of the United States, United Kingdom, or Belgium, and they will not mail their brochures to those countries.

The Dunn & Hargitt International Group offers complete confidentiality to all of its clients, and will not reveal any information on a client or on its accounts to any third parties.

Sources of Help in Forming Offshore Entities

Skye Fiduciary Services Limited

Skye Fiduciary Services Limited, based in the Isle of Man, are specialist consultants, designers and trustees and managers of offshore and international fiduciary structures.

They were established in 1991 by Charles Cain to provide specialist consultancy and management services in respect of offshore fiduciary structures, specializing in clients from or connected to the USA. The beginnings of Skye Fiduciary Services Limited go back over twenty years. In 1972, their Executive Chairman, Charles Cain, after some years working in international banking in East Africa and the United Kingdom, returned to his native country as the managing director of a merchant bank. Three years later he resigned to start his own business, which became, by 1989, the largest corporate and trust management business in the Isle of Man. In 1989, however, as a consequence of an illness, he sold out to a large financial services group.

In 1991, fully recovered, he established Skye Fiduciary Services Limited.

From its executive office in the Isle of Man, Skye Fiduciary Services Limited provides a design and management service relating to offshore companies and trusts.

Unlike many firms that simply provide offshore corporations, one of Sky's major functions is to provide trade management services. These include:

- *arranging and supervising appropriate banking and trade finance facilities and services.*

- *trade documentation*

- *exchange control planning*

- *double tax treaty planning*

- *administration of trading entities*

- *arranging bank Letters of Credit and other financial instruments*

- *arranging leasing, invoice discounting and credit factoring*

- *arranging tax efficient vehicles for transferring royalties and other income flows derived from intellectual property rights.*

- *offshore joint venture vehicles and holding structures for US persons*

- *international trading structures*

For more information contact:

> *Skye Fiduciary Services Limited*
>
> *Attn: New Clients Information*
>
> *2 Water Street*
>
> *Ramsey, Isle of Man 1M8 1JP*
>
> *Great Britain*
>
> *Telephone: +44 1624 816117*
>
> *Fax: +44 1624 816645; attn: New Clients Information*

ICS Trust (Asia) Limited

The other firm I can personally give my highest recommendation to is ICS Trust (Asia) Limited, based in Hong Kong.

The handover of the former British Crown Colony of Hong Kong to China is complete, and it is now called the Hong Kong Special Administrative Region, generally abbreviated to Hong Kong S.A.R., even on official documents.

As more than one local businessman has put it, "now that the politicians and journalists are gone (from covering the handover), we can get down to *business.*" This attitude is typical of Hong Kong, still a true capitalist center. In fact, many of the wealthy who left to obtain second citizenships in Canada, Australia, and elsewhere, have now returned home to continue building their fortunes.

Offshore re invoicing can be a very useful tool for exporters as well as importers, since it allows for the accumulation of tax free profits in an offshore environment.

Through re invoicing, an offshore corporation is established as an international intermediary between importers and their suppliers or between exporters and their customers. The offshore corporation can thus either 1) buy products, on behalf of the importer, at the negotiated price level and then sell, or re invoice, these same products to the importer at a higher price, thereby accumulating profits offshore where there is no tax liability and significantly

reducing profits in the country of destination where there is tax liability, or 2) buy products at discount prices from the exporter, thereby creating a very small profit in the exporting country with tax liability and sell, or re invoice, these same products at market value prices to overseas buyers, thereby accumulating profits offshore where there is no tax liability.

In order to be profitable, offshore re invoicing operations need to be situated in an environment where import export transactions are either tax free or low tax (in relation to the onshore portion of the operation).

Once the offshore company has been established, the management corporation needs to acquire the services of a post office box, a telex, a telephone, and a facsimile for its use. When all this is in place, the management company can begin re invoicing. An offshore service provider can arrange these services.

The merchandise can be sent directly to the exporter's client or to the importer. The only functions performed in the offshore haven are the preparation and dispatch of the new invoice and the management of the funds in the way instructed by the client and complying with local regulations.

The major advantage of Hong Kong is simply that it is a real business center, not just a tax haven. One of the consequences of that is the ability to add value to services that are provided in only skeleton form in other tax havens. The reinvoicing business is a prime example. Most tax haven jurisdictions host a number of trading companies that do nothing more than reinvoicing. But one Hong Kong firm has now developed this traditional service into a "real" business mode, with an ability to arrange local trade financing. This is a healthy step away from traditional tax havenry into a true offshore business center.

ICS Trust Company Limited is part of the ICS International group of companies headquartered in Hong Kong. This highly successful entrepreneurial group was started by Elizabeth L. Thomson. Elizabeth describes herself as "a lawyer by profession" (2 law degrees, a member of 4

Law Societies internationally), "an entrepreneur by choice"! She has helped innumerable people start new enterprises in many parts of the globe and is well known in Hong Kong for her work with women entrepreneurs.

With a staff of 40 at ICS, every aspect of your business is covered — from deciding to incorporate, to obtaining financing from the bank, to managing your paper work including Letters of Credit, to investing your hard earned profits! ICS is truly a "one stop shop" for entrepreneurs.

Their clients range from multinational companies for whom they run Direct Import Programs worth millions of dollars to individuals who seek tax sheltering and estate planning on an international scale. As an entrepreneurial group, they attract many entrepreneurs as clients — business people who have grown their business to a level of maturity and profits that requires expansion into Asia for many diverse reasons.

Instead of just a paper thin traditional tax haven reinvoicing company, with ICS you can develop a real business in Hong Kong. With their extensive banking contacts, ICS professionals will "shop" for the best letter of credit facilities that Hong Kong's competitive banking scene can offer, likely better facilities than you can find at home. Depending upon the client, ICS can often arrange letter of credit banking facilities for clients with either a low or zero margin deposit, usually required by the opening bank. By freeing up your collateral and capital, they provide you with more purchasing power to increase sales and gain higher profits.

Most of these reinvoicing transactions are usually effected such that they are tax free in Hong Kong. There is no withholding tax on dividends so it is often possible to engage in international trade through a HK company and obtain dividends from that company tax free.

ICS will also work with international banks and factors in Hong Kong and overseas to arrange financing, secured primarily on the strength of purchase orders from your clients. Working with banks, factories, shipping companies and freight forwarders, ICS will structure a transaction to increase the likelihood of obtaining flexible, low cost facilities.

The goods do not need to go through HK for us to use a HK vehicle to pass title. Most of their clients ship from a third country direct to their own country.

Although the traditional Hong Kong focus is on firms who trade in goods, it is also possible to use these structures in cases where services are to be provided from overseas. For example, a firm could contract out a study to a company in Hong Kong. This Hong Kong company could then sub contract out the work to a third party firm and the profit kept in Hong Kong, tax free.

If you import goods from Asia for sale to large chains, ICS can help you expand your credit facilities and increase your domestic sales by establishing and running a Direct Import Program for you. Combined with their international trade finance capabilities, the Direct Import Program is a powerful tool for generating more profits.

The primary goal of the Direct Import Program is to maximize your profits by making your customers perceive that they are buying "direct." This is achieved by:

- *setting up a subsidiary company in Hong Kong*

- *getting your buyers to open their L/C or orders to this subsidiary*

- *liaising with suppliers to ensure goods are to specification.*

The Direct Import Program works because of two powerful reasons:

- *The trend in the retail industry is for buyers to "buy direct" from the Orient. Having a subsidiary in Hong Kong which receives orders or L/Cs greatly enhances this perception.*

- *Large retail chains often can obtain freight and insurance at significant savings because of their economies of scale. Selling FOB Asia can often result in a lower selling price for the importer but with the same profit.*

ICS will set up and manage the subsidiary company for you, and prepare financing proposals for presentation to local banks. When everything is complete, goods are shipped directly from the Asian factory to the customer. The fact that you are now seen as an Asian supplier (and not the middleman) is often an important factor that clinches the deal. The added prestige of a Hong Kong office makes the customer think he or she is buying "direct" and therefore receiving the lowest price.

To get started, you should contact ICS with as much detail as possible about your business and its trading activities.

For further information, contact:

Mr. Kishore K. Sakhrani

Director

ICS Trust (Asia) Limited

8th Floor, Henley Building

Five Queens's Road, Central

Hong Kong

Telephone: +852 2854 4544

Fax: +852 2543 5555

Britannia Corporate Management Limited

A consulting business specializing in the formation of offshore corporations and trusts is Britannia Corporate Management Limited, located in the Cayman Islands. Its president, Gary F. Oakley, is a Canadian with 17 years of Cayman Islands residency. Britannia is licensed to manage investment holding and trading companies, real estate holding companies, patent holding companies, and insurance holding companies. It is licensed to incorporate and manage corporations registered in the Cayman Islands. As such, the firm can service as the registered office of a corporation, provide its secretary, officers and directors, or undertake any day-to-day functions that may be required. More information can be obtained by writing the following:

Britannia Corporate Management Limited

Attn: New Clients Information

P. O. Box 1968

Whitewall Estates, Grand Cayman

Cayman Islands

Britannia can be reached by fax at +1 345 949 0716, marking your fax to "New Clients Information."

You will be well-advised and well-serviced in the hands of any of these fine companies.

About the Author

Over the past 25 years, Adam Starchild has been the author of over two dozen books, and hundreds of magazine articles, primarily on business and finance. His articles have appeared in a wide range of publications around the world   including Business Credit, Euromoney, Finance, The Financial Planner, International Living, Offshore Financial Review, Reason, Tax Planning International, The Bull & Bear, Trust & Estates, and many more.

Now semi retired, he was the president of an international consulting group specializing in banking, finance and the development of new businesses, and director of a trust company.

Although this formidable testimony to expertise in his field, plus his current preoccupation with other books in progress, would not seem to leave time for a well rounded existence, Starchild has won two Presidential Sports Awards and written several cookbooks, and is currently involved in a number of personal charitable projects.

His personal website is at http://www.adamstarchild.com/

We also recommend this related book:

Passport to Tax-Free International Living

by Adam Starchild

ISBN: 1893713113

If you are like most people, you undoubtedly feel that you have paid enough taxes during your career to last several lifetimes, and you certainly don't relish the idea of paying taxes once you are retired. You may not have to. There are places around the world offering outstanding lifestyles that you can enjoy during your retirement (or even semi-retirement) where you may considerably reduce the taxes you would expect to pay in your home country. In some places you may be able to eliminate income taxes entirely. The opportunities exist; they are even promoted by some jurisdictions.

These places may be thought of as *retirement havens*, which is the subject of this book. Simply put, a retirement haven is a country, jurisdiction, or city that offers special tax incentives for their residents. While such places may be attractive to various individuals, they are especially so for retirees who wish to maintain their assets in the safest and most efficient manner possible. Unquestionably, one of the most effective methods for maintaining assets during the retirement years is to reduce your tax burden.

The author does not endorse any retirement haven over another. Included in the book are places around the world that may prove suitable for individuals who are retired, or are about to retire, and who wish to significantly reduce their tax burden in a land that is pleasant, safe, and where they can enjoy a superior style of life. The golden years can truly be golden with proper planning and wise decision-making.

You may find that you wish not to move to another part of the world during your retirement, or that you don't wish to live in any particular place. Perhaps you wish to travel the world perpetually. There is a term for this — Perpetual Traveler. Indeed there are people who have retired and bought yachts that they use as an "ocean-going mobile home." They visit ports and magnificent cities throughout the world, remaining for the length of time the country allows (which may be several months), and then sailing to the next destination. By not being a "resident" of a country, you are not liable for taxes. The sophistication of personal computers and Internet data links can keep you in touch with the world and informed about your investments.

No two retirement havens are alike. Each has unique characteristics that individuals must evaluate according to their own likes, dislikes, and expectations. What this book does is summarize the MANY countries that offer a significant escape from taxes.

Retirement need not be a mundane affair in which you watch your hard-earned savings and investments dwindle away due to a high cost of living and burdensome taxes. With the proper planning it can be a time of new opportunities and enjoyment, as well as a time in which you keep more of your assets by reducing your cost of living and taxes.

Over the past 25 years, Adam Starchild has been the author of over two dozen books, and hundreds of magazine articles, primarily on business and finance. His articles have appeared in a wide range of publications around the world — including Business Credit, Euromoney, Finance, The Financial Planner, International Living, Offshore Financial Review, Reason, Tax Planning International, The Bull & Bear, Trust & Estates, and many more. Now semi-retired, he has lived in a number of countries. His personal website is at http://www.adamstarchild.com/

www.ingramcontent.com/pod-product-compliance
Lightning Source LLC
Chambersburg PA
CBHW030014290326
41934CB00005B/334